Strengthening
Conventional Deterrence
in Europe

Strengthening Conventional Deterrence in Europe
Proposals for the 1980s

**Report of the
EUROPEAN SECURITY STUDY**

ESECS

STRENGTHENING CONVENTIONAL DETERRENCE IN EUROPE. Copyright ©1983 by The American Academy of Arts and Sciences. All rights reserved. Printed in the United States of America. No part of this publication may be reproduced or transmitted, in any form or by any means, without permission.

First published 1983 by
THE MACMILLAN PRESS LTD
London and Basingstoke
Companies and representatives throughout the world

Distributed in the Federal Republic of Germany, Austria, Switzerland and the German Democratic Republic by Nomos Verlags-Gesellschaft GmbH, Waldseestrasse, 3-5 Postfach 610, D-7570, Baden-Baden, FRG.

ISBN 0 333 36023 0 (hardcover)
ISBN 0 333 36024 9 (paperback)

Printed at Nimrod Press, Boston.

To Carroll L. Wilson

Contents

Preface ix

Part I - REPORT OF THE STEERING GROUP 1

Steering Group Members 2

Report of the Steering Group 7

The Need for Stronger Conventional Capabilities
for Deterrence and Reassurance
The Nature of the Soviet Conventional Military Threat
The Specific Requirements for Effective NATO
Conventional Defense
The Means for Enhancing NATO's Conventional
Defensive Capability
Summary of Conclusions

Part II - THE SOVIET THREAT IN THE 1980s 37

Workshop Members 38

Workshop Report 41

Military Power and Soviet Intentions
Soviet Doctrine and Strategy: Basic Guidelines
Warsaw Pact Operational Planning and Tactics
Warsaw Pact Capabilities for Military Operations
in Central Europe
Critical Factors for NATO Consideration

Supporting Paper — The Political Rationale of Soviet
Military Capabilities and Doctrine *by Hannes Adomeit* 67

Foreign Policy, Military Doctrine, and Military Strategy
Foreign Policy and the "Correlation of Forces"
The Stalin Era
The Khrushchev Era
The Brezhnev Era and Beyond

Supporting Paper — Soviet Operational Concepts in
the 1980s *by Christopher N. Donnelly* 105

War and the USSR: The Political Perspective
Soviet Studies of NATO Plans
Moving Towards the Outbreak of War
Hostilities: The "Initial Period" of War
The Soviet Offensive Against NATO
The Structure of the Offensive

Part III - REQUIREMENTS FOR CONVENTIONAL DEFENSE 137

Workshop Members 138

Workshop Report 141
Improving NATO's Conventional Posture
Correcting NATO's Deficiencies
Critical Issues for Improving NATO's Conventional Posture
Conclusions

Supporting Paper — Prospective Tasks and Capabilities
Required for NATO's Conventional Forces
by K.-Peter Stratmann 161
Conventional Forces and NATO Strategy
Some Divergent Philosophies: The Necessity for
Choice and Balance
Priorities for NATO's Conventional Forces

Part IV - CONTRIBUTIONS OF ADVANCED TECHNOLOGY 193

Workshop Members 194

Workshop Report 197
The Problem for NATO
Changing Roles for Conventional and Nuclear Weapons
New Non-Nuclear Options
Advantages of the Use of Advanced Non-Nuclear Technologies
Issues to be Resolved
Chemical Weapons
Conclusions

Supporting Paper — Potential Future Roles for
Conventional and Nuclear Forces in Defense
of Western Europe *by Donald R. Cotter* 209
Deterring Soviet Offensive Operations — How Much Do We Know?
The Need for a NATO Forward Defense
How Did NATO Get into this Nuclear Fix? — Needed Changes
Deterrent Roles for Future Conventional Forces
A Notional Concept for an Integrated Forward Defense of NATO
Changed Roles for Modernized Nuclear Forces
Candidate Modern Conventional Weapon Systems and Costs
Force and Policy Restructuring
Conclusions
Appendix

Preface

The European Security Study (ESECS), which has produced this volume, addressed an urgent issue: How can NATO improve its conventional capacity so as to enhance its deterrent to aggression and lessen its dependence on possible early use of nuclear weapons? The Study was initiated in the fall of 1981. The growing concern about nuclear weapons has made it even more relevant today.

The project originated with Professor Carroll L. Wilson, who had already organized and directed several international studies including the World Coal Study and the Workshop on Alternative Energy Strategies. In its methodology ESECS has built on those earlier studies.

For ESECS Professor Wilson assembled a Steering Group composed of twenty-six Americans and Europeans with experience in government, the military, defense analysis, and international relations. That group has been the governing body for the Study, and has been responsible for its structure and direction. It established three Workshops, each consisting of 10 to 12 experts, to analyze aspects of the topic. To assist each Workshop, papers were prepared by two or three individual specialists. Each Workshop met for five days and prepared a Report of its conclusions. The Steering Group had two meetings of three days each to discuss the issues and to prepare the Report of its conclusions and proposals in the light of the Reports of the Workshops, the individual papers, and other materials.

Carroll Wilson became ill in November and died in January 1983. By then the three Workshops contained in this volume had been held. His incapacity and death deprived the project of his experience, energy, tenacity, and leadership. Despite this severe loss, the Steering Group has completed its Report and presents it as a fitting tribute to him. We hope that this Study vindicates his belief in the value of tackling difficult problems by seeking to reconcile divergent views through discussion and analysis.

Many people have contributed to the work of the Study, and to this volume, as members of the Steering Group and Workshops, and as authors. This has been a truly group endeavor, combining the knowledge and expertise of over fifty people, civilian and military, from four NATO countries — the Federal Republic of Germany, Norway, the United Kingdom, and the United States. Much of the significance of the Reports of the Steering Group and the Workshops derives from the calibre and experience of their members. The Reports reflect genuine consensus among a group with diverse backgrounds. Their diversity was itself a source of strength. On specific military issues Steering Group members who are not military specialists were able to draw on the expertise of the military members and observers as well as on the Workshop Reports.

After Professor Wilson became ill, the Steering Group asked me to direct the completion of the Study and the Report. In fact, the task has been shared by various members of the Steering Group including McGeorge Bundy, Michael Carver, Andrew J. Goodpaster, Milton Katz, and Franz-Joseph Schulze. In addition, the project has benefited greatly from the invaluable contributions of Paul S. Basile, Donald R. Cotter, Daniel Gouré, John Keegan, and Charles J. Simmons. At our invitation an observer from Supreme Headquarters Allied Powers Europe (SHAPE) attended each Workshop; their participation was most helpful. We are indebted to Max Hall, our editor, who has imposed on the diverse components of the volume such coherence and consistency as they display. The ESECS staff members, Susan M. Leland, Sue Lena Thompson, and Martha J. Mason, have been outstanding in the handling of all practical aspects of the project. Their dedication, abilities, and teamwork have been indispensable to its completion.

The volume reflects the Study in its several components. Part I consists of the Report of the Steering Group, which presents the conclusions of its members. Parts II, III, and IV contain the three Workshop Reports, each followed by one or more selected supporting papers relating to the main topics. (For reasons of space, not all papers could be included.) Each Workshop Report embodies the consensus of those who participated in its sessions. The views expressed in the supporting papers are those of their respective authors. The names and affiliations of the members of the Steering Group and of each of the Workshops are set out before the respective Reports. The Steering Group, of course, assumes responsiblity for the overall direction and integrity of the project.

The process followed in the Study inevitably entailed substantial overlaps among its various levels: The Workshop Reports drew on the supporting papers, and the Steering Group Report on the Workshop Reports and papers. The Workshop Reports and individual papers make available to the reader most of the data and analyses underlying the reasoning and conclusions of the Steering Group.

Originally the project was to be continued into a second phase with more intensive analysis of selected issues. Because of the death of Professor Wilson, it is not expected that this second phase will be undertaken. This Report is complete in itself and stands on its own.

The European Security Study, with its distinctive process, required substantial funding for travel, staff, and other expenses related to the Workshops, Steering Group meetings, and preparation of papers and reports. The project would not have been possible without the generous support of the following: Cabot Corporation Foundation; Thomas D. and Virginia W. Cabot; Robert A. Charpie; The Ford Foundation; William T. Golden; Richard Lounsbery Foundation; John D. and Catherine T. MacArthur Foundation; David Rockefeller; Rockefeller Brothers Fund; Stiftung Volkswagenwerk; The Thomas J. Watson Foundation.

We are also indebted to the American Academy of Arts and Sciences for providing both the auspices and facilities for the Study.

April 1983   Robert R. Bowie

The American Academy of Arts and Sciences has been pleased to serve as the institutional base for the European Security Study. This is in keeping with our long tradition of contributing to the understanding of important policy issues through studies by scientists, scholars and people in public life.

The topic of the Study is important and timely, and related to international security and arms control, long-time concerns of the Academy. The participants from Europe and the United States are diverse, experienced and well-qualified. And the initiator of the Study, Carroll Wilson, was an active member of the Academy.

We hope that the ESECS Report will stimulate constructive public debate on the critical policy issues with which it deals by clarifying the basic need and possible means for improving conventional capabilities of NATO. In accordance with our custom, the Academy, while endorsing the intellectual quality of the ESECS Report, takes no position concerning its conclusions and policy recommendations.

Herman Feshbach
President

PART I

REPORT OF THE STEERING GROUP

In its Report, the Steering Group of the European Security Study has analyzed the need for improving NATO's conventional capability in order to serve NATO's basic purposes and to reduce reliance on early use of nuclear weapons, and has agreed on recommendations for doing so. Its analysis and conclusions have drawn on the Reports of three expert Workshops and the supporting papers (Parts II, III, and IV of this book) and on the knowledge and experience of its members.

STEERING GROUP MEMBERS

General Sir Hugh Beach
General (Ret.). Formerly: Master General of Ordnance, Deputy Commander in Chief, U.K. Land Forces.

Professor Robert R. Bowie
Guest Scholar, Brookings Institution; Dillon Professor Emeritus of International Affairs, Harvard University. Formerly: Director, Center for International Affairs, Harvard University; Director of Policy Planning, State Department; Deputy Director (Estimates), Central Intelligence Agency.

Professor Harvey Brooks
Benjamin Peirce Professor of Technology and Public Policy, Harvard University. Formerly: Dean of Engineering and Applied Physics, Harvard University; Member, President's Science Advisory Committee and Naval Research Advisory Committee.

Professor McGeorge Bundy
Professor of History, New York University. Formerly: Special Assistant to the President for National Security; President of the Ford Foundation.

Field Marshal Lord Carver
Formerly: Chief of the Defence Staff, United Kingdom; Chief of the General Staff.

Ministerial Director (Ret.) Hans L. Eberhard
Formerly: Director of the Armaments Directorate, German Ministry of Defense; staff and command positions German Army; Brigadier General.

Professor Lawrence D. Freedman

Professor of War Studies, Kings College, University of London. Formerly: Head of Policy Studies at the Royal Institute of International Affairs.

Dr. Alton Frye

Senior Fellow and Washington Director, Council on Foreign Relations. Formerly: Rand Corporation; Assistant to former U.S. Senator Edward Brooke (Senate Armed Services Committee).

General Andrew J. Goodpaster

General, United States Army (Ret.). Formerly: Commander in Chief, U.S. Forces in Europe and Supreme Allied Commander Europe (NATO); Superintendent, U.S. Military Academy.

Mr. Johan J. Holst

Director, Norwegian Institute of International Affairs. Formerly: State Secretary for Foreign Affairs; State Secretary for Defense.

Professor Michael E. Howard

Regius Professor of Modern History, Oxford University. Formerly: Professor of War Studies, University of London; Chichele Professor of the History of War, Oxford University.

Mr. Howard W. Johnson

Chairman of the Corporation, Massachusetts Institute of Technology; Director, Morgan Guaranty Trust Co. and E.I. duPont de Nemours & Co. Formerly: President of the Massachusetts Institute of Technology.

Professor Dr. Karl Kaiser

Director, Forschungsinstitut der Deutschen Gesellschaft für Auswärtige Politik (Research Institute of the German Society for Foreign Affairs); Professor at the University of Cologne; Specialist on European Integration, American-European Relations, Nuclear Energy.

Professor Milton Katz

Henry L. Stimson Professor of Law and Director of International Legal Studies Emeritus at Harvard University. Formerly: President of the American Academy of Arts and Sciences; U.S. Special Representative in Europe for the Marshall Plan; Chairman, Defense Finance and Economic Committee of NATO.

Professor William W. Kaufmann

Professor of Political Science, Massachusetts Institute of Technology; Consultant to the Secretary of Defense, National Security Council, Office of Management and Budget. Formerly: Rand Corporation.

Professor Catherine M. Kelleher

Professor of Defense Policy, School of Public Affairs, University of Maryland; Adjunct Professor of Military Strategy, National War College, Washington, D.C.

Mr. David Klein

Executive Director, American Council on Germany. Formerly: Foreign Service Officer in Moscow, Berlin, Bonn; National Security Council Staff; Assistant Director, Arms Control and Disarmament Agency.

Dr. Franklin A. Long

Henry Luce Professor of Science and Society, Cornell University; Co-Chairman of American Pugwash; Director of Exxon Corporation. Formerly: Chairman of the Chemistry Department; Member of the President's Science Advisory Committee; Director of the Arms Control Association.

Ambassador Dr. Rolf F. Pauls

German Diplomatist. Formerly: Ambassador and Permanent Representative to NATO; Ambassador to the United States, China and Israel.

Dr. William J. Perry

Investment Banker — Mathematician. Formerly: Undersecretary of Defense for Research and Engineering, Department of Defense; President of ESL, Inc.; Director of Electronic Defense Laboratories, GTE.

Professor Dr. Klaus Ritter

Director, Stiftung Wissenschaft und Politik (Research Institute for International Politics and Security); Professor of International Politics at the University of Munich.

General Franz-Joseph Schulze

General, German Army (Ret.). Formerly: Commander in Chief, Allied Forces Central Europe; Deputy Chief of Staff, Plans and Operations, Allied Command Europe.

Professor Marshall Shulman

Professor of International Relations, and Director, W. Averell Harriman Institute of Advanced Study on the Soviet Union, Columbia University. Formerly: Special Advisor on Soviet Affairs to the Secretary of State.

Air Chief Marshal Sir Alasdair Steedman

Air Chief Marshal, Royal Air Force (Ret.). Formerly: U.K. Military Representative to NATO; Air Member of Air Force Board (U.K.) for Supply and Organisation.

General Johannes Steinhoff

General, German Air Force (Ret.). Formerly: Chief of Staff, German Air Force; Chairman of the NATO Military Committee.

Professor Richard H. Ullman

Professor of International Affairs, Woodrow Wilson School, Princeton University. Formerly: Policy Planning Staff, Office of the Secretary of Defense; National Security Council Staff; Director of Studies at the Council on Foreign Relations; Editorial Board, *The New York Times*; Editor, *Foreign Policy*.

Professor Carroll L. Wilson*

Director, European Security Study (ESECS), Mitsui Professor Emeritus in Problems of Contemporary Technology, Massachusetts Institute of Technology. Formerly: Director, Workshop on Alternative Energy Strategies (WAES) and World Coal Study (WOCOL); Wartime Executive Assistant to Director of Office for Scientific Research and Development; General Manager, U.S. Atomic Energy Commission.

*Deceased

CONTENTS — REPORT OF THE STEERING GROUP

I. The Need for Stronger Conventional Capabilities for
    Deterrence and Reassurance   7

II. The Nature of the Soviet Conventional Military Threat   12

III. The Specific Requirements for Effective NATO
     Conventional Defense   18

IV. The Means for Enhancing NATO's Conventional
    Defensive Capability   24

V. Summary of Conclusions   31

Report of the Steering Group

We, the Steering Group of the European Security Study, twenty-six of us, civilian and military, on both sides of the Atlantic, have reassessed the relationship of the military posture of the North Atlantic Treaty Organization to its central purpose. This Report offers our analysis and conclusions.

I. THE NEED FOR STRONGER CONVENTIONAL CAPABILITIES FOR DETERRENCE AND REASSURANCE

The central purpose of the North Atlantic Treaty alliance is to maintain the security and political self-confidence of its members by assuring them against possible aggression, intimidation, or manipulation based on the military power of the Soviet Union. In so doing, NATO seeks to maintain peace and political stability.

The military needs of the Alliance can be properly understood only by recognizing its fundamentally political character. It was organized in an environment of turmoil following World War II, of political instability in Western Europe, and of deep concern over Soviet military and political pressure. Its objective was not to fight a war — not in defense and still less in attack — but rather to have and to make visible the defensive capabilities that would make the choice of war clearly and deeply unattractive to the Soviet Union, and thus also make Soviet attempts at intimidation unrewarding. The wisest leaders of the Alliance have never supposed that the Soviet Union would lightly choose the unpredictabilities of war against Western Europe. The primary object of the forces of the Alliance has been to present real and believable obstacles to any change in this Soviet caution, and to do it in ways that are also reassuring to the peoples of the Alliance.

Thus deterrence — the effective discouragement of resort to war — and reassurance — the maintenance of self-confidence among the peoples and nations of the Alliance — are intended as instruments of peace, and the object of military strength is to reinforce them both. The paradox is that all forms of military strength, even if dedicated to such peaceful purposes, must be designed and deployed in such a fashion that they do in fact deter and defend. Soviet military power must be countered in a manner that reassures NATO members as well as deterring the Soviet Union. Deterrence and reassurance are twin objectives that must be pursued together. Our study has led us to the conviction that a better balance between these objectives can be fostered by an improved conventional capability.

The need for attention to NATO's conventional defensive capability is not new, but for several reasons it has acquired new urgency in recent years. First, the Soviet Union has achieved full strategic nuclear parity with the United States. Second, Soviet theater nuclear forces aimed at Europe have rapidly grown far beyond NATO's capability in this category. Third, Soviet conventional capabilities have also continued to expand.

Finally, in response to these changes and others, there has been a growth in uneasiness and concern of the governments and peoples of NATO. The growth of vast and varied nuclear forces on both sides has brought home to both peoples and governments the risks and consequences of nuclear war. Our present reliance on possible early use of nuclear weapons threatens to undermine the two main purposes of the Alliance — the need for credible deterrence of adversaries and effective reassurance of our own peoples. We find ourselves in strong and unanimous agreement that the Alliance should now move energetically to reduce its dependence on such early use.

We recognize that the Soviet Union seeks to accomplish its purposes through a variety of instruments utilized in a combined and mutually supporting arrangement. It presumably prefers to pursue its aims by means other than a direct military attack. The Soviet Union seeks to use the hard and conspicuous fact of its military power as an instrument of intimidation and political manipulation to sway NATO governmental policies and popular attitudes toward compliance with Soviet aims and interests. Its military power looms as a setting for its diplomacy and arms control negotiations. Indeed, the Soviet Union's challenge to NATO and its peoples at present is primarily political.

Nevertheless the present imbalance of conventional forces on the Central Front might in some future crisis tempt the Soviet Union to aggression with conventional forces. If NATO should be unable to repel such an attack with its own conventional forces, or even if its members and their peoples should so perceive it, the situation could lead either to appeasement or to a bitter internal division over the possible use of nuclear weapons.

One critical measure of NATO's effectiveness has been its capacity to check any impulses to resort to force in a time of crisis, i.e. to contribute to "crisis stability." To achieve and maintain stability in a crisis generated by an apparent threat or risk of aggression, NATO must counter the threat in a manner that neither undermines the firmness of its own governments and peoples nor provokes a resort to force by others. We find it a particular value of improved conventional capability that it can contribute to crisis stability.

We accept the NATO doctrine of Flexible Response, under which the Alliance stands ready to use whatever level of strength may be needed to repel aggression. The doctrine postulates an initial and preferred resistance against conventional aggression with conventional weapons, while reserving a capacity for the possible use of nuclear weapons. Within this doctrine we firmly support stronger efforts to raise the nuclear threshold, i.e., to defer as long as feasible, and if possible to prevent, a situation in which NATO might be obliged to face a choice between surrender to aggression and resort to nuclear weapons with the attendant risk of provoking response in kind. The need to raise the nuclear threshold is a decisive reason for the development by NATO of a more robust, imaginative, and effective conventional capability.

We are mindful of the function of nuclear deterrent forces in countering any possible temptation on the part of any adversary to set loose a nuclear war, whether by initiating a nuclear attack or by forcing others to a possible desperate choice between resort to nuclear measures or surrender. We do not believe that the Alliance can hope to escape from the need for nuclear weapons in order to deter nuclear attack. Moreover, given the existence of nuclear weapons, we recognize that any armed conflict in Europe entails a risk of becoming nuclear. This very risk is itself a deterrent to war in any form. Nevertheless, we insist on the necessity for NATO to seek to reduce its present degree of dependence on a possible early recourse to nuclear weapons to deter a Soviet conventional attack.

We are also convinced that it is both necessary and wise to adhere to the established NATO doctrine of Forward Defense. The geographical distribution of NATO's peoples and the destructiveness of modern weapons preclude any policy of deliberately trading territory for time. This is especially true on the Central Front where any substantial withdrawal would signify the loss of large elements of the population and industry of the Federal Republic of Germany. Forward Defense is a corollary of collective security. NATO must plan to contain any possible attack well forward. We have kept this necessity in mind throughout our Study.

We have concentrated on NATO's conventional defensive military capabilities on the Central Front. NATO's function of deterring aggression and reassuring its peoples extends throughout the North Atlantic Treaty area, but its capacity to defend the Central Front is a necessary condition for the effective protection of the northern and southern flanks. Much of our analysis and many of our recommendations concerning the Central Region will also be applicable in the north and the south of Europe. The military means, however, must be fitted to the particular physical and political conditions of each area in which they are applied.

There are clearly many different ways in which NATO's conventional capability in the Central Region could be improved. Many of them have been recommended year after year by successive Military Committees, Supreme Allied Commanders and their subordinates. Some of the proposals would involve significant increases in defense budgets, some of them increases in enlisted manpower, and most of them both. Our Study has concentrated on those weapons systems and associated measures which would enable NATO to use conventional weapons systems to strike targets for which it now relies on nuclear systems both to deter and, if that were to fail, to counter Warsaw Pact military action.

In our analysis and recommendations we have taken account of the political and economic constraints in peacetime democracies. Yet within these constraints we have found reason for optimism. There are new technologies and new ways of using NATO conventional forces that can help to fulfill their mission. Changes in existing procedures for planning, training, operations, command and support can materially improve NATO's conventional force capabilities. In combination, new technologies and such other changes can help to counter the Soviet military threat. In our judgment, these improvements in NATO's conventional capabilities can be accomplished within the limits imposed by fiscal, political, and strategic necessities for setting priorities and making choices. We think there are specific and practical ways to deal with the particular problems and threats that most require attention.

We do not wish to give the impression that we regard technological improvements as providing the whole answer to the problem of defending Western Europe. When it comes to actual combat, they can greatly enhance the prospects that the NATO forces fighting on the ground will be able to repel the Soviet attack. But measures to ensure that these forces are not only adequately equipped, but also well trained, self-confident, and properly led, must always be given high priority. Both deterrence and reassurance depend on having a fighting capability that is seen to be effective.

We believe that the improvement of NATO's conventional military position shares a common purpose with the pursuit of effective arms control. Both are designed to reinforce security and political stability. Moreover, the pursuit by NATO of effective arms control concurrently with the upgrading of its conventional military posture can help to strengthen public support for both. It can also help to emphasize the defensive purpose of NATO's conventional weapons reinforcement.

Just as we should seek serious arms control, so we should seek better political relations with the Soviet Union. The pursuit of such improved relations is not inconsistent with the pursuit of deterrence and reassurance. While we want the Soviet Union to respect the dangers of aggression against us, we have no interest in giving it reason to fear attack of any sort from the West. In the past the steadfastness of the Alliance has been essential to the achievement of balanced agreements with Moscow, such as those which maintain the freedom of Austria and West Berlin. We hold that the effort to reduce political tension is a proper element in security policy.

In our inquiry, we proceeded from the hypothesis, to be tested by our studies, that important improvements in the conventional military capability of the Atlantic alliance are urgently needed to achieve its central purpose. In our judgment, our studies have confirmed our hypothesis. We are persuaded that NATO and its members can and should take prompt steps to improve their conventional defensive military capabilities; that such improvements can be effected at a reasonable and acceptable cost; and that such improvements can make a highly constructive contribution to deterring possible aggression and reassuring the NATO peoples.

The health and strength of the Alliance, and its role as an instrument of peace, depend ultimately on the understanding and support of its peoples. That support in turn depends on the ability of political leaders to explain the indispensability of the Alliance for peace and security and to persuade the electorate to support what is needed for its effectiveness. That function is especially important in the effort to enhance the conventional capabilities of the Alliance.

The succeeding sections of this Steering Group Report develop the analysis supporting our conclusions. We address first the nature of the Soviet conventional military threat; second, the specific needs for strengthening NATO's conventional capability in relation to the particular NATO missions that have high relevance to this threat; and third, the means for upgrading NATO's conventional defensive capability through new weapons and technologies and new concepts and modes of operation.

II. THE NATURE OF THE SOVIET CONVENTIONAL MILITARY THREAT

The Warsaw Pact currently has superiority in its conventional forces against NATO. Its strategy and operational concept seek to exploit surprise, speed, intense firepower, and numerical superiority for quick success. Heavily armored Warsaw Pact formations, supported by armed helicopters and tactical aviation, attacking with surprise against only partially mobilized and deployed NATO forces, pose the risk of rapid penetration into NATO territory to disrupt and destroy NATO defenses. Thus the Warsaw Pact resources in tanks, armored personnel carriers, artillery, and trained manpower constitute a particular threat to NATO; and it is in Central Europe, where they are most concentrated and where the terrain is favorable to high-speed armored maneuver, that the threat is most serious and the requirements for improved defense are the most urgent.

The Warsaw Pact's posture, strategy, and operational concepts do not necessarily imply plans for an early offensive against Western Europe. Soviet military power in Europe serves a variety of purposes including control over the nations of Eastern Europe, and — in Soviet eyes — deterring an attack by NATO on the Warsaw Pact. In the Soviet view, military power also has a major role in political relations between East and West. According to Soviet thinking, Soviet military power reduces the West's willingness to challenge Soviet political objectives and inhibits the West's ability to use its own military power for political purposes. The

Soviet Union believes its forces should be structured identically for the purposes of deterrence, political influence, or waging war. Consequently, the Soviet military posture supports its pursuit of political objectives without the actual use of force, to the degree that it successfully projects the image of a war-winning capability and appears to deny to adversaries the prospect of successful resistance. This military posture supports and is supported by such other facets of Soviet policy as proposals for "peace" and arms control.

We do not attempt to define with precision the circumstances which might impel the Soviet Union to accept the risks inherent in an attack on NATO. The Soviet Union appears most likely to initiate hostilities in reaction to the perception of a direct threat to its territory, its regime, its control over Eastern Europe, or other vital interests. In making such a decision the Soviet Union would be strongly influenced by a range of factors including: the political/military reliability of the Warsaw Pact, the degree of NATO cohesion, the prospects of success, and the military and political situation outside Europe. Such factors could constitute reasons to act or could restrain the Soviet Union from war.

Soviet military doctrine no longer asserts that war between East and West is inevitable, nor that any such war would inevitably become nuclear. Recent Soviet writings argue that the successful implementation of Soviet military strategy may allow a war to be kept conventional. Nonetheless, the Soviets recognize that any conflict between nuclear-armed opponents could escalate as one side or the other might seek to redress a deteriorating strategic situation.

Soviet strategy seeks to control outcomes. In Europe it focuses on preventing NATO from implementing its defense plans and in particular from having recourse to theater nuclear options. Soviet objectives in a war in Central Europe are strategic in character insofar as they require the destruction of the military potential of NATO, paralysis of NATO's theater nuclear capabilities, and occupation of NATO territory. Soviet military strategy, operational practices, and tactics have evolved in order to enhance Warsaw Pact capabilities to impose on NATO a Soviet-style campaign.

The preferred Soviet strategy for defeating NATO in Central Europe by conventional means emphasizes a short, swift campaign with a maximum use of surprise at the outset. NATO requires a period of warning in order to mobilize fully and deploy its forces in forward position. Early and effective mobilization by NATO would seriously complicate Soviet strategy and dim its prospects for a decisive victory. In the Soviet planners' view, a short, decisive campaign could catch NATO forces inadequately prepared and out of position, possibly outpace NATO release procedures for battlefield nuclear weapons, reduce potential problems concerning supply and the reliability of Soviet allies, and quickly confront the Alliance with the fateful risk of escalation to strategic nuclear war. Accordingly, Soviet strategy places high priority on adequate preparation of Warsaw Pact forces prior to the attack, and masking those preparations to the greatest possible extent from NATO.

Thus, Soviet strategy seeks to exploit NATO'S weaknesses and deny it the chance to make effective response to a Soviet offensive. It is based on the following principles:

- The achievement of strategic and tactical surprise, especially as to the specific time, locations, size, and character of an offensive operation.
- The imposition of the maximum shock against NATO defenses in the shortest amount of time, through a combination of superior numbers, air power, and firepower.
- The paralysis of NATO command and control and rear-area operations.
- The swift penetration of NATO's forward defenses followed by rapid advances along several axes deep into NATO territory to disrupt its defensive structure and deny NATO an effective response.
- The conduct of Warsaw Pact operations so as to allow a rapid transition to operations in a nuclear environment.
- The denial to NATO of the capacity for effective use of nuclear weapons by a combination of dispersal and continuous movement of Warsaw Pact forces, and the destruction of NATO nuclear capabilities.

Although these principles constitute the preferred Soviet strategy, Soviet forces are prepared to fight other types of campaigns. Soviet and other Warsaw Pact forces are equipped and trained to conduct conventional operations in a nuclear environment. The Soviet Union possesses an abundant war reserve, extensive stockpiles of military equipment and ammunition, and a large pool of military manpower. Moreover, Soviet military writings and exercises emphasize the need for flexibility in military planning in order to avoid a too rigid adherence to formal doctrine and strategy.

Soviet forces in general, but especially those in or near the Central Front, as well as some other Warsaw Pact formations, are being extensively modernized and restructured in order to meet the requirements of Soviet strategy against NATO. Among the most important qualitative changes in Soviet forces are:

- Increasing capability to conduct mobile, high-speed combat operations. Soviet forces possess firepower support systems of increased range and volume of fire; enlarged helicopter forces capable of operating with mobile ground formations; a more balanced divisional structure enabling both mechanized and armored divisions to undertake offensive operations; and improved logistical support for offensive forces.

- Increased capability to threaten NATO rear areas. New tactical aircraft of greater range and payloads are now operational and more are entering the inventory. Also Warsaw Pact Frontal Aviation has been reorganized to provide a concentrated "shock" capability in independent air operations. Additionally, the Soviets are deploying expanded warfare capabilities in heli-borne and airborne troops.

- Improved air defenses at all levels, imposing seriously enhanced obstacles to NATO's efforts to achieve effective air superiority.

- Massive investment in all forms of radio-electronic warfare for the purposes of paralyzing NATO command and control.

- Improved capabilities for theater nuclear warfare (the SS-20, 21, 22, 23, Backfire bomber and tactical aircraft).

The size of a Soviet offensive in Central Europe would depend heavily on whether Moscow chose to attack with forces in place, thereby maximizing the potential for strategic surprise, or sought to maximize its force superiority by mobilizing and deploying additional formations.

In the first case, the offensive would be conducted by two Fronts consisting of 19 forward-deployed Soviet divisions plus 11 additional divisions of the East German and Czech armies. (A Front in Soviet usage is roughly equivalent to two army groups). Such an attack would require from two to four days of visible preparation.

In the second case, the Warsaw Pact could deploy 90 and possibly up to 110 Warsaw Pact divisions in three Fronts with two or more Fronts in a second echelon. Of these, 59 or more would be Soviet divisions. Such a buildup would take approximately a month and provide NATO with a high degree of strategic warning.

The Soviet offensive is planned to be a highly integrated operation designed to assure the momentum of constant forward movement at pre-determined rates. It is based on attacks in waves by formations echeloned at each tactical level (i.e., battalion, regiment, and division) and oper-ational level (i.e., Army and Front). Under this method of attack, a de-pleted unit is completely replaced by a fresh unit and is itself withdrawn to the rear for renewal. The purpose of this offensive style is to maintain high pressure on the defender, to permit the deployment of overwhelming superiority at critical points along the battlefield, to enhance the ability of commanders to exploit breakthroughs, and to ensure a high degree of mobility and flexibility, at least at the operational level. The choice of how to allocate Warsaw Pact forces would depend on the depth and configura-tion of NATO defenses; the degree of surprise achieved; and the terrain.

Once combat started, the Warsaw Pact would seek to seize and retain the initiative by breaking through NATO forward defenses and thrusting forces into NATO rear areas. The direction, rate of advance, and momen-tum of Soviet tactical operations would be determined by a combination of the formation's pre-planned assignment and official norms and standards for successful completion of assigned tasks. Commitments of follow-on formations and reserves are explicitly defined in operational plans, al-though the actual course of the battle might result in changes in earlier directives. According to some projections, rates of advance for Warsaw Pact forces are planned to average as high as 50 kilometers a day during conventional operations and even higher in a nuclear environment. To achieve the requisite tempo of offensive operations, Warsaw Pact forces require close cooperation among all combat arms and adequate and sur-vivable command and control.

A recent Soviet innovation is the Operational Maneuver Group (OMG), designed for breakthrough operations to defeat NATO's strategy of Flexible Response and Forward Defense. The OMG is a specially se-lected unit of divisional strength assigned the task of rapidly penetrating NATO defenses on the heels of a breakthrough for the purpose of de-stabilizing the defensive line and destroying key targets, including com-mand and control centers, nuclear weapons, airfields, and supply depots. The objective of an OMG operation is to insert such a formation along each axis of a Front, behind NATO's forward defenses, on the first or second day of the offensive. While posing a potentially serious threat to NATO conventional defenses, the OMG concept is untested and would run counter to characteristic Soviet command and control practices.

In improving the Warsaw Pact's capability to conduct conventional operations, the Soviet Union has also continued to plan and deploy for the possible use of nuclear and chemical weapons. Soviet forces operate conventionally in a manner which would require relatively little transition in order to conduct operations in a nuclear or chemical environment. There is a substantial probability that if general nuclear release by NATO appeared likely, the Soviet Union would attempt to preempt this threat by massed nuclear strikes against key NATO nuclear and other targets. There is also a significant possibility that the Soviet Union would respond to even limited NATO first use by a Soviet theater-wide nuclear effort to destroy NATO's residual nuclear capability. Additionally, it is unclear whether the Soviet Union would risk a nuclear response by employing chemical weapons without also employing nuclear weapons.

Despite the substantial qualitative and quantitative improvements in Soviet and other Warsaw Pact forces over the past 15 years, Soviet planners still face severe uncertainties in planning a conventional offensive against NATO's Central Front.

- The most serious of these is whether the Warsaw Pact could achieve strategic surprise; otherwise NATO's forward defenses can be expected to be well manned and fully prepared.
- Second, there are questions concerning the quality and disposition of NATO's conventional forces and NATO's ability and willingness to use theater and battlefield nuclear weapons. This poses for the Soviet Union the problem of dealing with the uncertainties of escalation to nuclear exchanges.
- The Soviets must also be concerned that their forces have almost no experience in modern war and that their operational principles and weapons systems have not performed well in practice, for example, in the Middle East.
- Soviet military writings continually speak of the need for leadership, flexibility, and adequate command and control, and express dissatisfaction with capabilities in these areas.
- Also, planning for an offensive must consider the reliability of Soviet Warsaw Pact allies. Eastern Europe could constitute a weak link in Soviet capabilities, especially in case hostilities are extended. However, if the war is short and successful, political disaffection or

sabotage in Eastern Europe might not affect performance of Warsaw Pact allied armies or threaten Soviet supply lines.

Soviet decision-makers typically are calculating and cautious: they tend to avoid actions entailing serious risks which may get out of their control. Thus NATO can enhance deterrence by creating capabilities which magnify the uncertainties in the minds of Soviet leaders as to whether their strategy will work. In other words, deterrence may not require a capability to defeat the Warsaw Pact with certainty; it could be enough to deter if the NATO capability is seen to present unacceptable risks for the USSR.

By their nature, Soviet planned operations involve inherent elements of potential vulnerability:

- The highly pre-planned and rigid nature of Soviet offensive operations and their dependence on an uninterrupted forward flow of forces.
- The requirement for a swift victory.
- The reliance on adequate command and control in order both to ensure adherence to operational standards and norms, and to ensure close cooperation among all elements of the combined arms offensive.
- The dependence on lines of supply and communications westward from the USSR through Eastern Europe.
- The need to concentrate dispersed forces to effect breakthroughs, thereby offering potential high-value targets to NATO conventional and nuclear firepower.

III. THE SPECIFIC REQUIREMENTS FOR EFFECTIVE NATO CONVENTIONAL DEFENSE

The Soviet conventional military threat is serious and growing, but effective defense and deterrence are not beyond NATO's realistic capacity. In the previous section, we identified a number of vulnerabilities inherent in the Warsaw Pact doctrine and operational concept. The task of NATO is to develop its capacity to exploit these vulnerabilities. The need is not to match specific Soviet capabilities, but to deny them the operational possibilities on which any high confidence in rapid success must depend. In this section, we analyze the specific military missions which NATO must be able to perform for this purpose, and the military capabilities required to perform them. The next section will examine the means for doing so.

The nature of modern war in general and the specific character of the Warsaw Pact's force posture and doctrine require NATO conventional forces to be prepared to move rapidly from a peacetime posture to one of effective Forward Defense. NATO conventional forces must have the basic means, in adequate amounts, to sustain the intense, violent combat anticipated. Both the forces themselves and the NATO infrastructure must be sufficiently resilient, redundant, and survivable to withstand the shock of modern war at a level heretofore not experienced in Europe, and to maintain essential operations.

More specifically, NATO conventional forces must be able to perform five missions that stand out as critical for successful deterrence and defense. To be able to defeat an actual attack, NATO's conventional forces must be competent to perform these missions. To deter an attack, NATO's conventional forces must be at least strong enough to create for the Warsaw Pact planners a serious concern that they will be competent to do so. The five missions are: (A) countering the initial Warsaw Pact attack; (B) eroding enemy air power; (C) interdicting, attacking, and holding at risk the Warsaw Pact follow-on formations; (D) disrupting Warsaw Pact command, control and communications; and (E) ensuring secure, reliable and effective NATO command and control. Improvement in regard to each of these missions will reinforce NATO's capacity to perform the others.

Countering the Initial Warsaw Pact Attack

In order to improve its capability to counter the forward elements of a Warsaw Pact attack, NATO needs to accomplish three tasks.

(1) The first is to limit the likelihood and impact of surprise. NATO's peacetime deployment and state of readiness make it vulnerable to the Warsaw Pact's growing capability to initiate an unreinforced attack. Because of the inherent complexities, NATO intelligence cannot be certain to provide timely and unambiguous warning. NATO's political leaders must therefore be willing to authorize preparatory measures even in the face of some degree of ambiguity. By doing so they will provide NATO time both for alerting and deploying forces, and most important, for the preparation of their defenses. Furthermore a timely demonstration of

NATO's alertness and resolve will present the Warsaw Pact with uncertainties regarding the attainment of a swift victory. We note that the alerting of conventional forces could be less difficult politically than any visible increase of nuclear readiness.

NATO requires an integrated, theater-wide, all-weather capacity to acquire information and targets, together with a system for communications and data transmission that is resistant to Warsaw Pact electronic warfare measures. NATO also needs to improve the coordination of existing national reconnaissance assets. In both cases the objective is to coordinate all stages of the intelligence and warning function. Insofar as possible, these capabilities should be operated in peacetime in a manner consistent with wartime needs, so as to minimize the requirement for a change in command authority and operating procedures during a crisis.

To be able to respond to ambiguous warning, NATO requires response measures which are relatively cheap, repetitive, reversible, and non-provocative. Such measures might include heightened states of readiness for NATO tactical aircraft, dispersal of alternate command posts, and increases in reconnaissance activities and occasional low-level exercises, callable by the Supreme Allied Commander Europe.

(2) As a second task toward countering an initial attack, NATO must improve its capacity for target acquisition and data handling to ensure that adequate and accurate firepower is directed at critical targets in the close-battle area. Otherwise improving NATO firepower will not pay adequate dividends. In particular, this capability is needed to provide NATO with the means for the attrition and disruption of Soviet breakthrough operations. An adequate target-acquisition capability can also serve as an essential component of a surveillance and general intelligence capability. Focus on target acquisition rather than general battlefield surveillance would use resources most effectively.

NATO firepower will be a relatively scarce asset which cannot be wasted on low-value targets. An interoperable target acquisition and data-handling capability must be able to find and identify high-value Warsaw Pact targets, coordinate the information, and transmit it rapidly among the forces of different nations and services. In addition, such a system and its data-transmission elements must be resistant not only to direct electronic warfare but also, as far as feasible, to the electro-magnetic effects of nuclear blasts.

(3) The third task in the close-battle area is the neutralization of Warsaw Pact artillery. NATO forward-deployed forces, and particularly those

elements deployed in the covering-force area, are under increasing risk due to the massive growth in Warsaw Pact artillery and rocket inventories. These artillery and rocket concentrations are particularly threatening to those elements of NATO's forward defense which will have the task of countering Warsaw Pact armored breakthrough operations.

This task requires appropriate means for effective counter-battery fire (i.e., target acquisition, weapons delivery, area impact munitions) and measures to complicate Warsaw Pact targeting. NATO needs to prepare to conduct counter-battery fire at the very outset of a Warsaw Pact offensive, both to reduce the danger to NATO forces and also to act as a spoiler to complicate offensive operations. Specifically, there is a need for increased numbers of longer-range, improved, ground-based delivery systems, and multiple launch rocket systems in particular. Area impact munitions are available for such multiple launch rocket systems. NATO air power is likely to play an important role in performance of this task. Steps must be taken, however, to suppress the growing array of Warsaw Pact air defense systems (to be discussed below). For complicating Warsaw Pact targeting in forward areas, a combination of passive and active means is available. Concealment, mobility, deception, and electronic warfare are the most promising directions to pursue.

Attrition of Warsaw Pact Air Power

Warsaw Pact capabilities for offensive air operations and defense of its airspace against NATO air power continue to improve. NATO is unlikely to be able to counter the threat merely by adding air assets in large numbers. Therefore, NATO must identify and develop methods and capabilities which will multiply the effectiveness of available air power and impose high costs on Warsaw Pact air power.

Two approaches appear to meet the requirements for attrition of Warsaw Pact air power: (1) counter-air operations, and (2) enhanced NATO air defenses.

Counter-air operations seek to reduce the magnitude of the Warsaw Pact air threat. This can be done by large-scale and persistent attack on Pact airbases in order to reduce its capability to generate aircraft sorties. This offers the most effective means of defeating Warsaw Pact air power. Direct attacks on Warsaw Pact Main Operating Bases, particularly before the return of deployed aircraft, can force diversion to alternative airfields which are less well equipped, lack protective shelters, and have fewer

runways. On these alternative airfields, the greater vulnerability of Warsaw Pact aircraft could be exploited through attacks by manned NATO
aircraft. Together, these operations could materially reduce Warsaw Pact
sortie rates. The initial strikes on Warsaw Pact Main Operating Bases must
take place as an immediate response to the onset of a Warsaw Pact attack.
In order to defeat or destroy Warsaw Pact air defenses, NATO requires
improved stand-off weapons, fire-and-forget systems, and better electronic countermeasures.

At the same time, NATO must substantially improve its own air defenses. The existing missile defenses provide only partial coverage, particularly against longer-range Warsaw Pact aircraft and armed helicopters.
The most urgent need for NATO air defense is to improve air defense
management and interoperability. The internetting of fire units and control
centers, to provide real-time data-transmission capability, would not only
permit a better exploitation of available firepower but also enhance survivability. Airspace management must develop means to enable NATO
ground-based defenses to operate simultaneously and in the same space as
its air units.

Interdicting, Attacking and Holding at Risk
Warsaw Pact Follow-on Forces

Interdicting, attacking and holding at risk follow-on forces constitute
a part of NATO's Forward Defense. The delay and disruption thereby
imposed on the Warsaw Pact's offensive would reduce the scale and momentum of Warsaw Pact forces confronting NATO forward defenses.
Such interdiction requires deep attack against critical fixed targets, including river-crossing sites, transportation, logistical choke points, ammunition and fuel depots, airfields, air defense systems, and elements of Warsaw Pact command, control, and communications. Follow-on forces,
turned from mobile into stationary targets by being blocked behind choke
points close to the main battle area, offer the most lucrative targets. Such
deep attack aimed at the destruction of follow-on forces should be eval-
uated according to the primary criterion of where it can be done most
effectively, cheaply, and expeditiously.

In order to be able to perform such deep strikes against targets in
Eastern Europe, NATO requires the ability to identify and attack targets at
relatively long ranges (up to 300 kilometers beyond the battlefield). A
variety of delivery vehicles can serve the purpose, notably ballistic missiles and manned aircraft, discussed in Section IV below.

Disrupting Warsaw Pact Command, Control, and Communications

The rigidities of the Warsaw Pact's command structure and its reliance on absolute adherence to pre-planned norms and standards at the tactical level make the Warsaw Pact command, control, and communications (referred to by specialists as C^3) a potential vulnerability which NATO should seek to exploit. An effective NATO capacity to attack Warsaw Pact C^3 could leave Warsaw Pact commanders unsure and hesitant in regard to their ability to direct and coordinate forces, achieve and exploit breakthroughs, and maintain offensive air and ground operations at their planned rates of advance.

NATO requires an integrated concept of counter-C^3 operations. One component would be electronic measures to jam communications and surveillance systems. Another would be a capacity to disrupt divisional and Army headquarters, and control centers for air defenses and artillery fire. This requires the means to identify C^3 targets. Effective counter-C^3 would also be valuable for all other major missions.

Ensuring Secure, Reliable, and Effective NATO Command and Control

The Warsaw Pact has uniform organizational practices and procedures as well as equipment, on the Soviet model. NATO command and control must operate within a context of different national practices and styles. NATO, therefore, requires a common concept of command which would facilitate economy in communications, the delegation of authority, and coordination and consultation.

In addition, command, control and communications systems need to be improved to manage the immense volume of information which will flow to NATO commanders. Such systems should be oriented especially towards meeting the needs of lower-level combat formations for specific information, over and above the general requirements of higher command. It is vital that NATO communications systems be resistant to Warsaw Pact disruption efforts. NATO communications should not provide telltales for use by the Warsaw Pact in targeting NATO headquarters and communications centers. A variety of means should be employed to provide secure and survivable communications including concealment, reduced size and signatures of operating units, dispersal, redundancy, and hardening.

* * * * *

In sum, for effective deterrence and defense, NATO must be able in fact to perform its five critical missions and must be perceived by Warsaw Pact planners as able to do so. In their present condition and modes of use, NATO's conventional forces do not meet these criteria. For this reason, NATO now relies on the possible early use of its theater and battlefield nuclear arsenal. If, in some future crisis, the Soviet Union should be tempted to sudden aggression with its conventional forces, NATO might face a choice between defeat and the early use of nuclear weapons. In our judgment, NATO can upgrade its conventional forces sufficiently to perform the five critical missions and raise the nuclear threshold. In the next section, we analyze the ways of doing so.

IV. THE MEANS FOR ENHANCING NATO's CONVENTIONAL DEFENSIVE CAPABILITY

NATO can strengthen the capacity of its conventional forces to perform their five critical missions along two lines. One is by exploiting new advanced technology now available to provide target acquisition and more effective non-nuclear weapons. The other is through more effective use of the conventional forces now in place and under current procurement by applying new concepts and modes of operation. The improvements can be accomplished at a reasonable and acceptable cost.

New Advanced Technologies for Target Acquisition and Conventional Weapons

Advanced technologies for target acquisition and non-nuclear weapons offer the prospect of enhancing deterrence and reassurance and also of raising the nuclear threshold. In particular, they may provide more effective conventional means of performing certain tasks within the five critical missions.

Such new technologies can meet the requirements both for close-in battle and for striking Warsaw Pact forces in rear areas. Such systems and weapons can be located deep in NATO territory to reduce their possible vulnerability to preemptive attack.

Among the relevant technologies are: (1) area impact and guided conventional submunitions; (2) accurate means for delivering guided submunitions by surface-launched or air-launched non-nuclear missiles and other stand-off weapons; and (3) near real-time techniques for surveillance and target acquisition. In combination, these technologies could be almost as effective as theater or battlefield nuclear weapons for such purposes as:

— suppression of high-value fixed targets (airfields, command and control sites, supply depots, etc.);
— creation of choke points to impede Warsaw Pact forces;
— disruption of mobile formations;
— high rates of attrition for combat formations.

These technologies would be especially effective for the performance of three of the five critical missions for NATO forces: (a) attrition of air power; (b) attacking Warsaw Pact follow-on forces; and (c) countering the initial Warsaw Pact attack.

Attrition of Warsaw Pact Air Power

The needed capability for attrition of Warsaw Pact air power would be provided by medium-range conventional strike systems, preferably non-nuclear ballistic missiles, with a capacity to put at risk fixed targets deep in Warsaw Pact territory. Properly used, these could significantly reduce the threat from Warsaw Pact air power by their capacity to suppress air-bases and inflict losses on ground-based aircraft. This would entail further attrition by forcing surviving aircraft to operate from less capable and well-protected Dispersed Operating Bases which would be vulnerable to NATO attack. The attack on Main Operating Bases must be launched in immediate response to Warsaw Pact airstrikes. For reasons of timing and ability to penetrate, ballistic missiles are especially suited for this task. Attacks on Dispersed Operating Bases would occur over a period of one or two days and could be performed by manned aircraft which at these bases would face reduced Warsaw Pact air defenses.

Establishing and maintaining NATO air superiority over its own terri-tory, which is essential for the successful holding of ground, will require increased emphasis in NATO planning and deployment on air defense with both aircraft and missiles. Missile and air action against Warsaw Pact airbases and ground-based aircraft would, however, make a major and in-dispensable contribution toward such air superiority.

The Interdiction and Disruption of Warsaw Pact Follow-on Forces

The new technologies would provide a capability for attacks on both fixed targets and mobile formations behind the immediate battlefront.

Attacks on fixed targets could seriously disrupt and delay a conventional offensive by interdicting key logistical lines of communications, railheads, highway junctions, communications centers, and Warsaw Pact headquarters. These weapons could also create high-density targets by forcing mobile formations to mass behind interdicted choke points created by area munitions. The Warsaw Pact's need to cross natural barriers such as the Elbe, Saale, and Moldau Rivers, and further back, the Oder and Neisse, would create especially lucrative targets. Destruction of Warsaw Pact command, control, and communications assets could exploit the rigidities in Warsaw Pact attack planning.

Follow-on formations of both the first strategic echelons and the second strategic echelon also would be targeted. The objective would be to supplement the general attrition battle and reduce the forces confronting NATO forward defenses to manageable levels. This threat to follow-on formations could also disrupt Soviet strategy by denying to the Warsaw Pact the capability of massing overwhelming superiority on critical breakthrough sectors and exploiting breakthroughs if and when they occur.

The new technologies to provide these capabilities consist of a combination of long-range ground-launched and air-launched weapons armed with non-nuclear guided submunitions and area denial munitions. Advanced technology could also provide the necessary capability for real-time battlefield surveillance and targeting in order to acquire, identify, and track Warsaw Pact formations.

Countering the Initial Warsaw Pact Attack

The new technologies can give effective support to NATO forward defenses by the selective engagement of forward Warsaw Pact formations. A shorter range non-nuclear missile system, perhaps utilizing multiple-launch techniques, would furnish the needed capability. It would provide a capacity to deliver intensive firepower directly against forces confronting NATO defenses, supplementing existing capabilities. This added firepower could help to offset current Warsaw Pact advantages in numbers of tanks, armored combat vehicles, and artillery.

For the immediate future, NATO effectiveness could be dramatically increased against Warsaw Pact armored ground forces (and unsheltered Warsaw Pact aircraft) by equipping appropriate aircraft with modern dispensers and submunitions of a type which the Federal Republic of Germany has recently ordered into production. At a later date, when terminally guided submunitions become available, current estimates indicate that air force effectiveness against such targets could be increased by factors of up to 30 or more.

The new technologies are not merely in the realm of ideas and hopes. Many of them have been tested; some are being tested; and a few are even in production in the Federal Republic of Germany, France, and the United Kingdom, as well as in the United States. For political, economic, and technological reasons, close and sustained cooperation among the NATO countries in producing these advanced weapons is indispensable to the accomplishment of the program.

The new weapons technologies here recommended could use current infrastructures already in place on the Central Front, including bases and trained and organized personnel. There are possible trade-offs between the highly effective new technologies here recommended and other less effective conventional weapons within the current plans for procurement of several of the NATO countries. In due course, the reduced dependence on a possible use of theater and battlefield nuclear weapons could lead to a reduction in NATO's inventory of short-range nuclear weapons. Over and above its political and strategic significance, this reduction could have manpower and budgetary benefits.

We calculate that through decisive funding and imaginative, stable, and efficient planning and execution of procurement, the new technologies designed for the suppression of Warsaw Pact airbases and the interdiction of choke points could be acquired and deployed in 1986; and that those designed for the disruption of Warsaw Pact follow-on forces could be made effectively available by 1988.

The choice of specific systems to perform new missions will raise a number of questions which will need resolution. It must be recognized that a number of families of weapons currently in use both by NATO and by the Warsaw Pact already have or can have dual capability; and a number of components and technologies are common to both nuclear and conventional delivery systems. Dual capable aircraft, and more recently, cruise missiles, have already raised questions about blurring the distinction between conventional and nuclear systems. NATO will need to consider whether or not it should convert current nuclear missile systems to non-nuclear roles or develop separate systems.

Acquisition of capabilities to perform the missions outlined above would diminish the Warsaw Pact's prospects for implementing its optimal strategy and thereby winning a swift victory, and would raise the nuclear threshold. In particular, the technologies we have discussed would threaten the Warsaw Pact with high losses to valuable mobile combat formations at the forward edge of the battlefield, destroy the cohesion and power of Warsaw Pact air forces, and cause disruption in the offensive by interdiction of critical targets deeper in enemy territory.

For effective deterrence, as we have already stated, it is not necessary for these new NATO conventional capabilities to be perceived by the Soviet Union's leadership as insurmountable. It is enough that they could create grave uncertainty as to whether the Soviet forces could achieve and maintain the uninterrupted forward movement at predetermined rates contemplated in the pre-planned pattern of Soviet offensive operations.

More Effective Use of Conventional Forces
Now in Place and Under Procurement

As indicated in Section III, NATO's conventional capabilities can and should be strengthened by readjusting forces in place or under current procurement. Realistically, in the absence of a crisis call-up, NATO cannot count on increasing manpower in place. Moreover, for the immediate future in several NATO countries, economic conditions as well as domestic debate concerning the scope and nature of NATO's defense needs may even make it hard to maintain existing commitments. We believe, however, that the necessary improvement can be accomplished through a progressive implementation of corrective measures. A choice of the priorities to be observed will require a careful judgment between measures which are likely to have the maximum operational pay-off and those which can most easily and readily be implemented. The factors affecting this judgment will vary among different NATO nations.

NATO has been aware for some time of the need for such improvement and recently has undertaken some of the corrective measures. The rate and scale of improvement have been limited, however, by political and organizational impediments. Current popular anxieties concerning theater nuclear weapons and increasing recognition of the urgency of rectifying the imbalance in conventional forces may facilitate more rapid and extensive progress. This would be especially timely in regard to so high a priority need as enhanced interoperability, which could have a constructive effect across the entire spectrum of NATO operations, entailing changes in current procedures for planning, training, operations, command, and support. We have already emphasized the need for improved target acquisition and data handling, and for strengthened links between them and weapons controllers. We also draw attention to the need to remedy deficiencies in weapons stocks; to increase the number of direct fire anti-armor weapons; to prepare for the use of civilian assets for a quick execution of barrier plans; to exploit available reserve manpower more effectively; and to improve cooperation between German territorial forces and NATO forces.

We have stressed above the opportunities to exploit with advanced munitions such natural barriers as those created by major rivers. For this purpose, to the extent not already done, crossing points and bridging sites should be surveyed and targeted for destruction by weapons systems such as medium-range non-nuclear missiles as discussed above. Hostile follow-on forces required to mass behind such barriers would also offer targets suitable for attack by manned NATO aircraft equipped to deliver scattered mines effective against armored and soft-skin vehicles.

Implementation of these measures would not remove the necessity for NATO to retain a nuclear capability. The threat of nuclear weapons would still be important in compelling Warsaw Pact forces to operate in a "nuclear scared" mode and in deterring Soviet theater nuclear strikes. However, reliance on nuclear weapons for the execution of tactical missions in support of NATO forward defenses, or for the attrition of Warsaw Pact air power — with the attendant risk of nuclear responses — could be lessened or even avoided. In addition, NATO would reduce its reliance on possible early use of nuclear weapons to defeat Warsaw Pact forces attempting to achieve the penetration of NATO forward defenses at the early stages of an offensive.

Arms Control and Diplomacy

As already stated, our proposals for improving NATO's conventional military position are consistent with efforts for arms control, confidence building, and similar measures. Improved NATO conventional forces, effective arms control, and carefully directed diplomacy can be mutually supporting toward their common objectives of defusing tensions and maintaining political stability. Public support for defense will be enhanced if it is clear that serious arms control initiatives are also being pursued.

Measures for arms control and confidence building might also contribute to a reduction in the risk of military surprise. The 1975 Helsinki Agreements on prior notification of, and observers at, maneuvers involving more than 25,000 personnel are an example. Accordingly, we support the proposal for a NATO-Warsaw Pact standing committee to exchange information, especially in crises; to discuss questions concerning the respective force postures; and to explore other possible measures to promote stability. Such measures could not in themselves prevent surprise attack, but failure to observe them could in some circumstances furnish some warning of imminent danger.

Costs

Mindful of the budgetary constraints within which NATO defense planning must go forward, we have examined the costs of the advanced non-nuclear weapons technologies which we now recommend. Given the inherent complexities and uncertainties, we have made our calculations within a range of possible error, but we believe them to be realistic and meaningful for indicating the scale of expenditure involved.

For this purpose we have sought to estimate the acquisition and operating costs of the new advanced weapons systems here recommended over a ten-year period for the NATO countries as a group. The supporting paper on this topic (in Part IV of the book) makes a *minimum* estimate of under $10 billion. We consider it prudent to base our calculations on a median estimate of $20 billion, recognizing that the actual costs could be 50 percent higher or lower.

Within this aggregate estimate, drawing on the supporting paper, we offer a breakdown of some of the principal components on an essentially illustrative basis, using the same wide range of possible costs in each case. For the suppression of the Warsaw Pact's 30 to 40 Main Operating Bases on which their ground-attack air units are maintained, and the interdiction of some 100 choke points, we have assumed a requirement of some 900 non-nuclear missiles. The cost of the missiles, which we take to be approximately $2 to $6 million each, and the supplementary costs for missile shelters on existing air bases and operating personnel, over a ten-year period, amount by our estimate to some $3 to $7 billion. For the interdiction of follow-on echelons, we assume a requirement of some 5,000 non-nuclear missiles with appropriate "smart" warheads. The estimated cost of these missiles together with the cost of surveillance and targeting for the Central Region is approximately $6 to $18 billion. For other aspects of the missions previously described, particularly the close-in battle, we assume a requirement of some 1,000 salvos of multiple launch rocket systems with terminally guided warheads at an estimated cost of $200 to

$600 million. We also include a requirement of $1 to $3 billion in related research, development, and testing.

Aside from the new technologies, we believe that the improvements in the present posture of NATO's conventional forces by readjustments suggested above can largely be accommodated within the current NATO norm of an annual real growth of 3 percent in defense spending. Whatever increases may be required for such readjustments, together with the costs of the new technologies, could be accommodated within a level of expenditure about 1 percent higher than the present NATO commitments, if such commitments are sustained and extended beyond 1986.

Taken together, the readjustments of NATO conventional forces now in place and under current procurement through new concepts and modes of operation, and the new conventional target acquisition and weapons technologies here recommended, would provide NATO with more effective defense and deterrence through a conventional capability to perform its five critical defensive missions. They would steadily reduce the degree of NATO's present dependence on a possible early use of nuclear weapons.

We recognize that political pressures generated by the current economic situation in the NATO countries make it difficult to achieve even the present NATO commitments. Nevertheless, we reaffirm our conviction that even at the top of the range the estimated costs of the new programs we now propose are moderate in relation to the overall level of NATO current defense budgets and in relation to the benefits from raising the nuclear threshold, enhancing the deterrent, and strengthening the self-confidence of the Alliance.

V. SUMMARY OF CONCLUSIONS

In this Report, we have addressed:

First, the political and strategic significance of the current imbalance in conventional military capabilities in Europe between NATO and the Warsaw Pact, and the consequent dependence by NATO on possible early use of nuclear weapons.

Second, the significance of the present Soviet conventional forces in Europe and the Soviet doctrine for using them.

Third, the specific needs for strengthening NATO's conventional defensive capability.

Fourth, the means for enhancing NATO's conventional capability at reasonable and acceptable costs and in such a manner as to enhance deterrence, raise the nuclear threshold, reassure the NATO peoples, and contribute to political stability.

Our conclusions can be summarized as follows:

The Political and Strategic Significance of the Present Imbalance in Conventional Military Capability in Europe between NATO and the Warsaw Pact

1. The central purpose of the North Atlantic Alliance is to maintain peace and political stability in the North Atlantic Treaty area. To do so, the Alliance must assure its members against aggression and against intimidation or manipulation based on the military power of the Soviet Union.

2. To accomplish its central purpose, NATO must have defensive military forces capable of deterring aggression and intimidation in ways that can reassure its own people and do not augment instability. Deterrence and reassurance should be pursued as twin objectives.

3. NATO's objectives are gravely threatened by a serious imbalance between its conventional defensive military capability and the conventional military forces of the Soviet Union and its Warsaw Pact allies. In some future crisis this imbalance might tempt the Soviet Union to aggression with its conventional forces. If NATO should be unable to repel such an aggression with its own conventional forces, NATO could be forced to choose between defeat and the use of its nuclear weapons.

4. We accept that NATO should maintain its doctrine of Flexible Response, which calls for an initial resistance against aggression with conventional weapons but reserves a capacity to use nuclear weapons. Within this doctrine, NATO should move promptly to upgrade its conventional capability in Europe and "raise the nuclear threshold," i.e., make it practicable to defer as long as feasible, and if possible prevent, a situation in which NATO might be obliged to face a decision on the use of its nuclear weapons.

5. The upgrading of conventional defensive forces is compatible with measures for arms control and confidence building. Together, they can help greatly to promote political stability and reduce the risk of war.

The Significance of the Soviet Union's Conventional Forces in Europe and its Doctrine for Using Them

6. With strategic nuclear parity, the main threat to peace and to NATO is the offensive potential of the large and steadily increasing Soviet and Warsaw Pact conventional capabilities in Europe, governed by a strategy and operational concept that emphasize surprise, speed, intensive fire-power, and numerical superiority. It is in Central Europe that the threat is most serious and the need for improved NATO defensive capability most urgent.

7. The Soviet Union regards its military power as a primary factor in a variety of instruments which it seeks to use in a combined and mutually supporting arrangement to accomplish its objectives. It structures its military forces identically for the purposes of deterrence, political influence, psychological maneuver, or waging war.

8. The Soviet strategy and doctrine emphasize a short, decisive offensive and call for constant pressure through an intense initial attack, supplemented by follow-on forces intended to provide momentum for constant forward movement at predetermined rates. Soviet military planners face serious uncertainties, however, concerning their capacity to achieve their objectives.

9. The Soviet concept and plan of operations entail inherent vulnerabilities which NATO can exploit for defense. These relate to the Soviet need for achieving strategic surprise; the highly predetermined and rigid nature of the Soviet planned offensive operations and their dependence on an uninterrupted forward flow of forces; the need for a swift victory; dependence on long lines of supply and communications through Eastern Europe; the vulnerable targets arising from the Soviet necessity to concentrate forces in order to seek breakthroughs.

The Need for Enhancing NATO's Conventional Defensive Capability

10. NATO needs a conventional capacity adequate to deter and defeat a Soviet conventional military threat. This can be based on exploiting vulnerabilities.

11. NATO must adhere to the present doctrine of Forward Defense. The geographical distribution of NATO's peoples and the destructiveness of modern weapons preclude any policy of deliberately trading territory for time.

12. Five specific missions stand out as critical for successful defense and deterrence by NATO. These missions are: (A) countering an initial Warsaw Pact attack; (B) eroding Warsaw Pact air power; (C) holding at risk and attacking Warsaw Pact follow-on formations; (D) disrupting Warsaw Pact command and control; and (E) ensuring secure, reliable, and effective NATO command and control. It will be necessary to disrupt Warsaw Pact air power within hours and halt the initial ground assault and disrupt the forward flow of Warsaw Pact reinforcements within a few days.

13. The needed improvements in NATO's conventional capability can be accomplished within the constraints imposed by fiscal, political, and strategic necessities for setting priorities and making choices within the NATO countries.

The Means for Enhancing NATO's Conventional Military Capabilities

14. It is feasible for NATO to upgrade its conventional defensive capability to the degree needed for an actual and perceived capability of performing the five critical missions.

15. The upgrading can be accomplished through (A) new advanced target acquisition and conventional weapons technologies that are realistically available; and (B) an improvement of the conventional forces now in place and under procurement through new concepts and modes of operation.

16. The improvement in the effectiveness of NATO conventional forces can be accomplished through a progressive implementation of corrective measures. In recent years, NATO has undertaken some of the required measures but there is a need for more rapid and extensive progress. Among these measures, a high priority should be given to greater interoperability among NATO forces through changes in current procedures for planning, training, operations, command, and support.

17. New advanced technologies for target acquisition and conventional weapons can provide a far more effective conventional means than is now available for carrying out NATO's critical defensive missions. These include area impact and guided conventional submunitions; accurate delivery means for guided submunitions by surface-launch or airlaunch non-nuclear missiles and by other stand-off weapons; and techniques for near real-time surveillance and target acquisition. These new technologies would be particularly useful for the attrition of Warsaw Pact air power; interdicting and disrupting Warsaw Pact follow-on forces; and

helping to counter the initial Warsaw Pact attack by the selective engagement of forward Warsaw Pact formations. In addition, they can greatly enhance the effectiveness of NATO aircraft against Warsaw Pact armored ground forces by equipping the aircraft with modern dispensers and submunitions.

18. These advanced conventional technologies have been designed; many have been tested and others are being tested; and a few are already in production in the Federal Republic of Germany, France, and the United Kingdom, as well as in the United States. We calculate that the new technologies to provide a capability to suppress Warsaw Pact air bases and interdict Warsaw Pact choke points could be acquired and deployed by 1986. Those that would provide a capability for the disruption of Warsaw Pact follow-on forces could be made effectively available by 1988.

19. For political, economic, and technological reasons, close and sustained cooperation among the NATO countries in producing advanced weapons is indispensable to the accomplishment of the program.

20. In the development of advanced conventional technologies, questions will arise affecting the choice of specific weapons systems to perform new missions.

21. We have calculated costs within a wide range of possible error. Nevertheless, we believe our estimates to be realistic and meaningful for indicating the general scale of expenditure required. We estimate that the costs of procuring and operating the new target acquisition and conventional weapons systems here recommended over a ten-year period could amount to about $20 billion (with a possible variation of 50 percent higher or lower) for the NATO countries as a group.

22. These costs, together with those entailed by paragraph 16, could be accommodated within a level of expenditure approximately 1 percent higher than the current NATO norm of 3 percent annual real growth in defense spending, if that norm is sustained and extended after 1986, as we believe it should be.

23. While we recognize that certain NATO countries face political and economic problems in meeting even their present NATO commitments, we are convinced that the costs of the new programs we now propose are moderate in relation to the overall current NATO defense budgets. They are fully justified by the benefits from raising the nuclear threshold and fostering political stability.

PART II

THE SOVIET THREAT IN THE 1980s

How would the USSR plan to use its forces in case of an offensive against the NATO Central Front? What would be its weak points or vulnerabilities which might be exploited to disrupt or counter it? Those were the questions considered by the Workshop on the Soviet Threat.

The members of the Workshop had available three supporting papers — one by Hannes Adomeit, a second by Christopher N. Donnelly, and a third by Ennis C. Whitehead. This Part contains the Report of the Workshop and the supporting papers by Adomeit and Donnelly.

WORKSHOP MEMBERS

Dr. Hannes Adomeit (Author)

Staff, Stiftung Wissenschaft und Politik, Ebenhausen; author of *Soviet Risk Taking and Crisis Behavior*. Formerly: Lecturer, Institute of Soviet and Eastern European Studies (University of Glasgow); Deputy Director, Center for International Relations, Queen's University (Kingston, Ontario).

Professor Robert R. Bowie (Chairman)

Guest Scholar, Brookings Institution; Dillon Professor Emeritus of International Affairs, Harvard University. Formerly: Director, Center for International Affairs, Harvard University; Director of Policy Planning, State Department; Deputy Director (Estimates), Central Intelligence Agency.

Mr. Christopher N. Donnelly (Author)

Director, Soviet Studies Research Centre, Royal Military Academy Sandhurst; specialist in Soviet defence.

Colonel Charles R. Fox (SHAPE Observer)

Colonel, U.S. Air Force; Deputy Assistant Chief of Staff for Intelligence at SHAPE.

General Andrew J. Goodpaster

General, United States Army (Ret.). Formerly: Commander in Chief, United States Forces in Europe and Supreme Allied Commander Europe (NATO); Superintendent, U.S. Military Academy.

Mr. Daniel Gouré (Rapporteur)

Senior Associate, Jeffrey Cooper Associates Inc.; Consultant on Space Issues to the BDM Corporation; Ph.D. Candidate, Soviet Studies Department, Johns Hopkins University, School of Advanced International Studies.

Air Vice-Marshal W. J. Herrington

Air Vice-Marshal, Royal Air Force (Ret.), Director of Service Intelligence. Formerly: Senior Directing Staff, Royal College of Defence Studies; Defence Attaché Paris; Air Operations Directorate, Ministry of Defence.

Colonel Reinhold Heuermann

Colonel (Ret.); Engineer in electronics. Formerly: Chief of General Situation and Forces Comparison Branch, Military Intelligence Production Division, German Intelligence Service (BND); Intelligence Division, International Military Staff, NATO Military Committee; Armed Forces Staff of Ministry of Defense (Warsaw Pact economy, armaments technology, logistics).

Dr. David Holloway

Department of Politics, University of Edinburgh. Formerly: Guest Scholar, Cornell University.

Colonel Guenther Lehmann

Colonel (Ret.). Formerly: Deputy Assistant Director Intelligence, NATO; Chief, Warsaw Pact Forces Branch of Intelligence, Ministry of Defense, Bonn; Headquarters Allied Forces Central Europe.

Professor Marshall Shulman

Professor of International Relations, and Director, W. Averell Harriman Institute of Advanced Study on the Soviet Union, Columbia University. Formerly: Special Advisor on Soviet Affairs to the Secretary of State.

Lieutenant General Charles J. Simmons

Lieutenant General, United States Army (Ret.); Consultant. Formerly: Commander 3rd Armored Division and Deputy Commander in Chief, United States Army Europe.

Major General Ennis C. Whitehead (Author)

Director of Analysis, Burdeshaw Associates. Formerly: command experience with tank and armored forces in Korea, Vietnam and several tours in West Germany; service with Joint Chiefs of Staff in Washington, D.C. and in intelligence in DIA; NSA abroad; and NIO for General Purpose Forces in CIA.

Professor Carroll L. Wilson

Director, European Security Study (ESECS), Mitsui Professor Emeritus in Problems of Centemporary Technology, Massachusetts Institute of Technology. Formerly: Director of the Workshop on Alternative Energy Strategies (WAES) and World Coal Study (WOCOL); Wartime Executive Assistant to Director of Office for Scientific Research and Development; General Manager, U.S. Atomic Energy Commission.

Supporting Papers:

1. Hannes Adomeit, *The Political Rationale of Soviet Military Capabilities and Doctrine*.
2. Christopher N. Donnelly, *Soviet Operational Concepts in the 1980s*.
3. Ennis C. Whitehead, *Warsaw Pact Threat in Central Europe*.

The Soviet Threat in the 1980s

The mission of the Workshop on the Soviet Threat was to examine and assess the Soviet threat to Europe in the 1980s. In order to provide subsequent workshops with sufficient insight into Soviet military policy and planning, the participants described and analyzed the central factors that would bear upon a Soviet decision to go to war, the Soviet military posture in Europe, and the character of Soviet military operations following the outbreak of hostilities. It was evident from the earliest discussion that to describe the Soviet threat solely in terms of gross military capabilities or Soviet operational planning would be inadequate for the purpose of conveying the complex nature of Soviet decision-making for war in Europe. Soviet strategy, posture of forces, and tactical operations were discussed both in the broader context of political-military doctrine and objectives as defined by Soviet leaders, and in the context of Soviet views of the utility of variegated military power.

Rather than simple quantification or technical descriptions, this report seeks to characterize the threat in terms of its operational features, strengths, and vulnerabilities. The use of static numerical comparisons does not adequately encompass the character of the Soviet threat nor illuminate its particular vulnerabilities. Focusing on NATO's quantitative inferiority to the Warsaw Pact obscures the existence of qualitative offsets and all too readily guides military planning in the direction of methods for reducing gross force imbalances. A fundamental conclusion of this Workshop report is that NATO can best bolster its conventional deterrent by concentrating on defeating Soviet strategy, rather than on simply attriting Soviet forces.

Whether arising from aggressive designs or motivated by defensive interests, a Warsaw Pact decision to go to war with NATO would undoubtedly be realized through some sort of offensive operations. It is difficult to define precisely the circumstances or rationale which would impel the Soviet Union to accept the enormous risks inherent in a major conventional offensive on NATO's Central Region. Such an event is possibly the least likely threat confronting NATO today. Threats against NATO's flanks, sea lanes, or vital interests elsewhere, which may be more plausible, could be catalysts for a confrontation in the Central Region. Nevertheless a central offensive would be more serious.

MILITARY POWER AND SOVIET INTENTIONS

Soviet military power in Europe serves a number of purposes and responds to a number of imperatives: strategic, political, offensive, and internal. The most effective Soviet military posture is one which projects the image of the capability to use military power successfully and thereby denies an adversary any expectation of victory or successful resistance. Such a posture provides an inherent high-confidence deterrent, serves to restrain fissiparous tendencies within Eastern Europe, and can influence the political relationship between East and West. The successful enhancement (qualitative or quantitative) of Soviet military capabilities has, in Soviet eyes, changed the military balances which, in turn, influence international relations and increase Soviet freedom of action. According to Soviet thinking, the loss by NATO and the U.S. of their military superiority has reduced their willingness to challenge Soviet vital interests and inhibited their ability to use their military capabilities as a political instrument.

Though the posture of Soviet forces in Europe is a reflection of the kind of war the Soviets believe they will have to fight, this is not seen by Moscow as limiting the political utility of military power. The Soviet Union does not believe that its forces should be structured differently for the purposes of deterrence, political influence, or waging war. A serious capacity to wage war is viewed as an extremely credible deterrent posture. Such a posture would be desired by both sides in the event of war. So it is logical in Soviet thinking, and not contrary to deterrence rationales, to deploy such a posture in peacetime.

Thus the first threat to confront NATO is "the threat of force." Soviet military strengths can provide a means for political intimidation of NATO not only in peacetime, but in a crisis and even sometimes during hostilities. The Soviet military machine has been structured and modernized with an eye to restricting NATO's options to counter the threat of force — or the use of force. And it should be remembered that the character of the Soviet political system, and in particular its making of foreign policy, may permit the use of the threat of force without risks equal to those faced by the West.

The ongoing Soviet modernization of its conventional forces in Europe places additional pressures on NATO's conventional and theater nuclear forces to carry the burden of deterring Soviet aggressiveness in Europe. NATO's strategy of Flexible Response is increasingly constrained by Soviet superiority in conventional and theater nuclear forces. A particular objective of the Soviet military buildup and political pressure on NATO is to make NATO reliance on nuclear weapons less credible and, in the event of war, to make a NATO nuclear response more problematic.

The Soviet Union would prefer to achieve its objectives by peaceful means (including the threat of war). For what objectives would it be willing to accept the risks of war? That is a central issue. How does it evaluate the risk of war versus the risks from not acting and thereby deferring or abandoning its objectives?

A Soviet attack on NATO out of the blue is extremely unlikely. It was the view of the Workshop that the Soviet Union would be most likely to initiate hostilities in the event it believed war to be inevitable or in response to what it perceived as a direct threat from the West to its vital interests. These vital interests were identified as: (1) the security of the territory of the Soviet Union; (2) the Soviet position in Eastern Europe — including the stability of the Warsaw Pact; and (3) Soviet access to areas of vital concern. It is true, however, that war in Europe could break out unexpectedly as a result of superpower confrontations external to the region (e.g., in the Middle East).

Many circumstances would influence both the Soviet decision to employ forces against NATO and the character of its military actions. These factors include the state of the Soviet Bloc, the degree of NATO cohesion, and the military and political environments outside NATO.

As for the state of the Bloc, large-scale insurrection in Eastern Europe might cause the Soviet Union to use military force against NATO if it felt NATO was about to intervene. In the Soviet view their action would be one of preempting an attack by the West. For others it would be an an aggressive move cloaked by propaganda as a defense stance. The questionable reliability of some or all of its Eastern European allies could complicate the Soviet decision.

The permeability of geopolitical membranes suggests increasing possibilities for conflicts in one region to expand into others. For example, conflict elsewhere in the world might lead to increased Soviet military activities on the Continent, perhaps for the purpose of immobilizing NATO's strategic reserves. These activities, in turn, could result in a crisis in Europe. Increased NATO preparedness might also precipitate a Soviet military move in Central Europe.

It seems clear that the Soviet Union now makes and will continue to make aggressive political use of its military power. The further growth of that power and continuance of the adverse trends in the NATO-Warsaw Pact military balance cannot but weaken deterrence, strengthen Soviet political influence, and possibly increase the likelihood of that event against which the Alliance was expressly founded.

SOVIET DOCTRINE AND STRATEGY: BASIC GUIDELINES

Soviet military doctrine encompasses the official State view of the nature of future war, the preparations undertaken for war, the organization and preparation of the armed forces, and the methods of conducting war. In Soviet thinking, war is an instrument of State policy to be employed when it best serves the objectives of the State.

Soviet doctrine initially viewed an East-West war for decisive purposes as the ultimate clash of Capitalism and Socialism from which only one emerges. As such it would be total war, inevitably involving strategic nuclear weapons. However, Soviet doctrine no longer views war between East and West as inevitable — this change due primarily to the increase in Soviet military power, particularly strategic nuclear power. And because of changes in NATO doctrine, in particular the strategy of Flexible Response (established in NATO Military Committee document MC 14/3), the Soviet Union was faced with an expanded range of NATO military responses to extant Soviet threats. As a result, Soviet doctrine now encompasses the possibility of greater flexibility and a wide range of options in conflicts with the West. It reflects uncertainty about the ability to limit or control escalation in case nuclear weapons are used.

Soviet strategic objectives in Europe, in military terms, are broadly:

- To neutralize the West's strategic option by
  — improvements in their own systems;
  — political pressure and propaganda;
  — decoupling the tactical theater option;
  — arms control.
- To paralyze, neutralize or destroy NATO's theater nuclear capabilities by
  — political pressure and propaganda;
  — a balance of nuclear force in their favor, e.g., the SS-20 mobile missile system with three warheads;
  — military preparedness for a conventional phase of the war involving air power, diversionary forces, helicopter assault, sabotage, ground forces;
  — the use of their own preemptive nuclear strikes against NATO if required.
- To destroy NATO forces in Western Europe as rapidly as possible before they can be reinforced, thus to avoid a possible stalemate in the land battle which might then escalate to nuclear war, might have an adverse effect on the Warsaw Pact allies, might be a temptation to the Chinese.
- To occupy NATO territory in the Central Front.

The Soviets regard nuclear weapons as war-fighting weapons and thus as part of both NATO's and the Warsaw Pact's combat capability. At the same time, they regard them as instruments of terrific destruction the use of which carries with it great uncertainties and risks. Soviet writings show that they may contemplate the use of tactical nuclear weapons at any stage of a general war — at the outset to achieve surprise and an instant change of force in their favor; during the battle to break down enemy resistance or maintain the momentum of the advance; to preempt NATO's use of weapons as outlined in NATO strategy; or not at all.

The Soviets have stated on numerous occasions that they would not be the first to use such weapons. It is clear that they believe it would be difficult to control escalation once the weapons have been used, and therefore they would hope to win without recourse to the nuclear option. In the Soviet view the ability to control the course and outcome of a conflict employing nuclear weapons is, at best, uncertain. The Soviets seek to reduce the uncertainty by managing the degree of freedom of the threat, i.e., NATO's nuclear forces. The risks from a failure to anticipate an enemy's nuclear attack or destroy his nuclear forces is high. There is also the danger of escalation, especially in view of the U.S. commitment to defend NATO Europe with strategic weapons, if necessary. Therefore, the Warsaw Pact would seek, to the extent possible, to reduce these risks through a short, swift conventional campaign. Neutralization or destruction of NATO's nuclear means during the conventional stage of war would be a high priority.

But if they decided to use nuclear weapons, then, according to their military writings and public statements, they would use them on a massive scale against NATO nuclear forces, airfields, headquarters and ground targets. Whether they would in fact behave in this manner is something which cannot be determined with certainty in advance.

In the event nuclear release by NATO appears likely, whether in limited or large numbers, there is substantial probability but not a certainty that the Soviet Union would attempt to preempt NATO use of nuclear weapons. There is a similar likelihood, but again not a certainty, that the Warsaw Pact would respond to NATO's initial use, even a demonstration use, by a massive counterblow.

A European war with an initial conventional phase — a possibility now accepted by Soviet doctrine and strategy — is the most desirable form of conflict with NATO, from the viewpoint of the Warsaw Pact. By winning in the initial conventional phase, the Soviet Union might prevent NATO from resorting to its nuclear weapons. But Warsaw Pact forces would still anticipate the use of nuclear weapons by dispersing reserve formations and by their readiness to shift rapidly to nuclear operations.

Operational factors also contribute to the Soviet insistence that a conventional war in Europe be short and swift. A short, decisive campaign may literally outpace NATO nuclear release procedures, deny NATO the advantage of mobilization, reduce the potential for problems of supply and Eastern European reliability, and enable the Warsaw Pact to secure objectives in NATO without incurring excessive casualties or inflicting excessive destruction on captured territory. Also, a short time frame reduces the chances of catastrophic errors and an opponent's capacity to capitalize on those errors.

The essential requirement in the attainment of a short, swift victory is surprise. The main means of achieving surprise is by deceiving the enemy as to the time, place, weight, or mode of attack. Soviet leaders, after deciding to go to war, would seek to use the crisis period to place their forces in the most advantageous position to achieve surprise and exploit NATO vulnerabilities.

The operational requirements of Soviet strategy arising from the need to achieve a short, swift, and decisive victory (thereby avoiding the threat of escalation to nuclear conflict) are:

— achieve surprise, seize the initiative, dislocate NATO;
— impose the maximum amount of shock in the shortest amount of time;
— paralyze enemy command and control;
— penetrate deep into enemy rear areas, with continual movement, thereby maintaining surprise;
— deny NATO effective first use; be able to destroy NATO theater nuclear forces either during the conventional phase or in anticipation of their release.

In Soviet thinking, the offensive is the most important form of combat action. It provides the means to carry the battle to the enemy, fix and destroy his forces, and eliminate him as a threat. The Soviet concept of seizing the initiative centers on maintaining the offensive, the constant flow of forces forward. While recognizing the need to plan for defensive operations, even here Soviet strategy emphasizes the essential operational advantages of using offensive means in the defense and the need to regain the initiative by counter-attack. Nonetheless the Soviets are conscious that the worst position is to be caught on the defensive with an offensive posture and strategy. The greatest danger is a halt in the momentum of Soviet operations. The operation begins to fail when momentum ceases. However improbable it might appear to NATO planners, the Soviets plan for the possibility of a NATO "spoiling attack" at the start of their offensive.

It is important to recognize that Soviet military doctrine gives considerable weight to the so-called "preparatory phase" of war in which the armed forces and political will of potential opponents are weakened, perhaps sufficiently to make war itself unnecessary. Current Warsaw Pact force programs, whatever their military value, may serve the additional purpose of reducing NATO's sense of its own capacity to defend itself. NATO should look for ways to counter Soviet efforts to vitiate NATO's defenses during any such preparatory or crisis phase.

WARSAW PACT OPERATIONAL PLANNING AND TACTICS

Soviet operational strategy and tactics appear to be undergoing an evolution in response to the change in NATO strategy in 1967 to Flexible Response. Over time, the Soviets have developed a series of tactical and operational means of countering NATO's strategy. This effort is continuing today. The threat of the limited employment of nuclear weapons in support of NATO's conventional defense required a change in Soviet strategy and operational concepts. The battle needed to be carried into the enemy's rear and his use of theater nuclear forces made more problematic if not impossible. For example, the Operational Maneuver Groups (OMGs), flexible, highly mobile maneuver formations with heavy firepower, are being developed to allow high-speed penetration into enemy defenses (see supporting paper by C. N. Donnelly in this volume).

Discussions of Soviet doctrine and strategy often give a misleading impression that the military system is based on absolutely rigid adherence to formulaic interpretations of political and military circumstances. It would be a mistake to view Soviet strategy and operational planning as fixed and immutable. At the strategic and operational command levels, the Soviet Union maintains a high degree of flexibility, including the ability to bring Soviet forces to the brink of war and then retreat from confrontation or conflict. In part this flexibility is due to the nature of decision-making in the Soviet system, and in part it is a by-product of possessing a highly structured, controlled military machine. To repeat, it is a mistake to assume that the decision to initiate hostilities or the timing of such an act would be made solely on the basis of doctrinal specifications or norms.

At the tactical level, Soviet command and control procedures and attack planning remain, at least for now, fairly rigid, and flexibility is curtailed. Military objectives are specified in detail according to space and time. Furthermore, tactical doctrine (for example, duration and weight of artillery support to breakthrough operations, operations of helicopters in support of ground operations, and timing of special landing operations following a chemical-nuclear strike) requires highly specific pre-planning and execution. According to official norms and standards, the performance of commanders and units is judged against these norms and success defined in terms of timely completion of designated tasks in strict accordance with the operational or tactical maneuvers set down in attack orders from higher command echelons. Soviet operational and tactical planning is dependent on highly centralized decision-making and rigidly-adhered-to tactical norms and drills. Once set in motion the offensive must run unimpeded to be successful.

Initiative and Surprise

The basic means for seizing and retaining the initiative are surprise and continuous momentum.

First there is strategic surprise. In order to achieve this, it is necessary to deceive NATO as to the time, place, or mode of attack. The Warsaw Pact will attempt to achieve strategic surprise regardless of the character or length of the crisis preceding hostilities or the extent of Warsaw Pact mobilization. In particular, as suggested earlier, the Soviet Union will seek to conduct itself during a crisis — once the decision to go to war has been made — so as to delude NATO as to the time, direction, and character of such an attack. In the past, the Soviet Union has utilized a variety of strategies to confuse opponents as to its strategic intentions.

At the operational level, surprise is obtained by the selection of the axes of advance — the main routes forward — and the identification of breakthrough sectors. The timing of commitment of forces and reserves also contributes to operational-tactical surprise. The initiative is to be achieved and maintained through a combination of massive shocks against enemy defenses to paralyze his forces, the attainment of a breakthrough along each selected axis, and the passage of mobile forces into the enemy's rear areas. However, if the Soviets commit themselves to deploying follow-on forces in breakthrough efforts, perhaps as Operational Maneuver Groups, then the second echelons will be considerably weaker. Thus, in the event the initial blow is unsuccessful the Warsaw Pact will be faced with a serious difficulty. For NATO, the problem of whether to concentrate on defeating the first or the second echelon will depend critically on NATO's ability to identify the timing of the commitment of the breakthrough units, including potential Operational Maneuver Groups.

Once combat has been initiated, Soviet operational principles call for maintaining the initiative through "continuous operations." This is the most intense form of combat action, requiring day-and-night combat in order to effect the progressive disruption of enemy forces and destruction of enemy positions. The use of continuous operations is particularly important in the event Pact forces are unable to achieve a rapid breakthrough by other means.

Therefore, it is critical that NATO tactical commanders have the capability to identify and track Soviet maneuvering units, including those by

OMGs and follow-on forces. Intelligence systems must be responsive to this information-collecting requirement, and procedures must be established to share the collected information among NATO formations at all levels. It is essential that this system also operate in peacetime to allow intelligence personnel and commanders to observe Warsaw Pact exercises and gain familiarity with, and confidence in, the collected information.

Speed and Movement

For the Warsaw Pact to ensure that the war is short and decisive, the course of battle may require early commitment of follow-on formations, OMGs, reserves, or even second-echelon formations. These forces can exploit a sudden unexpected successful breakthrough or block a counterattack. This "follow-on" system, though tactically rigid, is intended to permit operational momentum.

Follow-on forces, however, are intended to go into action according to a pre-planned timetable. At the start of an engagement, in order to ensure speed and movement, the military is expected to achieve its objectives with the forces at hand. This places a premium on those forces maintaining forward movement, in order to retain the battlefield from which to retrieve damaged equipment for repair. The actual time of deployment and location of the follow-on forces could be a significant factor in the Warsaw Pact's ability to achieve surprise.

An important form of movement in Soviet operations is "maneuver by fire." The ability to place heavy concentrations of firepower, including artillery, multiple rocket launchers, helicopters, and tactical air, on selected targets or zones and to shift fire from one zone to another is critical to attaining the required shock and mass for successful breakthroughs. Increases in the numbers of artillery tubes and multiple rocket launchers in Soviet divisions have greatly expanded the Soviet capability to place large volumes of fire on NATO targets.

Mobility is critical to the ability of Warsaw Pact forces to successfully implement their operational strategy. Mobility permits Warsaw Pact forces to remain dispersed until required to concentrate prior to commitment. For example, the period of massing of an OMG is expected to be extremely brief (four hours) because it is at this time that Warsaw Pact forces are most vulnerable. The shorter the massing period the less the threat of destruction. Obviously, mobility is affected by geographic conditions, especially the presence of roads or terrain obstacles.

Warsaw Pact forces project average rates of advance as high as 50 kilometers a day during conventional operations and even higher in a nuclear environment. In order to maintain these rates, they will have to avoid points of resistance and move into weakly defended rear areas. Warsaw Pact "norms" for operations by breakthrough would place substantial forces behind NATO's forward defenses at the end of the first day. The actual rates of advance would depend on terrain and NATO resistance.

To achieve the requisite tempo in offensive operations, Warsaw Pact forces require, besides mobility: adequate and survivable command and control; close cooperation of all arms; surviving NATO's fire (if Pact formations are identified and targeted).

In summary, the overriding tactical requirement of assault forces is to maintain high-speed continuous momentum. Sustained combat 24 hours a day is designed to ensure that Pact armies retain the initiative.

In Soviet planning to maintain this continuous momentum, the most important feature is proper force echelonment. The depth of echelonment permits fresh troops to pass through depleted assault elements on a battle drill schedule, night or day, to maintain the initiative. The OMG can do the same, but is specifically intended to exploit the efforts of the assault elements and force a breakthrough; it is, therefore, a force drawn from elements of the attacking echelon.

Soviet forces are equipped and trained to operate at night. Infrared driving devices, tank searchlights, and night sights on weapons provide the technical means for continuous night operations. Night operations are considered particularly important in maintaining Warsaw Pact initiative. Night contributes to surprise.

Operational Directions of Advance

As mentioned earlier, an objective of initial Warsaw Pact operations would be to develop a number of distinct axes of advance along which to penetrate NATO defenses and move into its rear areas. The Pact would endeavor to attain definite superiority in all combat arms along these axes. Along the remainder of the front, the Pact might conduct diversionary attacks at force ratios even below 1:1. This use of force would require adequate intelligence as to the disposition of NATO forces and the character of its defensive operations.

The number of axes which may be developed depends on circumstances, including the state of NATO and Warsaw Pact preparedness, the degree of surprise, and the use (or non-use) of nuclear weapons. Generally, from six to nine axes are to be expected along the entire Central Front.

A Front most likely will deploy along two or three axes. Each Army within the Front can deploy one OMG along two operational axes to create a breakthrough. Once initial breakthroughs have been accomplished, it is expected that advancing forces will spread out into NATO's rear.

NATO may have to respond to a series of offensives occurring both simultaneously and sequentially along different axes. This could severely strain NATO's ability to shift its forces laterally along the front to meet emerging attacks.

The Structure of the Offensive

Warsaw Pact forces are trained to deploy in successive waves at each tactical level (i.e., battalion, regiment or division) or operational level (i.e., Army and Front) so as to maintain the pressure on the defender while retaining a high degree of mobility and operational flexibility.

Each tactical or operational level can, in theory, deploy in one, two, or three waves for attack. The first wave is organized as the "first echelon," and the second and third waves will constitute the "second echelon" and "the reserve," respectively. The commanders' choice would be determined by three considerations: (1) the depth and configuration of the enemy defense, (2) the extent of surprise gained and the consequent degree of preparedness of the enemy, and (3) the ground.

In practice, the shape of the terrain, and thus the space available for deployment, is the deciding factor at the divisional level and below. At the operational level, consideration of the enemy's defense has the greatest importance.

If strategic or operational surprise can be assumed, then the Front will usually deploy its armies in one wave, maintaining a small (20 percent) uncommitted reserve. If the defenses are well prepared, then the attack sectors will be narrowed and the Front will attack in depth, formed in two successive waves at both Army and Front level. When the defenses to be breached are organized in one belt, then the attacking forces will put the bulk of their combat formations into the first wave. Where the defense is organized in several successive belts, the attacking forces will attack in several waves, on a narrow frontage.

At each tactical level a second echelon usually constitutes about 30 percent of the total force available. When a two-echelon structure is adopted, a reserve of 10 percent of the force, or less, is usually maintained. A second echelon always operates to a prepared plan or alternative plans, limiting it to specified axes, objectives, and timing. Alternatively, when information as to the nature of the defense is insufficient to permit prior planning or the situation is fluid, instead of a second echelon a substantial reserve of 30-35 percent could be maintained. The disadvantage of a reserve is that more time is usually required to plan its action and to commit it to the battle.

Second echelons are employed to build up pressure on the main axis so as to ensure the breakthrough of the enemy's zone of defense. They are also used to: repel counter-attacks; cover flanks; create the external front of an encirclement; widen the breakthrough; or replace exhausted first echelons.

The Mobile Group was developed at the operational (Army and Front) level in World War II as an alternative to the massed echelon assault. It normally comprised the best equipped armored or mechanical formation (corps) in the Army. (A World War II Soviet tank corps was almost identical in size to a modern Soviet tank division.) Mobile Groups were formed either instead of or in addition to second echelons and had different tasks.

Mobile Groups were designed to develop the breakthrough by penetrating into the tactical and operational depth of the enemy; to break out into enemy routes of withdrawal and so complete the encirclement of an enemy; to destroy reserves moving up, pursue the defender withdrawing, and seize important lines and objectives in depth. In Soviet terms, they were primarily exploitation forces, whose use was designed to turn tactical success into operational success.

The Operational Maneuver Group, normally of divisional size, is the modern version of the Mobile Group. It was developed by Soviet operational planners from recent exercise experience and a study of World War II practices. When making the decision to incorporate an OMG, the Army commander is committing himself to increasing substantially the weight of his effort on the first day of the battle and reducing accordingly the weight of his second echelon, if indeed he deploys one at all. When the first echelon had completed or nearly completed the breakthrough of the defensive belt, the OMG would be committed, normally on the first day of the operation. The idea is to push on into the depths of the enemy so as to exploit success and jeopardize the stability of the defense. This is a most important consideration, as it will hinder the defender's ability to make effective use of his nuclear weapons.

The employment of the OMG has several important characteristics:

- It is a concept of employing existing forces in a novel way.
- Its committal demands a large amount of fire support to ensure the neutralization of opposition.
- Its committal takes place at the most critical moment of the battle and is therefore a potential vulnerability.
- If its committal is successful the Army commander will have inserted a powerful armored division behind the NATO defensive belt *on the first day* of the operation.
- Each Army may deploy an OMG and their actions will be coordinated by the Front staff.
- Because the decision to deploy a division as an OMG rather than as a second echelon will change the ratio of forces in each wave of the attack, and will jeopardize the stability of the defense by threatening the rear and the system of command and control, NATO's identification of the OMG and its location (especially the location of its sector of committal) must be considered one of the most important tasks of the NATO divisional intelligence staff.
- Conversely, any NATO weapon system capable of rapid and devastating response (rocket launchers and helicopters are identified in Warsaw Pact writings as the most effective conventional weapons) will be a prime target for Soviet forces supporting the OMG.
- The division operating as an OMG will be allocated maximum air and artillery support. The corridors of committal of the OMG may well coincide with the corridors established by the air operation.

Several other features characterize the structure of the Soviet offensive. Its efficient operation depends to a large extent on (1) continuous and efficient command and control by the operational commander, and (2) an adherence to well-rehearsed tactical drills by the tactical formations. Thus the Soviet operations commander achieves a high level of operational flexibility at the expense of tactical flexibility. The imaginative raiding tasks being evolved for the OMG and the wide latitude of maneuver allowed to it are exposing a need for a new type of Soviet low-level officer, capable of a greater degree of initiative than was previously necessary. The need to reconcile these two opposing requirements, especially in the light of Soviet tradition and obedience, is causing the Soviet military some considerable anguish.

The concepts of echeloning and force structuring apply whether or not a degree of buildup has been achieved before the start of the war. Whatever the degree of buildup, Soviet doctrine makes it clear that surprising the enemy as to the timing, form, and location of the main effort is essential if victory is to be assured. A Soviet attack on NATO is almost inconceivable without some degree of surprise. Without it, Soviet leaders could not be certain of a quick victory; and failure to win quickly could hasten the release of nuclear weapons to NATO forces, with potentially disastrous consequences.

Because the whole Soviet military system is primarily organized for the offensive, it must maintain a forward advance to enable repair and supply systems to function efficiently in war. Although Soviet defensive tactics and defensive operational plans are soundly based, defense is considered as a temporary expedient to protect flanks or provide a breathing space for the organization of counter-attacks.

Nuclear, Chemical, Biological Warfare

Nuclear, chemical, and biological weapons are all considered to be weapons of mass destruction. The use of nuclear weapons by NATO would pose the greatest potential threat to the conduct of Warsaw Pact operations and the viability of Pact forces. Conversely, the correct and timely employment of nuclear weapons by the Soviet Union would permit the Warsaw Pact to influence the military balance decisively and achieve strategic and operational objectives. However, their use in the theater would be a significant escalation of the level of conflict and raise the potential for unrestrained escalation up to strategic exchanges.

Soviet operational commanders are prepared to conduct operations at all times as though nuclear weapons might be employed without warning. Soviet forces operate conventionally in a manner which necessitates little transition in order to conduct operations on the nuclear battlefield and exploit nuclear strikes. Operational practices may also reduce Soviet vulnerabilities to nuclear strikes. In the event the war cannot be kept conventional Soviet forces would seek to destroy nuclear and nuclear-related targets in a preemptive strike.

In addition to tactical nuclear weapons, Warsaw Pact forces have the option to employ chemical or biological weapons, or both. If nuclear weapons have been used, then the use of other weapons of mass destruction is likely. But chemical and biological weapons are not effective substitutes, as yet, for nuclear weapons. In light of the significant risk of NATO responding to chemical attack with nuclear weapons, it is unclear whether the Warsaw Pact would take the risk of attempting large-scale employment of chemical or biological weapons on the battlefield prior to the use of nuclear weapons.

WARSAW PACT CAPABILITIES FOR MILITARY OPERATIONS IN CENTRAL EUROPE

Basic Force Posture

Soviet forces are organized and deployed to meet a range of contingency options within specific time periods. Plans are prepared to reflect such contingencies (including a NATO attack on the Warsaw Pact). These plans specify forces to be mobilized and committed; timing for mobilization and initiation of military operations; and contribution of forces from or to adjacent military theaters.

A portion of the Soviet armed forces is at a high state of readiness and could be employed without the mobilization of reservists or civilian resources. The rest is at reduced stages of readiness and would require preparation time prior to commitment to combat. At a high state of readiness are the following:

— 100% of the Strategic Rocket Forces (including SS-20);
— One-third of the ground forces (100% in the forward area opposite NATO);
— About 70% of the Air Force;
— About 25-50% of the Naval Forces;
— About 80% of the Home Air Defense Forces.

On the other hand, most of the ground-force divisions and supporting rear services are in a low readiness category. To become operational they depend on the mobilization of reserve manpower, trucks and other civilian-related equipment and supplies. This would require between two and four weeks of mobilization and movement.

Comparison of Standing Forces and Mobilization Capabilities

It is not known under what conditions the Warsaw Pact might attack NATO, but Soviet doctrine stresses the importance to a successful operation not only of surprise, speed, and the use of echeloned forces attacking in successive "waves" along independent axes of advance, but also of force superiority. If the Pact were to opt for an initial attack without lengthy mobilization, only the combat-ready divisions in non-Soviet Eastern Europe could be used initially. However, if the Soviets chose to seek the maximum available force superiority this would require that they deploy additional forces before an attack.

This deployment would in turn require time to mobilize and deploy ground formations and rear services from the Soviet Union and fill out Warsaw Pact cadre formations. Mobilization would significantly expand Soviet and Warsaw Pact force totals but would limit Soviet capabilities to achieve strategic surprise. The Soviets could deploy additional forces up to a total of 110 Warsaw Pact divisions and 4,600 aircraft within one month. Some mobilization could take place under various guises including the biannual rotation of troops to Soviet forces deployed in Eastern Europe.

If the Soviets chose an option with the highest possible surprise they would initiate an attack in an early stage of the buildup and probably use only the combat-ready divisions in non-Soviet Eastern Europe in the first-echelon Fronts. The initial attack would then be conducted by two Fronts with ten Armies. The second-echelon Fronts (one Polish coastal Front and three Soviet Fronts) would follow and be deployed at a later stage of the attack. Such an attack could be initiated with two to four days of visible preparations.

If the Soviets chose to rely on numerical superiority at the beginning of the offensive they would start the attack after completion of a large buildup. They could then deploy three Fronts in the first echelon, followed by two second-echelon Fronts assembled in Poland and eastern Czechoslovakia.

The problem for NATO is that an extended crisis with indications of mobilization and movement of formations could create ambiguity about Soviet intentions which would provide NATO with difficult choices. The problem for the Soviets would be that such an enormous assembly would offer targets for NATO's nuclear weapons and the achievement of strategic surprise would be impossible. The risk of losses and the warning of the enemy would probably prevent the Soviets from choosing this option. The other option — highest possible surprise — would possibly not be used because the initial superiority would be considered not high enough. The Soviets would very likely choose an option that was somewhere between these two described.

Soviet Force Modernization

Soviet theater forces in Europe are currently benefitting from a sustained modernization effort which encompasses nuclear as well as conventional air and ground forces. This program of modernization involves not only increased numbers of better-quality weapons but the restructuring of Soviet forces to provide greater offensive power. Among the most significant improvements are:

1. Theater nuclear forces have been improved considerably in recent years:

— SS-20 mobile missile system replacing older SS-4, SS-5, bringing improved accuracy, greater range (4,400-5,000 km) and ability to reach all targets within Europe and the U.K.;
— SS-21, 22, 23 replacing older tactical launchers;
— 135 Backfire bombers in service, bringing longer range (5,500 km); also new bomber in development-production.

2. Ground forces:

— divisions have been restructured, with more infantry, artillery, and more transport (larger trucks);
— improved nuclear, biological and chemical protection; improved reconnaissance vehicles; anti-tank guided missiles; and air defense.

3. Air forces:

— improved ground-attack aircraft (longer range, greater payload);
— improved attack helicopters;
— improved airlift capability.

Air Power

Significant developments are taking place in the re-equipment and organization of Soviet air forces. New types of aircraft (Fencer and Flogger, for example) with greater range and weapon-carrying capability are entering service in increasing number. The restructuring is designed to exploit the full operational potential of the aircraft and to provide air support from the immediate battle area to the full depth of the theater. Close support of the ground forces remains the task of Frontal Aviation, short-range aircraft and helicopters. Newer, longer-range aircraft will be employed in an air campaign independent of ground-force commanders against distant targets — NATO nuclear resources, airfields, headquarters and lines of communications. These would be supported and augmented, when required, by centrally controlled air units whose aircraft have the range to reach targets in the United Kingdom and France.

Especially significant is the increased reliance by the Warsaw Pact on helicopters. Soviet ground forces in particular are employing large numbers of helicopters of Army Aviation for a great variety of tasks — fire support against fixed defenses, protection of flanks during attacks, independent air assault on objectives in enemy rear areas (nuclear targets, headquarters, airfields, communication choke points), and assistance in river crossing. The ability of helicopters to operate in poor weather and at night has been greatly enhanced. Helicopters are assigned to Operational Maneuver Groups to provide mobile fire support, moving forward with the OMGs as they advance into NATO rear areas.

These developments have considerably increased the scale and effectiveness of the Soviet air threat throughout NATO.

Logistics

Soviet leaders recognize that adequate logistical support is essential for high-speed, sustained attack operations. To meet their perceived tactical needs within the Armies they have:

- increased the ammunition and fuel transporter capacities within the divisions and Armies;
- strengthened vehicle repair capability within the Army;
- increased the tank transporter fleet for moving tanks to the battle area;
- restructured the battlefield logistics system.

Soviet divisions in East Germany, Poland, and Czechoslovakia are fully manned and stocks of fuel and munitions in the forward area have been very greatly increased. Nevertheless, the bulk of Soviet ground forces and their logistic support have to come from the Soviet Union, distances of some 900 kilometers. They are dependent on lines of communication across Poland, Czechoslovakia, and East Germany, and though they utilize aircraft, water, roads, and pipelines, the capacity of the railways remains a key element. There are choke points such as transloading stations, river crossings, road junctions, and other spots which are vulnerable to attack.

Electronic Warfare

Soviet military doctrine recognizes that control of the electronic environment is critical in winning the land, air, and sea battle. They have developed their electronic warfare capabilities into an integrated system called Radio Electronic Combat (REC). This system includes the full spectrum of electronic warfare encompassing signal intelligence, electronic countermeasures, and electronic warfare support measures.

The purpose of Radio Electronic Combat is to limit, delay, or nullify the enemy's use of his command and control weapon communication systems while protecting Soviet systems by electronic "counter countermeasures." The system uses electronic jamming, deception, warning, protection, direction finding and intelligence collection. It is practiced by all branches of the armed forces with new systems on aircraft, helicopters, land vehicles and ships. This system poses a significant threat to NATO forces.

Chemical Warfare

The Workshop cannot predict whether the Soviets would use chemical weapons in an attack in Europe. However, we do know that they possess a sizeable offensive capability with several types of agents and weapons for their delivery. We also know that they train their troops in defense against such weapons. We might expect the Soviets, if they use such weapons of mass destruction, to use them in breakthrough attacks, against airfields, and on command posts. But the Soviet military considers chemical weapons less effective in most circumstances than tactical nuclear weapons.

Airborne Forces

The Soviet airborne forces are the only parachute-deliverable forces in the world which have mechanized mobility after landing. With seven divisions available, the Soviets could launch a number of successive airborne attacks to seize key bridges, control centers, and airfields and other objectives that depend on airlift capability. Once on the ground, these forces can move and fight like a miniature motorized rifle division. Their contribution in an initial attack could include an element of surprise and confusion which might be difficult to counter.

Special-Purpose Forces

Soviet success with small detachments against the Germans and against Japanese rear areas in World War II augurs well for the similar use of "diversionary" troops in the first days of a NATO war. Likely targets would include communication centers, radar sites, and, most important, nuclear weapon systems. The ability of such detachments to disrupt and delay should not be underestimated. Special-purpose units have been organized in the Soviet Army and several Eastern European countries and continually practice for a variety of special operations against NATO installations.

CRITICAL FACTORS FOR NATO CONSIDERATION

The Workshop on the Soviet Threat, summarizing its findings, offers the view that planners of a more effective NATO deterrent in Europe must give attention to the following critical factors in the Soviet military machine.

Improvements in Soviet Forces

First, there is the extensive modernization of Warsaw Pact forces in general, and particularly of those in or near the Central Front. This is significantly increasing the threat to NATO. Among the most important features of this modernization process which NATO must consider are:

- An increasing capability to threaten NATO rear areas, by new tactical aircraft, new capability for independent air operations, massive growth of helicopters, and expanded unconventional warfare capability (airborne, heliborne, special operations forces).
- An increasing capability to conduct mobile, high-speed combat operations, by improved firepower support (both range and volume of fire), a more balanced divisional structure permitting more flexible employment, and the introduction of the OMG concept.
- Improved air defenses at all levels, seriously reducing NATO's ability to penetrate.

- Improved theater nuclear capabilities: improved range, accuracy, and number of warheads.
- Massive investment in all forms of radio electronic warfare.

Soviet Operations

In addition to those improvements in Soviet forces, certain critical factors in operations should be especially noted. Implementation of Soviet strategy and doctrine depends upon:

- Proper timing and sequencing of operations.
- Adequate command and control.
- Knowledge of NATO dispositions and operations.
- Synchronized combined arms operations to include: rapid deployment of forces, sustained air operations in NATO's depths, breakthrough tactics and exploitation, development of the OMG, sustained continuous combat (echelonment of forces), and powerful air defenses.
- Adequate and responsive logistical support.

We will take up each of those operational factors in turn.

The Importance of Time

A failure of the Warsaw Pact to achieve a rapid victory would open up the very problems which caused the Warsaw Pact to pursue the rapid-victory option: reliability of Soviet allies, supply, NATO mobilization, and nuclear escalation. The extreme requirements in Soviet operations for speed and high rates of advance noted in this report stood out as critical issues. The Warsaw Pact offensive is a highly integrated system dependent on maintaining a constant flow at a predetermined rate. Any interruptions of that flow threaten the entire operation. The ability to create uncertainty for Soviet commanders also has the potential to disrupt the operation by increasing the potential for decision errors.

The Vulnerability of Command and Control

The Soviets rely on a strict, centralized system of control with the application of battle drills, standards and norms to achieve objectives in prescribed time intervals. Since there is little room for tactical initiative (division and below), disruption of the command-and-control system could have a significant effect on the outcome of operations. Command, control, and communications capabilities are made intentionally redundant just because of this vulnerability. NATO can seriously impede the Warsaw Pact's ability to succeed in offensive operations by selected attacks on command-and-control targets and by interfering with communications between command echelons.

The Importance of Intelligence

The Soviets expect to know the location of enemy defenses and supporting artillery. Soviet planning specifies amounts of supporting firepower, rates of advance and battlefield tactics in offensive operations. NATO deceptions and shifts in defensive positions could waste Soviet firepower and confuse Soviet attack planning. NATO needs to restrict the Warsaw Pact's ability to gain useful battlefield intelligence and to deny the Pact easy opportunities to target NATO forces and defenses.

Synchronized Combined Arms Operations

To achieve rapid advances, the Soviets must mass quickly and then execute attack plans without delay. Any NATO attacks on assembly areas and deployment routes could severely disrupt and delay the scheduled scheme of maneuver and fire.

The creation of the Operational Maneuver Groups is a recent development in this area. OMGs are well-suited to perform breakthrough and exploitation operations.

Indeed, "breakthrough" is the key Soviet attack maneuver. The Soviets expect to mass and attack quickly, with high force ratio advantages on the main axes. Such an attack, to be blunted, must be denied the mobility essential to a breakthrough operation. Once Pact forces are fixed, the tanks and infantry carriers must be destroyed in large numbers and the supporting artillery must be located and neutralized. The use of terrain, obstacles, fortifications, and mines should be studied for their effect on the mobility of the breakthrough force.

Following the breakthrough, the OMG and second-echelon forces may be employed to achieve decisive operational results deep into the NATO defense. Thus at the same time that NATO must meet the breakthrough, it must also attack and disrupt the OMG and second echelon — either before its commitment or as it passes through the first echelon. Disruption of routes of advance, destruction of command-and-control centers and attack on massed vehicles can achieve this goal.

Air operations must be synchronized with the others. The Soviets would desire to paralyze, disrupt, and destroy NATO theater nuclear capability with shock aviation attacks. The initial air campaign, assisted by sabotage and diversionary forces, could be decisive in reducing NATO nuclear response. Airfields, storage sites, and missile launchers would be the key targets. NATO must be able to counter this serious threat by both defeating Warsaw Pact air power over NATO territory and denying the Pact the ability to deploy freely on its airfields.

Air defense is another part of synchronized combined operations. The Pact has given a special emphasis to improved air defense: interceptors, surface-to-air missiles, anti-aircraft artillery, radars and control centers. If NATO aircraft are to penetrate Pact airspace in interdiction or for close support, they must have a counter to the massive air defense force.

Logistics

The lines of communication from the USSR are essential lifelines for Soviet forces. Any disruption will weaken their offensive capability. Likewise, the storage and distribution system and repair workshops in the forward area provide vulnerable targets for NATO attacks. If the initial offensive can be contained, then attacks on Warsaw Pact lines of communication could seriously degrade further combat operations.

There are other critical Soviet factors to consider in strengthening NATO's conventional deterrent, besides Soviet improvement of its forces and the ways in which the forces would be expected to operate in battle.

One of these is the factor of the USSR's European allies. Dependence on those allies is an important potential strategic problem. More than half of the ready Pact divisions in Central Europe are non-Soviet. These forces have older equipment, possess less firepower, lack mobility, possess no nuclear weapons, and may be lacking the motivation to carry out a Moscow-directed attack.

Additionally, a major concern for Moscow is the recognition by its Pact allies that NATO nuclear weapons probably would be used on their soil if the war escalated.

If hostilities were precipitated by unrest in Eastern Europe, the Soviet Union would have to be seriously concerned about the security of its lines of communications. This would complicate Soviet military planning.

Though it is difficult to judge the overall reliability of non-Soviet Warsaw Pact forces, they are likely to perform their required missions so long as the Pact is perceived to be winning the war.

One final critical factor needs mentioning — manpower.

The Soviets will experience a dip in available manpower in the latter part of the 1980s. There are several ways of solving the shortfall but some reduction in the number of active military personnel may well be required.

The ethnic heterogeneity of the Soviet population poses problems. During the 1980s the non-Russian (particularly the Muslim) population will become more significant, posing problems within the armed forces. Among the problems created by non-Russian conscripts are language and communications difficulties, lower educational levels, and discrimination.

The great emphasis on political-patriotic education in the Soviet and Pact armed forces reflects concern for the reliability of their troops. This education is particularly geared to maintaining their reliability and morale in war. There is a concern for the potential use by NATO of psychological warfare.

The Political Rationale of Soviet Military Capabilities and Doctrine

by
Hannes Adomeit

Dr. Adomeit is on the Staff of the Stiftung Wissenschaft und Politik in Eben-hausen, Federal Republic of Germany.

The momentum of the Soviet military buildup of the 1960s and 1970s shows every sign of being carried over into the 1980s. Serial production of modern tanks, armored personnel carriers, artillery pieces, fighter air-craft, medium-range bombers and missiles, as well as cruisers and aircraft carriers, is continuing. New weapons are being developed and tested. New large military production plants and assembly buildings are being con-structed. The technological gap in weapon systems has been closed in many areas, and in some areas the Soviet Union has taken the lead.

At the military-strategic level, the Soviet Union (at long last from its point of view) has achieved parity. It has been engaged in a thorough modernization program of its medium-range nuclear delivery systems and simultaneously is about to modernize its shorter-range systems. It has been widening the margin of superiority in practically all aspects of the con-ventional military balance — in Europe, in Central Asia, and in the Far East. It has, finally, developed capabilities for military intervention in areas far beyond the Soviet homeland: a blue-water navy and long-range air transport to move and support two airborne divisions.

Soviet foreign policy has reflected, or at least has seemed to reflect, a new sense of confidence and assertiveness based on such newly developed military capabilities.[1] Soviet military power was an important factor in

Notes are at the end of the paper.

defeating the purposes of the American military involvement in Vietnam and ultimately in Hanoi's victory over Saigon in 1975, as well as in reunified Vietnam's expansion of control over Laos and its invasion of Cambodia in 1978/79. The Soviet-Cuban military intervention turned the tide of the civil war in Angola in 1975/76, and of the war between Somalia and Ethiopia in 1977/78. And, finally, Soviet combat troops were used on a massive scale to forestall the impending collapse of the revolutionary regime in Kabul and hence to prevent the erosion of Soviet control over Afghanistan. Care needs to be taken, however, not to draw simple conclusions from these developments.

First, whereas there may very well be a straightforward correlation between growth in Soviet military power — in Europe and globally — and growing political ambitions, it is not at all clear whether there is also a direct relationship between growing military power and an increasing tendency by the Soviet leadership to take risks. The Soviet advances in the 1970s may very well have taken place less because of the "objective" shifts in the military balance in favor of the USSR than because of "subjective" Soviet perceptions of American indecisiveness and American inability or disinclination to use force in the wake of Vietnam and Watergate.

Secondly, although Soviet behavior in the past shows that the Soviet leaders do not regard nuclear war as an appropriate and effective means of furthering their foreign-policy objectives, it does not provide a clear answer as to the utility they attach to military power in peacetime and crises, to the use of force short of nuclear war, and to their confidence that they could control the dangers of escalation. It does not, above all, answer questions as to the primary rationale of the Soviet military buildup. It does not reveal whether this rationale is primarily military or political; whether the military effort serves primarily "defensive" needs ("to safeguard Soviet security") or "offensive" goals ("to assure the victory of socialism on a world scale"); or, finally, whether the buildup is "simply" the end result of specific features inherent in the Soviet system: bureaucratic inertia, the preeminent position of the military and orthodox Party leaders in Soviet domestic politics and the priority of the military over the civilian sector in the economy.

Thirdly, even if firm answers could be provided to all or some of these questions it may be incorrect to assume that the answers would still be valid in the future. More than ever before, current trends cannot be taken for granted and extrapolated without qualification. The reasons for this are found, on the one hand, in the economic and political costs incurred by the Soviet Union by emphasizing the military instrument in foreign policy and, on the other hand, in the requirement for the Soviet leadership to find entirely new solutions for the chronic ills of the Soviet system.

The rate of growth in defense spending has remained constant for the past fifteen years or more (at 4-5 percent according to the estimates of the CIA, or 9 percent in W. T. Lee's calculations).[2] No matter whether one takes lower or higher Western estimates, the rate of growth in the last portion of this period has exceeded that of the economy as a whole. The burden of military expenditures on the economy, therefore, has been growing year after year. This cannot continue indefinitely.

Also, whereas in the past more than 400,000 more men a year have been available for military service than have been drafted, soon there will be 200,000 fewer than are being drafted at present.

Finally, the shift in the "correlation of forces" in favor of socialism, which was interpreted by Soviet spokesmen in the late 1960s and early 1970s as having provided the basis for the turn to "realism" and acceptance of the "principles of coexistence" by Western leaders (more of this later), has led — as if by delayed reaction — to a considerable upsurge in U.S. defense efforts and to a policy of economic sanctions against the Soviet Union. This, too, advises caution against the assumption that past and present Soviet policies can be projected into the future.

Nevertheless, politics and policies in the Soviet Union (and in Russia) traditionally have changed very gradually;[3] and such major changes as have been attempted — as, for instance, by Malenkov in 1953 and Khrushchev after 1955 — very quickly were overturned or significantly modified. This is a point that will have to be borne in mind by Andropov and, for that matter, by any other leader to emerge at the top after him.

A closer look at past and present policies, therefore, is warranted. For this purpose, first, some essential definitions of doctrine, strategy, and "the correlation of forces" will be provided. An attempt will be made then to examine the interplay of (1) Soviet military capabilities, (2) Soviet military doctrine, (3) verbal and nonverbal threats, and (4) Soviet foreign-policy objectives in different phases of East-West relations since 1945. The primary focus of this examination will be on Europe. However, even though the scope of the present endeavor does not always permit this to be made explicit, Soviet policies and military strategy toward Europe are only *part* of global Soviet policies and overall Soviet military doctrine; they are, in particular, to a very considerable degree a function of Soviet-American relations and the Soviet-American strategic relationship.

FOREIGN POLICY, MILITARY DOCTRINE, AND MILITARY STRATEGY

The most striking features of Soviet definitions of military doctrine and strategy are the earnestness with which such definitions are pursued and the emphasis on their "inevitably" political character — their "class essence."

As to the difference between the two terms, the editors of the book *Voennaia strategiia* (Military Strategy), whose chief editor was Marshal V. D. Sokolovskii, insisted: "Military strategy occupies a subordinate position with regard to military doctrine. Military doctrine determines overall policy in principle, while military strategy, starting from this overall policy, develops and investigates concrete problems touching upon the nature of future war, the preparation of a country for war, the organization of the armed forces, and the methods of warfare." [4]

Military doctrine is thus said to constitute a single system of guidelines of the leadership of the state in the military sphere. "Military doctrine, therefore, is state doctrine." [5] Another authoritative Soviet book calls military doctrine "a system of guiding views and directions of a state on the character of wars in given specific historical conditions, the determination of the military tasks of the state, the armed forces and the principles of their structuring, and also the methods and forms of solving all these tasks, including the armed struggle, which flow from the goals of war and the socio-economic and military-technical possibilities of the country." [6]

There are, according to Soviet definitions, two aspects to any military doctrine: political and military-technical. [7] As for *Soviet* military doctrine, "its political aspect was formulated by V. I. Lenin. The Leninist theses on the attitude of our state toward war, the nature of our military tasks, and the political aims of war are still valid today. They were further developed in the decisions of the Congresses of the Communist Party." [8] Indeed, the source materials on this aspect of doctrine can be considered as fairly rich.

As for the "military-technical" aspect of Soviet military doctrine, information is scarce. Certainly, the documents adopted at the Party Congresses are at such a level of abstraction when it comes to military affairs that the formulation of strategy could take almost any direction. Also, Soviet sources do not make it altogether clear who is or should be responsible for codifying military doctrine. Whereas the editors of *Voennaia strategiia* unambiguously state that the political leadership of the state is responsible for it,[9] a Soviet *Dictionary of Basic Military Terms* rules that "a nation's political *and* military leadership" is responsible.[10]

It is highly unlikely that the political leadership rules on important questions of doctrine without consulting the military, and the institution where such consultation takes place most likely is the Defense Council (*Sovet oborony*).[11] It would make sense, therefore, to include "the military" in all of the Soviet definitions. On the other hand, in keeping with the traditional primacy of the Party over the military as well as with the Leninist emphasis on the necessity of "subordinating the military point of view to the political,"[12] it must appear preferable to *exclude* "the military" from the definition. This must appear advantageous even to the military, because if doctrine is held to lie within the prerogative of the state, that is the Party, "strategy" — because of its subordinate role — becomes primarily a matter of responsibility by the military, or at least the military may interpret the relationship between doctrine and strategy in these terms.

The broad political content of military doctrine, its character as a single system of political guidelines, and its origin in the class nature of the state account for misunderstanding and misperception in the strategic debate between East and West. Soviet writers generally do not consider Western strategic doctrine in military professional or "military technical" terms. They see it primarily as an instrument of foreign policy, as an expression of Western thinking on the use of military power in the nuclear age. "Brinkmanship," the "strategy of deterrence" (*strategiia ustrasheniia*), the "doctrine of containment" (*doktrina sderzhivaniia*), "doctrine of liberation," the special interest in limited wars and the theory of "escalation of war" are referred to as imperialist "military strategic theories and doctrines."[13] The Western (alleged or real) strategic doctrines of "preventive war," "massive retaliation," and "Flexible Response" are called "military political doctrines."[14]

In theory, thus, there are clear distinctions in Soviet military science: "Doctrine" belongs primarily to the political realm. "Strategy," as well as military operations and tactics, is part of "military art" (*voennoe iskusstvo*); its "laws are objective and apply impartially to both hostile sides."[15] But then the distinctions between doctrine and strategy do remain largely an abstraction (though, an important abstraction for political and ideological reasons). This is so because military strategy is said to encompass a whole range of pursuits which go far beyond the confines of simple "implementation" and very much overlap with doctrine. According to Sokolovskii's *Voennaia strategiia,* for instance, the theory of military strategy includes:

— the laws governing armed conflict;
— the conditions and nature of a future war;
— the theoretical foundations for preparing the country and the armed forces for war and the principles of war planning;
— the services of the armed forces and the basis of their strategic utilization;
— the fundamentals of civil defense;
— the methods of conducting armed conflict;
— the basis of the material and technical support for armed conflict;
— the bases of leadership of the military forces in war;
— the strategic attitudes of the probable opponents.[16]

In addition, the practical side of strategy is said to include the following:

— the development of a strategic concept and practical realization of plans dealing with the preparation of the armed services for war;
— guidance of the preparation of the armed services for war;
— provision of leadership to the armed forces during war.[17]

Interestingly, Soviet military theoreticians do *not* discuss the problem of possible differences between declaratory and operational doctrine (or strategy). They do not explore the possibility that Western concepts may have the exclusive or supplementary quality of verbal communications transmitted to the adversary so as to achieve foreign-policy objectives. Western concepts are generally taken very seriously and held to be genuine expressions of a search of how to use force without risk of destruction to the capitalist system. Conversely (and not at all surprisingly), Soviet sources are silent on the topic — to be explored here — of how the USSR has used doctrine or strategy as a form of verbal communication to enhance *its* foreign policy.

FOREIGN POLICY AND THE "CORRELATION OF FORCES"

Perhaps the most important concept for the theory and practice of Soviet foreign policy is that of the "correlation of forces." This is not a new concept. Soviet political leaders, ideologues, and international relations experts rightly stress that Lenin constantly pointed to the necessity of taking into account "all the forces, groups, parties, classes and masses operating in a given country,"[18] and that he emphasized that in foreign policy, as in politics in general, "one must be able to calculate the correlation of forces . . . This is the core of Marxism and Marxist tactics."[19] To that extent the assessment of the "correlation of forces" prior to taking any major political initiative is part and parcel of what Nathan Leites called the "operational code" and what Richard Pipes and Alexander George refer to as "operational principles" in Soviet foreign policy.[20] To these rules of procedure belongs the principle — in Lenin's words — of "reviewing as precisely and as soberly as possible" the forces opposing Soviet power and of answering questions such as: "What are these forces? How are they grouped against one another? How are they deployed at present?"[21]

The importance which is attached to the correct assessment of the distribution of power is indicated, among other things, by the care and the frequency with which various Russian terms are employed in the political discourse, e.g., *sootnoshenie sil* (literally, correlation of forces, the term most commonly used), *rasstanovka sil* (distribution or disposition of forces), *gruppirovka sil* (the grouping of forces, less frequently used), and *balans sil* (the balance of forces, often employed pejoratively to refer to traditional Western "balance of power" theories).[22]

But what is the role of military power in the Soviet assessments of the correlation, distribution, or balance of forces? For several decades Soviet commentators have been stressing that their concept differs from the Western approaches on this very issue. Whereas Western theoreticians are said to think of the correlation of forces in purely military terms and in terms of international *state* relations, Soviet analysts see themselves engaged in a much more complex and differentiated task. They, so they say, look at the correlation of forces as an expression of international *class* relations. They take into account, in addition to military factors, political, economic, social, and ideological dimensions of power, as well as psychological factors, such as morale. Also, contrary to the persisting tendency among "bourgeois" theoreticians to assess the correlation of forces by comparing the power potential of the main or leading states or military alliances, Soviet analysts assert that they themselves weigh the influence of medium-size and smaller powers and the strength of the non-aligned countries in the international system.[23]

All these factors, in the Soviet view, became much more important after 1917. Ever since then powerful forces have been created which have been able to exert a significant influence on world affairs. These forces, it is argued, include the socialist countries, the communist and workers' parties, the national-liberation movement, significant portions of the non-aligned movement, as well as certain sections of social democracy, the labor unions, scientists, and intellectuals in the capitalist countries.[24]

It is these factors which, in the Soviet perspective, account for change. "The changes which have taken place in the system of contemporary international relations," one Soviet analyst summarizes, "can fully be regarded as the result of international class struggle, the result of the class and socio-political battles that have been going on in the world and inside individual countries in the course of the last decade . . ."[25] Conversely — and completely in keeping with the claim and the reality of a power and policy bent on changing the international status quo — Soviet writers emphatically reject the Western notion of "stability" as they see it. "Stability," they claim, is typically but wrongly understood in the West as flowing from "the balance of military power among powers or blocks, thus ignoring the real processes of class struggle, which are constantly injecting, and will continue to inject, new elements into the international situation."[26]

In examining the significance of the Soviet assertions quoted it is necessary to bear in mind their timing. Although it is correct, as noted, that the concept of the "correlation of forces" (in contrast, for instance, to the theory of coexistence) can directly and unambiguously be derived from Lenin, it is nevertheless curious that 1974/75 would see the sudden appearance of a number of authoritative articles on that subject. Evidently, the Soviet leadership and the Central Committee departments responsible for international questions felt obliged to "clarify" something. It is not coincidental that such clarification should come precisely at a time when, in the view of many Western analysts, detente had failed its first important test during the October 1973 war, and when the meaning of detente was being seriously eroded by the Soviet arms buildup. Western critics of Soviet intentions were quick to point out that detente had been explained by the Soviet leaders as the result of a significant shift in the "correlation of forces" in favor of socialism — that is, for all practical purposes, of a shift in military power. They quoted Soviet sources to the effect that this shift had *forced* or *compelled* the West to adopt a more "realistic" attitude in world affairs and, above all, to abandon its traditional policy from "positions of strength." "Could it be," one of the Western critics asked, "that the Kremlin hopes to engage the West in moves toward detente that will prove disarming, both literally and psychologically, while the East becomes militarily preponderant in the expectation of translating this military might into political influence at some point in the future?"[27]

Not surprisingly, in view of questions such as these, efforts were deemed opportune in the Soviet Union to "clarify" the matter. The verbal emphasis on military power was being reduced and the military component in the "correlation of forces" de-emphasized.[28] But even though such efforts were made (and are still being made), they were (and are) not entirely convincing. Whatever the reason — pride in the military achievements, the influence of vested bureaucratic interests, or simply an inability or unwillingness to hide genuine perception — de-emphasis in some contexts is invalidated by re-emphasis in others. The very same authors who stress the importance of "class forces" still regard the "steady growth and build-up of the forces of socialism, of its military potential, and the enhancement of the political prestige of the Soviet Union and other socialist countries" as one of the "most pronounced trends in the confrontation between the two world systems."[29] They argue that although the "correlation of forces" cannot be reduced to the military factor alone, it is nevertheless true that "military strength of a state is by all means a decisive element of its position in the world."[30] Although there were many factors in the struggle for peace, there could nevertheless be "no doubt that all the other factors could not play their role if the powerful armed forces of the socialist states, and above all the Soviet Army and Navy, did not exist."[31] With these "clarifications of clarifications" concerning the "correlation of forces" in mind it is now possible to examine more closely the actual use of Soviet military power and military doctrine for political purposes in Europe under Stalin, Khrushchev, and Brezhnev.

THE STALIN ERA

The role of military power during the Second World War was perceived by Stalin as straightforward and direct. This was expressed in his remark of April 1945 — part statement of accomplished fact, part prophecy — that "This war is not as in the past; whoever occupies a territory also imposes on it his own social system."[32] The course of the war conformed to these perceptions: Stalin advanced the Soviet armed forces as far as possible into Eastern Europe, Germany, and the Balkans in the west, into Iran in the south, and into northeast China, Manchuria, Korea, and Sakhalin in the Far East. Powerful Soviet military offensives were not halted until after the announcement of Japanese capitulation. In recurring conflict over saving Soviet lives and resources versus speedy military advances Stalin invariably overruled the caution and hesitation of his generals to maximize territorial gains. And almost everywhere, with the exception of Iran and the Soviet occupation zone of Austria, the Soviet military presence was translated into Soviet political control or predominant influence. Years after the war Stalin was still to regret: "The reason why there is now no communist government in Paris is because in the circumstances of 1945 the Soviet Army was not able to reach French soil." [33]

Stalin's military advances and occupation of territory in Europe, Iran, and the Far East, however, were operations without risks of confrontation with the United States. Such risks only arose after the break-up of the wartime alliance. They were present in all those Soviet attempts at using military force or the threat thereof to gain additional territorial advantage and/or predominant political influence: in Turkey (1945), in Iran (1946), in Berlin (1948-49), and in Korea (1950-52). [34] These probes are noteworthy for the fact that, first, they were made in conditions of U.S. nuclear weapons monopoly, U.S. superiority in economic and technological resources, U.S. naval supremacy and U.S. strategic invulnerability relative to the USSR; and, secondly, that they were made at all — despite the (in military terms) patently unfavorable "correlation of forces" and, connected with it, the high probability of failure.

One possible explanation for the Soviet probes to have taken place at all is a failure by Stalin to appreciate the military and political significance of nuclear weapons. This explanation, however, must be rejected. Stalin almost certainly realized that nuclear weapons had endowed international relations with an entirely new quality. Most importantly, in the specific conditions of the early postwar period these weapons had put the Soviet Union decidedly at a disadvantage *vis-à-vis* the United States. This was acknowledged by Stalin. "The equilibrium has been destroyed" (*ravnovesie narushilos'*), he is reported as having stated in a closed meeting in Moscow shortly after the use of American nuclear weapons against Japan. [35] The United States, he reiterated later, in 1948, is "the most powerful state in the world." [36]

It is most likely that Stalin for this very reason (sensitivity to the actual distribution of power) was careful to limit the risks of his military probes. The mere display of American determination to resist was, in every case of Soviet probing, sufficient to cause Soviet retraction and withdrawal.[37]

What is of significance in the present context is the Soviet reaction to the unfavorable military-strategic balance. Three interrelated levels need to be distinguished: the political level; the declaratory, doctrinal, or propagandist level; and the military level. At the political level, the character of Soviet reactions has already been noted. It was that of an offensive probing that was to recur, in its intensity, only under Khrushchev, in 1958-62. Such probing was not only backed by the threat of military force but also, wherever Soviet control permitted, by militant action of local communist parties. The seizure of power by the communist party in Czechoslovakia, the attempt to isolate and depose Tito in Yugoslavia, and the blockade of Berlin were all indications of Stalin's conviction that constant pressure — military threats from the outside and militancy of local communists from within — would ultimately wear down the adversary's will to resist and transform the political conditions in the target country.

Since this trust in the effectiveness of "shaking the little finger," as Khrushchev critically but euphemistically was to call it,[38] proved unwarranted both in Yugoslavia and in Berlin, the militancy of violence (including that of violent strikes in Italy and France) was replaced by a militant Peace Movement. This phase, however, was not to endure. A shift in the "correlation of forces" in favor of socialism (explosion of the first nuclear weapon in August 1949 and the victory of the Chinese communists over the Kuomintang in the course of the same year) led Stalin to resume the armed probing, although its center had by then shifted from Europe to Asia.

All this is not merely of historical interest. It is to suggest that *trust in the effectiveness of combined external military and domestic political pressure to achieve Soviet objectives has characterized Soviet foreign policy in Eastern and Western Europe without interruption ever since Stalin.* It is also to suggest that the purposes of pressure have remained the same: *to consolidate gains that have been made while at the same time attempting to expand Soviet influence.*

Activity at the second level — doctrinal, declaratory, and propagandist — was closely tailored to enhance these dual purposes of Soviet foreign policy. Primary examples of this are Zhdanov's "two camps" doctrine in Soviet ideology and, until after the end of the Berlin crisis, the strict adherence of Soviet ideologues and propagandists to the Leninist thesis of the "inevitability of war." [39] Soviet military doctrine and strategy fit into the very same pattern. In the postwar era the development of military strategy had practically come to a stop. "Thought was reduced to silence, and genius reduced to Stalin." [40] The emphasis in military strategy thus remained where it had been since the 1930s: on offensive operations in war. This was corroborated by Stalin's admonition that military science had to follow closely the experience of the recent war where "temporary" reverses had been overcome and the war had been carried to the territory of the enemy.

To the extent that changes had taken place since the war, they were held to be of no major consequence. This was applied to nuclear weapons, too. Such weapons were regarded simply as one of the many "temporary" or "transitory" factors affecting the initial phases of war. They were not counted among the "permanently operating" factors *deciding* the outcome of the war. This doctrine was clearly reflected by Stalin in an "interview" (replies to questions put in writing) with the British correspondent Alexander Werth in September 1946, where he had stated:

> I do not believe the atomic bomb to be as serious a force as certain politicians are inclined to regard it. Atomic bombs are intended to intimidate the weak-nerved, but they cannot decide the outcome of war, since such bombs are by no means sufficient for this purpose. [41]

Again, an important lesson for the present is to be derived from this stance. Since Stalin knew perfectly well that the atomic bomb had destroyed the equilibrium of power between East and West, and since after all — in the case of Japan — such weapons *had* decided the outcome of war, [42] official Soviet doctrine did not reflect actual Soviet thinking. *Soviet military doctrine was used then, and has been used ever since, as a device with which to influence Western perceptions and policies.* This is not to say that this is the only purpose of Soviet military doctrine. It is, however, one of its purposes, and one that has become increasingly important.

The Soviet response to the military-strategic advantages enjoyed by the United States at the third level, that of military forces and armaments, followed the very same offensive pattern noted in the first two contexts. Its primary focus was Europe. Demobilization in the USSR (from about 11 million men at the end of the war to — according to various estimates — between 2.5 and 5 million men in 1948) had been carried out in such a way as to provide 175 divisions with a more flexible command

and control structure, more professional leadership, and more firepower and greater mobility. Soviet forces in Germany numbered over 300,000. They had at their disposal several thousand tanks, and many of the units were part of "guard" (*gvardia*) or "shock" formations drawing on the best personnel and equipment available. These forces (Group of Soviet Forces in Germany) and the Northern Group of Forces in Poland consisted of no less than seven armies with twenty-four maneuver divisions, thirteen supporting divisions (nine anti-aircraft, two artillery and two internal security divisions) and forty independent brigades or regiments. Although three of the six mechanized armies deployed in East Germany were merely on cadre status, the reorganization of the armed forces referred to above allowed for rapid mobilization and conversion to combat readiness. But even without such measures, the size, equipment, and readiness of the forces actually deployed conformed to the offensive strategic and operational concept. They appeared (and were) entirely sufficient to overrun the weak defenses of Western Europe.[43]

Again, to mention all this is not just to satisfy academic historic interest. Soviet conventional superiority in Europe and the offensive strategy connected with it have remained one of the most important military and political facts of life in Europe. *Their utility as a political instrument with which to influence American and Western European perceptions and policies has never really diminished.* The instrument itself has never been allowed to become blunt. This is also true for the Khrushchev era.

THE KHRUSHCHEV ERA

The successors of Stalin, with Khrushchev emerging by 1955 as the *primus inter pares,* initially continued the shift from confrontation to a certain relaxation of tensions begun by Stalin in Europe after the end of the Berlin blockade in the Spring of 1949 and in Asia after the stalemate reached in the Korean war. The post-Stalin "thaw" and the "Spirit of Geneva" appeared at the time to be lasting and to exclude the outbreak of serious crises and military confrontations.

In 1956 and 1957, however, developments in missile technology and the twin crises of Hungary and Suez converged to arrest and reverse the swing from confrontation to coexistence.

Soviet intervention in Hungary was an important factor in this context. It shattered the hope, even among many Western communists, that a fundamental change in the Soviet system and Soviet foreign policy had taken place.

The Suez crisis, however, heralded some important *changes in the directions* of Soviet foreign policy. New Soviet political commitments in the Middle East were helping to speed up the process of decolonization and undermining the Western economic and military position in that area. At the same time, the Suez crisis initiated important *changes in the conduct* of Soviet foreign policy, notably in the way in which new military capabilities, military threats, and military doctrine were employed for foreign-policy purposes. The frequent invocation of the dangers of escalation, the declaration of a readiness to send Soviet "volunteers" and, finally, Bulganin's letters of 5 November 1956 to Eden and Mollet (asking how Britain and France would have felt if they had been attacked "by more powerful states possessing every kind of destructive weapons" and reminding them that there were countries which "could have used other means such as rocket techniques") — all these were innovations in the style of foreign policy.

The departure from Stalinist diplomatic practice consisted not only of the fact that verbal threats were being employed against Western European member countries of NATO but that for the first time Soviet leaders were backing these threats by invoking Soviet nuclear weapons and medium-range missile capabilities. In the years thereafter, the Soviet threat posture under Khrushchev was to be systematically developed by integrating these three elements (verbal threats, nuclear weapons, and missiles) in one unified approach. Its main purposes: militarily to counteract the United States' strategic systems based in Western Europe, and politically to utilize and deepen "intra-imperialist contradictions," notably those between the U.S. and its European allies.

At the same time, the function of Western Europe as hostage to U.S. political restraint and military caution was being enhanced by the "nuclearization" of the Soviet threat to Europe.[44] Between 1957 and the early 1960s Soviet forces at tactical air army level were being equipped with nuclear weapons, and by 1960 guided missiles (*Scud*) were being deployed at front and army levels and artillery rockets (*Frog*) at division level.

Nuclearization of the armed forces was one of the factors which made it possible for Khrushchev to implement a good portion of his troop reduction program. This program was also to affect the Soviet forces in Central Europe. Two mechanized divisions were withdrawn from Germany. However, given the fact that simultaneously two mechanized divisions were converted to tank divisions, and four infantry divisions to full mechanization, and given the fact that all six of the latter were deployed forward within the immediate proximity of the border between East and West Germany, the threat posed by the combined conventional and theater nuclear capabilities had actually increased.[45]

If superiority in conventional forces and matching of NATO short-range theater nuclear systems are considered two main pillars of the Soviet threat posture in Europe, medium-range and intermediate-range nuclear delivery systems must be regarded as a third important pillar. Whatever the reason — prohibitive cost, technical deficiencies of the first-generation weapon systems, or opposition by the more traditional branches of the Soviet armed forces — the Soviet Union under Khrushchev, contrary to American fears of a "bomber gap" and a "missile gap," never did embark on a large-scale program of producing long-range bombers and intercontinental ballistic missiles. It opted instead for large serial production and deployment of medium-range and intermediate-range capabilities. Thus, another asymmetry of military power was being created in Central Europe.

Attempts were made by the Western Alliance to compensate for the Soviet advantages. Soviet superiority in conventional weapons was met by the deployment of a large number of battlefield nuclear systems, mostly artillery, and the threat of a first use of nuclear weapons; and it was, in part, to the Soviet advantages in medium-range and intermediate-range nuclear systems that the Western Alliance responded with an increased reliance on U.S. superiority in strategic nuclear weapons. Soviet military doctrine, in turn, was used to counter this Western concept.

Thus, at the conventional/tactical nuclear level, Soviet doctrine asserted — as early as the mid-1950s — that it was impossible to limit nuclear war or control escalation; that the explosive power of nuclear weapons was such "that it *completely excludes the possibility* of their employment *only* on a 'tactical' scale";[46] and that it was "quite clear that the first attempt to use this 'tactical' weapon would lead to the mass use of atomic and hydrogen bombs."[47] In the late 1950s and 1960s there were good reasons to consider such a view as valid since neither the Soviet nor the American delivery systems had the necessary accuracy to make limited nuclear war feasible. But even then lack in accuracy of the systems did not rule out nuclear strikes limited in location and the number of weapons employed. Moreover, particularly in the latter half of the 1960s, there were important modifications, exceptions and contradictions in the published sources of Soviet doctrine, which must lead the careful analyst to conclude that the official rejection of any significant distinction between tactical and strategic nuclear weapons in doctrine does not preclude recognition of such a distinction in war. The reason for the Soviet refusal, then as in contemporary circumstances, is relatively simple. As Raymond Garthoff has pointed out, "so long as the Soviet Union gains most by *complete* abstention from the use of nuclear weapons it will do nothing to encourage an alternative whereby the *limited* use of nuclear weapons relieves the enemy from facing a choice between a strategy of defeat and one of suicide." [48]

At the level of central strategic or intercontinental nuclear systems, Soviet doctrine — as authoritatively put forward by Khrushchev in his speech to the Supreme Soviet in January 1960 — provided for a comprehensive program of minimum deterrence and military sufficiency. In the later view of his domestic critics, Khrushchev relied "on one weapon, and that an untried one." [49] More precisely, Soviet doctrine relied on a combination of nuclear weapons and their delivery systems as the *decisive* weapon for deterrence and war-fighting. This doctrine was based on increasingly exaggerated claims by Khrushchev. Such claims began with the statement in November 1958, that "The production of the intercontinental ballistic rocket has been successfully set up." [50] They continued with the assertion in January 1959, at the XXI CPSU Congress, that "*Serial* production of the intercontinental ballistic rocket has been successfully organized," [51] went on with the report to the Supreme Soviet in early 1960 that the USSR had achieved superiority over the U.S.A. "in the creation and mass production of intercontinental ballistic rockets of all types," [52] and finally led to the blunt suggestion in March 1960 that "the Soviet Union is now the world's strongest military power." [53]

At the same time, Khrushchev announced in his January 1960 speech that he intended to reduce the manpower level of the armed forces from 3.6 to 2.4 million. "Today," he said, "the defense potential of the country is not determined by how many soldiers we have under arms, by how many people wear the uniform." It rather depends to a decisive degree, he continued, on the firepower (e.g., nuclear weapons) and the means of delivery (e.g., ballistic missiles) available. [54] In conjunction with the troop reductions already made, the cutbacks in naval programs, the stagnation in the *overt* defense expenditures, and the declarations that the center of gravity in the competition between the two systems had now shifted from the military to the economic sphere, it appeared — for a time — that the "new look," which Malenkov had unsuccessfully tried to provide for the Soviet military posture, was now being adopted and implemented by Khrushchev.

The Soviet "new look," however, soon collapsed — for a variety of reasons. Foremost among them is the fact that doctrine had anticipated developments on the "hardware" side by about a decade. The discrepancy between projected image and reality was becoming ever more pronounced as the U.S. was beginning to embark on a large-scale expansion of its strategic weapons program and, in its turn, claiming strategic superiority. Another important reason is the confrontation in Berlin in 1961 which clearly demonstrated the undiminished role of the ground forces in local conflicts (just as, one year later, the Cuban missile crisis was to underline the important role naval forces could play in such conflicts).

Of primary significance in the present context, however, is the fact that the newly won nuclear *capabilities,* to the extent that they existed, and the new over-extended *doctrine* developed on their basis were immediately integrated into an ambitious *foreign policy*. The aim of this policy went far beyond the rationale of the Soviet military posture and doctrine as stated by Khrushchev: "where there are equal forces, there must also be equal rights and equal opportunities." [55] It was rather meant to achieve a decisive breakthrough at the very center of East-West competition: in Europe.

Initially, starting from 1958, this aim was pursued with confidence. "No longer were we contaminated by Stalin's fear," Khrushchev was to say later. "No longer did we look at the world through his eyes. Now it was our enemies who trembled in *their* boots. Thanks to our missiles, we could deliver a nuclear bomb to a target at any place in the world. No longer was the industrial heartland of the United States invulnerable to our counter-attack." [56] By 1961, however, the U.S. superiority claims and the dissipation of the "missile gap" myth were seriously eroding the effectiveness of Krushchev's campaign. Soviet superiority claims were changing to claims of parity. The attempt at achieving a breakthrough in the East-West struggle at the center of competition yielded to the taking of emergency measures in order to prevent the collapse of the East German regime. Troop reductions were replaced by troop increases. Overt stagnation in defense expenditures gave way to the announcement of a dramatic rise in defense spending. The moratorium on nuclear weapons testing was broken. And, finally, direct deterrence of the United States by emphasizing Soviet strategic power and doctrine was increasingly being supplemented, almost supplanted, by threats to selected West European member countries of NATO.

Thus, Khrushchev threatened that in the event of war NATO military bases in Italy would be destroyed ("even if they are in orange groves"), and in Greece as well ("reportedly located among olive groves").[57] Six H-bombs, he thought, would be quite enough to annihilate the British Isles, and nine would take care of France.[58] Germany, he warned, would be "reduced to dust";[59] "the very existence of the population of West Germany [would be] placed in question."[60] In retrospect, Khrushchev held such threats to have been effective:

> "If a third world war is unleashed," Adenauer often said, "West Germany will be the first country to perish." I was pleased to hear this, and Adenauer was absolutely right in what he said. For him to be making public statements was a great achievement on our part. Not only were we keeping our number one enemy in line, but Adenauer was helping to keep our other enemies in line, too.[61]

The political purpose of the nuclear threats, even without Khrushchev's frank admission, was quite obvious. By bringing pressure to bear on the most exposed and most vulnerable NATO members, and by deepening their anxiety about war, the attempt was made to induce them to urge restraint on the United States. Since the United States did not make any effort to challenge the building of the wall, it is doubtful that the outcome of the Berlin crisis was interpreted by Khrushchev as a "setback" or "failure," as many Western analysts believe. Gains had been made. The West had "swallowed one bitter pill."[62] Provided the United States could be put under more direct pressure and faced with a more credible threat, provided its consciousness of vulnerability could be raised to the European level, and provided doctrine could match capabilities, conditions in Central Europe would perhaps get "more mature"; the West might be prepared to swallow yet another bitter pill. Undoubtedly, this was part of the reasoning underlying Khrushchev's venture to deploy medium-range and intermediate-range missiles in Cuba. His successors were to draw the appropriate lessons from the failure of this venture.

THE BREZHNEV ERA AND BEYOND

The Overall Military Effort

Marshal M. V. Zakharov, who was reinstated as Chief of General Staff by the new leadership, expressed previous criticism by military leaders and the spirit of the new times by saying, in obvious reference to Khrushchev, that "subjectivism is dangerous in any activity," but "particularly dangerous in military affairs which deal with problems of the country's defence." These observations applied especially to persons who claim "strategic far-sightedness" but lack a "rudimentary knowledge of military strategy."[63] While Zakharov warned against over-emphasis on strategic weapons, he also ruled out the complete dismantling of the new look and warned against those "leaders who are under the spell of the old experience, who turn this experience into a fetish and, by their authority and high position, obstruct the coming into being of everything that is new, progressive and outstanding."[64]

What came into being were not only substantial modernization programs for the ground and air forces, new types of naval vessels, the equipment of the armed forces with greater firepower and mobility, new types of aircraft and a great airlift capability — in short, significant quantitative and qualitative improvements in Soviet *conventional* power — but also a vast expansion and modernization of the *chemical* and *nuclear* weapons arsenal. As a result, the three pillars of the Soviet military threat to Europe mentioned above (conventional, battlefield, and intermediate-range nuclear weapons) and under Krushchev the still very shaky fourth (central strategic) pillar were strengthened, and a fifth one added: the buildup of intervention and power projection capabilities beyond the traditional reach of Soviet military might.

It could be argued that NATO, too, has expanded and modernized its forces. Such an argument, however, misses the point. Concerning expansion, the argument is simply wrong: numerically, by far most of NATO's conventional or nuclear weapons programs have stagnated;[65] increases in some areas have been negated by decreases in others. Concerning modernization, as noted, the improvements made by NATO have, in most categories, been matched by the Warsaw Pact, and in some categories the Pact has moved ahead. The central points, however, are, first, that the *qualitative* lead which NATO still enjoys in some weapons systems has for all practical purposes been invalidated by Warsaw Pact *quantitative* superiority; and, secondly, that the Pact has opened up new asymmetries of power where none previously existed, and widened those which had been created earlier.

The primary burden of the effort to achieve this state of affairs was borne by the Soviet Union. The number of men in its armed forces increased steadily from 3.4 million in 1964 to approximately 4.4 million in the late 1970s. (In the same period U.S. military manpower declined from about 2.7 million to 2.0 million.) Over the same period Soviet ground forces expanded from 148 divisions to over 170 divisions.[66] To keep pace with the manpower expansion as well as the increase and restructuring of the Soviet divisions, the Soviet Union stepped up its output of major weapons systems. Thus, in the mid-1970s the USSR annually produced 2,600 tanks (U.S.: 450), 950 tactical aircraft (U.S.: 575), 1,100 helicopters (U.S.: 506) and 1,400 artillery pieces (U.S.: 156).[67]

By far the biggest emphasis and the largest share of Soviet resources went to improving the threat posture *vis-à-vis* Europe.[68] Soviet forces stationed in Eastern Europe increased from 475,000 in the early 1960s to over 600,000 men in the late 1970s. (Over the same period the strength of U.S. land, sea, and air forces in Europe declined from 434,000 men to 300,000 men.) Although the total number of Warsaw Pact divisions in Central Europe remained practically unchanged between 1965 and 1980 (at 57 divisions), total ground force manpower deployed in the region grew by 150,000. (In contrast, NATO armed forces decreased by almost 50,000 men).[69] The most dramatic change, however, occurred in the wake of the Soviet invasion of Czechoslovakia when the USSR created the Central Group of Forces and stationed five divisions in that country. Because, simultaneously, four Czech motorized rifle divisions and an infantry regiment were abolished, the net result of the invasion was to increase the Warsaw Pact division total by only one. (Later, in 1980, this was to be negated by the withdrawal of one tank division from East Germany.) However, since five Category I Soviet divisions had been deployed instead of low-category readiness Czech divisions, Warsaw Pact force capabilities and readiness for combat in Europe had substantially improved. Such improvement was enhanced by the formation of additional combat units at army and front levels of subordination, expansion of manpower at division level, and, associated with that, a significant expansion of weapons assets.[70]

The emphasis on improving force capabilities *vis-a-vis* Europe is evident also in the area of short-range and intermediate-range nuclear systems. The Warsaw Pact divisions deployed in Europe (as far as, but excluding, the three western Military Districts of the USSR, Moscow, Volga, and Ural) are supported by 650 *Frog*/SS-21 short-range missiles (as against about 100 *Lance* and *Honest John* on the NATO side) and by another 650 SS-12/22s and *Scuds* (as compared to NATO's 180 *Pershing IAs*), by up to 2,500 aircraft that could be employed in a nuclear role (as against 800 on the NATO side), a new, expanding strike capability based on the Backfire supersonic, semi-strategic bomber, and a large force of longer-range land-based missiles of the old SS-4 and SS-5, and the new SS-20 type.[71] The Warsaw Pact, thus, increased its traditional numerical advantages over NATO over the whole spectrum of intermediate-range aircraft and missile systems. Taken by itself, this would not be of particular concern. More significant, however, is the fact that the new systems deployed represent a substantial improvement over their predecessors in terms of speed, mobility, survivability, range, and accuracy. With their help the Soviet Union has provided itself with the capability to destroy most of NATO's nuclear systems and targets of strategic importance either in a nuclear or (since many of the systems are "dual capable") conventional/chemical strike.

Simultaneously, the Soviet Union undertook a massive program to catch up with (and — wherever possible — overtake) the United States in the strategic arms competition. The enormous scale of the Soviet effort is indicated by the fact that Soviet deployments leapt from 200 land-based intercontinental ballistic missiles (ICBMs) in 1964 to 800 in 1968, and to numerical superiority over the United States during SALT I (1,530 missiles as against 1,054 American land-based missiles). Similarly, the number of submarine-launched ballistic missiles jumped from little more than 100 in 1964 to over 1,000 at the end of the 1970s. The number of deliverable warheads rose from about 450 to, at present, more than 8,500.[72] As a result of this, and in particular as a result of the deployment of a large number of ICBMs of the SS-18 and SS-19 type equipped with multiple warheads (up to ten), yet another asymmetry has developed in favor of the Soviet Union. That country now has a greater capacity to destroy ICBM sites than the United States. By the mid-1980s, the USSR will have, at least in theory, the capacity to destroy about 90 percent of American ICBMs in their silos.

Finally, the Soviet Union has significantly improved its power-projection capabilities. These are based mainly on the expansion of the long-range airlift capacity of the Soviet air force and the civilian *Aeroflot;*[73] eight airborne divisions; new long-range naval combat capabilities with ever new types of ship;[74] an expanded naval and civilian sea transport capacity;[75] and about 12,000 men in naval infantry, most of whom are deployed in four regiments. Western experts note that the naval deployments of 1978-1981 (the result of political decisions made at the end of the 1960s) conformed to a "new strategic concept."[76] The central role of the forward-deployed Soviet naval forces was no longer combat against U.S. strategic nuclear submarines but anti-carrier tasks.[77] If so, the purpose of Soviet naval deployments would have shifted even further to a war-fighting role in local and limited conflict; they would add to the effectiveness of future long-range airlift operations, of the kind successfully demonstrated in Angola and Ethiopia in the latter half of the 1970s. Certainly, they have already enhanced the effectiveness of Soviet power projection in areas contiguous to the USSR but vitally important to Western Europe — for example, the Mediterranean and the Persian Gulf.[78] Is it sound to conclude, therefore, that the role of combined Soviet naval and air power is and probably will be even more political than ever before? Does it follow that there is a grand political design underlying the Soviet military buildup?

The Overall Declaratory Effort

Any attempt to answer these and the related questions posed in the introduction on the basis of Soviet sources immediately runs up against a paradox: the more evident the superiority in the various dimensions of the East-West arms competition, the more pronounced are the Soviet claims of "parity," "equilibrium," and "essential equality of forces." The more doubt is being expressed in the West whether the Soviet military buildup could still be considered as just merely serving legitimate defensive needs of the Soviet Union, the more insistent the Soviet assertions that the purpose of Soviet military efforts is only to "safeguard Soviet security." The more explicit the Western suspicion that the Soviet Union has been taking one initiative after the other to gain unilateral advantage, increasingly relying on the military instrument — that the USSR has been "cashing in" on its newly developed capabilities — the more insistent the Soviet denial that this has been the case.

In the late 1960s and early to middle 1970s one could still read that "It is clear that if the aggressive forces of international imperialism were to continue their policy of the arms race and preparation for war, the socialist states *must have a military potential that is quantitatively superior* to the potential of the imperialist countries."[79] In that period it was also frankly admitted that "The historic function of the Soviet armed forces at present is *not* limited to the defense of the motherland and the other socialist countries."[80] It was also openly acknowledged that Soviet strategic power by itself was not an effective means to deal with local-war contingencies affecting the interests of the USSR and other socialist countries:

> From the point of view of meeting the task of preventing local wars, and in such cases, in which the necessity arises militarily to support such peoples as are fighting for their freedom and independence against the forces of internal reaction and imperialist intervention, the *Soviet Union may need mobile, well trained and well equipped forces.* [81]

To the extent that the national-liberation struggle could be supported more effectively by the USSR, *"expansion of the Soviet military presence and aid by other socialist states even now constitutes an important factor* of international relations." [82] Since even a cursory examination of naval history showed that major powers attained important strategic aims in wartime and in peacetime, using their navies as weighty arguments in the battle with their adversaries, the Soviet Navy, too, could be used accordingly. It could further Soviet "state interests." It could be an "instrument of the policy of peace and friendship of peoples, of *deterring military adventures and of resolute opposition to threats against the security of peace-loving peoples* by imperialist powers." [83] As for Europe in particular, as late as 1977 statements as frank as the following still could slip by the censor:

> The representatives of the NATO countries deny [that] an equilibrium of strength [exists] in Central Europe. Judging by some of their statements, the "balance of forces" that would suit the Western countries in that area is one which would rule out the possibility of the socialist countries influencing international events *beyond their frontiers.* [84]

By that time, however, the official line for the second half of the 1970s and the early 1980s had already been firmly set by Soviet political leadership. According to Brezhnev, the concern expressed in the West that the Soviet Union was building up its military potential quantitatively and qualitatively, systematically and consistently to an extent that exceeded the requirements of defense had "no basis." He said, "A Soviet military threat does not exist and cannot exist for Europe or for any other parts of the world." Assertions to the effect that the USSR and the other countries of the Warsaw Pact had achieved in Europe some kind of "military superiority" (*voennyi pereves*) over the NATO countries and were continuing to build up their armed forces were, "to put it mildly, tendentious and misleading." As for the alleged increases in Warsaw Pact strength, "the Soviet Union over a number of years has not expanded or built up its armed forces in Central Europe." As for alleged Warsaw Pact military superiority over NATO, "at the talks in Vienna the [two] sides exchanged official information which shows that no 'superiority' or 'disproportion' exists."[85]

These assertions clearly demonstrate that there are limits to attempts at distilling the rationale of the Soviet military effort and military doctrine from published Soviet sources. They also underline the fact that in the period from the late 1960s to the early 1980s there is an inverse relationship between growing Soviet military strength and its open verbal invocation. The reasons for this are fairly obvious.

The first reason has been already touched upon in the discussion above concerning the Soviet clarifications about the relative importance of military power in the overall "correlation of forces." This reason is: Since detente in Western perceptions was predicated upon Soviet *restraint* in the arms competition, since SALT I had, for many Western observers, ratified *parity* in the military-strategic sphere, and since the negotiations on mutual balanced reductions of forces meant, in the Western view, asymmetrical reductions by the Warsaw Pact to achieve an *equilibrium* of forces in Central Europe, any major Soviet arms effort could only be interpreted as a quest for newly gaining or widening existing *superiority*. Thus, the logic of Soviet participation in arms control negotiations required the denial of superiority already achieved or any intention to acquire superiority.

Secondly, in the course of the 1970s the necessity of openly invoking Soviet strength was largely becoming obsolete. The realization was beginning to gain ground in Western public opinion — in the United States more so than in Western Europe — that the Soviet Union was, in fact, engaged in a major arms buildup. Western publications, official and non-official, were reflecting this very fact. NATO governments were becoming ever more aware of the relative military weakness of the alliance and were beginning to look for means to redress the military balance (as evident, for instance, in the 1977 Long-Term Defense Program and in the discussions in 1977/78 about countering Soviet superiority in tanks by the deployment of enhanced radiation weapons in Central Europe). They were also becoming more conscious of the need to provide NATO military doctrine with greater credibility (as apparent in the 1979 decision to deploy new intermediate-range nuclear delivery systems in Western Europe unless tangible results of arms control negotiations were to make such deployment unnecessary).

Thirdly — and very much connected with the previous point — as the NATO countries possess significantly higher economic and technological resources, the Soviet leaders evidently thought that everything possible had to be done at the verbal, declaratory level in order to prevent these resources from being mobilized for major military research and development, arms production, and manpower expansion programs.[86]

Fourth, perhaps paradoxically at first sight, opportunities were opening up for the Soviet Union in the course of the 1970s to influence more thoroughly a new Western "peace movement." They were connected with the fact that the very plans and programs by NATO governments to redress the balance and restore credibility to NATO military doctrine, in the view of important sections of Western public opinion and, most important, among left-wing sections of major political parties in Western Europe, were threatening to lead to additional *Soviet* military efforts, to a new round in the arms race, to higher inflationary rates in the Western economies, and to cutbacks in social welfare programs. Soviet claims about military superiority, as accomplished fact or intended end result of the buildup, and open acknowledgement of far-reaching political purposes would have seriously undermined the potential effectiveness of this movement.

Whereas there have been changes in emphasis in Soviet interpretations of the reasons for and the significance of the military buildup of the USSR, there are also some themes which have remained constant. These themes center upon the thesis that Soviet military programs are defensive and that they constitute a reaction to military developments abroad which threaten Soviet security. To the extent that the military efforts of the USSR are acknowledged by Soviet spokesmen to have a political purpose, such purpose, in Europe, is said to consist of the requirement of defeating "imperialist policies from positions of strength" and to frustrate attempts at "pressuring" or "blackmailing" the Soviet Union. Outside Europe, but including the Mediterranean, it is portrayed as the need to constrain Western political options.[87] In areas where "national-liberation struggles" are taking place, in Africa (e.g., Angola), Asia (e.g., Afghanistan) and Latin America (e.g., Nicaragua), Soviet military power is held not to be instrumental in the export of revolution but designed to "prevent the export of counterrevolution."[88] These defensive, status-quo, and security-oriented explanations may have some validity in individual cases. However, they by no means cover the whole rationale of the Soviet military effort.

The Military and Political Rationale

In an attempt to explain the rationale of the Soviet military effort, the argument has been put forward by a careful Western specialist on Soviet affairs that there existed a "severed link" — a "discontinuity" — between Soviet military capabilities and military strategy, on the one hand, and political rationale, on the other; that the Soviet leaders in all likelihood have *not* "set out systematically to undermine all of NATO's defense options, knowing that at a certain point they [the Soviet leaders] will undermine political options as well"; that "the most immediate explanation for the systematic growth of Soviet military power is [a Soviet] response to requirements of war"; and that, finally, "the Soviet Union has the military machine it has because it is principally the work of military men." [89] Each and every one of these propositions must be regarded with great reservation.

To begin with, one should not discard lightly Western conventional wisdom that Soviet military policy, doctrine, and foreign policy are shaped by the *Party,* i.e., the *political leadership,* alone or in conjunction with military leaders. [90] The military establishment, of course, will do its best to secure for itself a large share of economic resources (and has not done badly at it), and it will also attempt to prejudice allocation decisions by suggesting military strategies favorable to that end. There is, however, no evidence that the above-mentioned Leninist precept concerning the necessity of subordinating the military viewpoint to the political has been abandoned. In the Soviet system of government, perhaps more than in any other system, military affairs are regarded as too important to be left to the generals. Party control and secret police supervision at each and every level of the military hierarchy are a constant reminder of this. Even in instances, notably under Khrushchev, where there is conflict over military policies, it would be erroneous to conceive of it as conflict pure and simple between the military and the Party. More often than not it is conflict between different sections *of* the Party and *among* the political leadership, with one section supporting and more successfully utilizing the military for its political purposes. Also, all the well-known facts that (1) the military enjoys a privileged position in society, (2) high-ranking military officers are prominently represented in arms control negotiations, (3) military requirements have a priority in the economy, and (4) military power plays a large role in Soviet foreign policy should not be considered as evidence of the ascendancy of the military at the expense of the Party/political leadership. They should rather be regarded as an indication of the high value which the Party/political leadership places on the military instrument to support its external policies, and on military virtues, norms and principles as an aid in nation-building.[91]

If it is correct that the borderlines between political and military viewpoints are fluid and if both political and military leaders recognize the important role of military power in international affairs, it follows that the current force posture which the Soviet Union has developed most likely constitutes the end result of a dynamic process, in which military and political rationales are mixed; in which long-term ("strategic") and short-term ("tactical") considerations overlap; and in which "defensive" and "offensive" motives are difficult to disentangle. There are, however, three consistent developments.

First, whereas from the second half of the 1940s until the first half of the 1960s the Soviet leaders were reacting primarily to perceived dangers and constraints, they were, from the second half of the 1960s to the late 1970s, acting more often than not in response to *new opportunities.* Whereas, in the first period, the Soviet leaders were — as their foreign affairs specialists write — engaged primarily in an effort to first constrain and then deny political and military options to the adversary superpower and its allies, they have, in the second period, been creating *new options* for themselves. Whereas they were initially concerned most of all with the security and defense of the USSR and the other members of the Warsaw Pact, they are now engaged in a much more difficult and ambitious endeavor at "protecting" and "aiding" *new allies and clients* from Cuba via Angola and South Yemen to Mongolia and Vietnam.

Secondly, it is difficult to avoid the conclusion that military developments fit into an overall *political design.* This design was in all probability not clearly conceived by Stalin in 1945, and perhaps not even by Brezhnev in 1964. Yet the evolution of the Soviet force posture — particularly after 1964 — does have the appearance of consistency, not of a coincidental, random series of events. The logic of this consistent development can be summarized as follows:

— creation of preponderance in conventional weapons in Europe with the intention of counteracting U.S. strategic superiority and the result of making this region "hostage" to good American intentions;
— "nuclearization" of the Soviet conventional forces and establishment of superiority in intermediate-range nuclear systems, thereby redoubling the threat to Western Europe;

— achievement of parity, perhaps "parity plus," in the strategic sphere
with the result of neutralizing U.S. "overhang" strategic capabilities, and weakening the U.S. nuclear "umbrella" for Western
Europe, as well as enhancing the importance of the military asymmetries at the conventional and theater nuclear level in favor of
the USSR;

— modernization and expansion of the conventional and theater nuclear forces and improvements in the speed, accuracy, survivability, and range of the systems deployed in Europe with the
result of achieving escalation dominance at each and every level of
the arms competition up to the central strategic systems and thereby
seriously eroding the credibility of NATO's doctrine of "Flexible
Response";

— enhancement of regional superiority along the southern and Far
Eastern borders of the USSR, establishment of a naval presence in
the Mediterranean and the Indian Ocean, and creation of power
projection capabilities with the effect of extending the reach of
Soviet arms and reinforcing their effectiveness in areas contiguous
to the Soviet Union but vital to Western Europe.

Thirdly, a corresponding, equally *consistent pattern as regards military doctrine* can be noted. In each and every phase of the development
of the Soviet force posture, doctrine was designed to maximize the political effectiveness of capabilities. Since Soviet relative strengths have always been in the conventional sphere, the maximization of this Soviet
military advantage under Stalin, as noted, took the form of denying the
political and military importance of nuclear weapons. Under Khrushchev
and Brezhnev, when the decisive importance of the growing arsenals of
nuclear weapons on both sides could no longer be ignored, it took the form
of stressing automaticity of nuclear escalation and castigating theories of
limited war. Quite obviously, however, in each phase of Soviet policy the
adoption of a purely deterrent and defensive posture (doctrine and capabilities) would have had a minimal political effect, or none at all. Such a
posture, moreover, would have completely contradicted the ideological
basis on which the Soviet leadership operates: the emphasis on being part
of a forward movement of history and on having the historic obligation to
create a framework in which such movement can take place.

Thus, the politically most effective posture for "deterring" (*sderzhi-
vat'*) and "intimidating" (*ustrashit'*) potential and actual adversaries has,

in the Soviet view, always been one that makes Soviet preparedness for fighting and winning wars credible. The politically most promising doctrine and strategy has been regarded as one that stresses the offensive, that threatens to carry the war to the territory of the enemy, and that postulates a brief military campaign and a resounding victory for the Soviet armed forces. It is one that is able credibly to rule out all of the opponent's defensive options. The Soviet leaders, for these reasons, do not make a clear-cut distinction between the prevention of war and the preparation for war.[92]

Preparation for war, however, does not mean that the Soviet leaders "really believe that they can fight and win" nuclear war. Even a belief in general that victory in conventional war is possible, assuming the Soviet leaders hold such a belief, does not mean that they are confident about their ability to control the risks of conventional war *in Europe*. The United States and its allies still retain enormous deterrent and defensive capabilities. Furthermore, Western Europe is an area vital to U.S. security, and the American determination to defend this area cannot be overestimated or overlooked. The risk of escalation from conventional to general nuclear war, therefore, is always present. It cannot be ignored, and is not ignored, by the Soviet leaders. What they can (and do) attempt to achieve, however, is to create concern on the part of Western European public opinion and political leadership that the link provided by "Flexible Response" between conventional and nuclear war, as well as between war in Europe and general war, has been weakened and can be broken altogether.

This warrants the conclusion that the main purpose of the Soviet military buildup in Europe is not first to prepare for and then fight war, conventional or nuclear, but to influence Western perceptions. It is to change the psychology of Western European and American public opinion and political leadership. It is to maintain and enhance, rather than alleviate, Western European insecurity; to create an atmosphere in which the first use of nuclear weapons by NATO is seen as militarily counterproductive and morally reprehensible; and to convey the impression that Western Europe *cannot* and therefore, *will not* be defended. The protracted process of European arms control negotiations is just as much a part of this purpose[93] as the formation of ever more specialized and ever more effective institutions designed to exploit Western attempts at rectifying military imbalances.[94]

One of the many constant features of Soviet perceptions and policies after 1945 has been the ideologically conditioned view held by the Soviet leadership that "socialism" is engaged in an historically ordained, long-term competition with "imperialism," of which the United States is the most powerful exponent. Western Europe, according to this view, is the most important as well as the most promising area, the control of which will ultimately decide the outcome of the struggle of the two world systems. It is an area of utmost importance because of its highly developed economic and technological base and its role as a bridgehead for U.S. military power and political influence. Despite its predominantly Western orientation, it offers opportunities for penetration by the Soviet Union. This is due, in Soviet calculations, to Western Europe's close proximity to the USSR; its political fragmentation, social differentiation and ideological diversity; and its lack of viable autonomous defense options. Thus, in order to rise to a dominant position in Europe, Soviet leaders — from Stalin to Andropov — have attempted to remove U.S. influence and the U.S. military presence from Europe and have tempted the Europeans with an "all-European" destiny, with a "zone of peace" or a "pan-European security system" which would make U.S. military guarantees superfluous.

The all-European temptation has been skillfully manipulated by the Soviet leaders. Over the years they have refined their traditional dual-track approach, i.e., the combination of diplomacy with propaganda; the fueling of the Western Europeans' fear of war, while seemingly meeting their desire for peace and cooperation; the gradual establishment and further improvement of regional military preponderance in Europe while taking one arms-control initiative after another; and, finally, the involvement of the Western European governments in arms control negotiations at the state level while simultaneously attempting to undermine the negotiating stance of these governments by appealing to oppositional factions and forces outside and inside the government.

This last approach, in particular, has gained in importance. Its most recent manifestation are the vigorous efforts made in order to reverse NATO's dual-track decision (deployment of intermediate-range nuclear systems in Western Europe unless the results of negotiation make this unnecessary) by relying on a variety of mechanisms and organizations: local communist parties, communist and non-communist trade unions, meetings between the Communist Party of the Soviet Union and Western European Social Democrats, conferences of concerned scientists and physicians, and support for marches and demonstrations by "progressive" and "peace-loving" forces, including pacifist, religious and environmentalist groups. Another part of this approach is the preferential treatment accorded to those factions of non-communist ruling parties or coalition partners in Western European governments which are more favorably inclined to accepting the Soviet point of view. With the help of parties, factions and groups such as these the Soviet leaders evidently hope to bring pressure to bear on Western European governments and to constrain their freedom of action on security matters. They quite obviously strive to deepen fear and anxiety among the Western public at large and to enhance a — justified or unjustified — sense of vulnerability among governments about the strength of domestic opposition.

There can be no doubt: Feelings of external as well as internal insecurity and vulnerability, heightened awareness of a changed and changing power balance in favor of the Soviet Union and perceptions that the defense of Europe is impossible, were they to gain ground, do matter. In regions outside or adjacent to Europe, such perceptions, combined with disunity in the Western Alliance, local political instability, superior Soviet force projection capabilities and Soviet realization of a lack in U.S. determination, would in all likelihood induce greater Soviet risk-taking propensities. In Europe, such perceptions could spread a spirit of accommodation to Soviet demands and ultimately transform the political conditions in that region. Responsible leadership in the West would consist of adopting measures which can effectively counteract these political purposes of Soviet military capabilities and doctrine.

NOTES

1. As early as 1971, Marshall Shulman noted that "the Soviet leadership is in a chesty mood, prepared to enjoy the advantages of a rising power position," and that the Soviet Union was "now pressing outward for a role commensurate with its status as one of the two superpowers in the world" (Marshall D. Shulman, "What Does Security Mean Today?" *Foreign Affairs*, July 1971, pp. 612-13).

2. According to the CIA, the estimated dollar costs of Soviet defense activities "grew at an average annual rate of over 3 percent from 1965 through 1980" (National Foreign Assessment Center, *Soviet and U.S. Defense Activities, 1971-80: A Dollar Cost Comparison*, SR81-10005, January 1981, p. 1). "When valued in rubles, this growth rate is 4-5 percent, reflecting the different pricing structure in the Soviet Union" (the corresponding report for *1970-79*, SR80-10005, January 1980, p. 3n). For the very different methodology and results by William T. Lee see his *The Estimation of Soviet Defense Expenditures, 1955-1975: An Unconventional Approach* (New York: Praeger, 1977), esp. fig. 10.2, p. 147.

3. This is a point made by Seweryn Bialer, "The Harsh Decade: Soviet Policies in the 1980s," *Foreign Affairs*, Summer 1981, p. 1003.

4. *Voennaia strategiia,* 3rd edn., [Marshal] V. D. Sokolovskii, ed. (Moscow: Voenizdat, 1968), p. 57.

5. *Ibid.,* p. 55.

6. *Spravochnik ofitsera,* S. N. Kozlov, ed. (Moscow: Voenizdat, 1971), p. 73.

7. *Slovar' osnovnykh voennykh terminov,* [General-Colonel] A. I. Radzievskii, ed. (Moscow: Voenizdat, 1965), entry "Voennaia doktrina."

8. *Voennaia strategiia,* p. 55.

9. *Ibid.*

10. *Slovar' osnovnykh voennykh terminov* (italics mine).

11. The Defense Council dates back to 1938 (then called Main Military Council). Its membership typically includes the General Secretary of the Party, the Prime Minister, and the Defense Minister. Other members are selected according to the power and standing they may have at any given point in time (this would, at present, almost certainly include Foreign Minister Gromyko). Yet another set of participants may be included because of particular decisions to be adopted, necessitating, for instance, the presence of officers from the Defense Ministry and the General Staff; the Central Committee secretary in charge of the armaments industry; the heads of the Military Department of *Gosplan* and of the Military-Industrial Commission; and, finally, experts from the Academy of Sciences.

12. *Leninskii sbornik,* 2nd ed., Vol. XII (Moscow, 1931), p. 437.

13. *Voennaia strategiia,* p.61.

14. *Mezhdunarodnye konflikty,* Zhurkin and Primakov, eds. (Moscow: "Mezhdunarodnye otnosheniia," 1972), p. 16. Sokolovskii's *Voennaia strategiia* is more precise on this issue. It speaks of "massive retaliation" as a "strategy" developed on the basis of the "policy of deterrence" (*ustrashenie*), p. 68. Later, "Flexible Response," too, is called a "strategy" rather than a "military political doctrine" (pp. 73 and 75).

15. *Voennaia strategiia,* p. 17. This statement has to be distinguished from assertions that Soviet and "bourgeois" military strategy respectively reflect a "class essence."

16. *Ibid.,* pp. 16-17.

17. *Ibid.,* p. 19.

18. V. I. Lenin, *Pol. sobr. soch.,* Vol. XLI, p. 65, as quoted by A. Sergiev, "Leninizm o sootnoshenii sil kak faktore mezhdunarodnykh otnoshenii," *Mezhdunarodnaia zhizn',* 4 (1975), p. 102.

19. V. I. Lenin, *Pol. sobr. soch.,* Vol. XXXVI, p. 288, as quoted by Sergiev.

20. Nathan Leites, *The Operational Code of the Politburo* (New York: McGraw-Hill, 1951); Richard Pipes, "Some Operational Principles of Soviet Foreign Policy," in *The USSR and the Middle East,* Michael Confino and Shimon Shamir, eds. (Jerusalem: Israel University Press, 1973), pp. 5-30, and Pipes, "Operational Principles of Soviet Foreign Policy," *Survey,* Spring 1973, pp. 41-61; Alexander L. George, "The 'Operational Code': A Neglected Approach to the Study of Political Leaders and Decision-Making," in *The Conduct of Soviet Foreign Policy,* Erik P. Hoffmann and Frederic J. Fleron, Jr., eds. (London: Butterworths, 1971), pp. 165-90 (reprinted from *International Studies Quarterly,* June 1969, pp. 190-220).

21. V. I. Lenin, *Pol. sobr. soch.,* Vol. XLIII, p. 131, as quoted by A. Sergiev, "Leninizm o sootnoshenii sil," pp. 102-3 (note 18 above). Lenin was speaking at the All-Russia Congress of Transport Workers on March 27, 1921. "Only when we are able to estimate these forces correctly and quite soberly, irrespective of our sympathies and desires," he said, "shall we be able to draw the proper conclusions concerning our policy in general, and our immediate tasks in particular."

22. These terms and their significance were first explored by Raymond Garthoff, "The Concept of the Balance of Power in Soviet Policy Making," *World Politics,* October

1951, pp. 85-111. The changes in their employment and emphasis were further examined by William Zimmermann, *Soviet Perspectives on International Relations, 1956-1967* (Princeton University Press, 1968).

23. G. Shakhnazarov, "K probleme sootnosheniia sil vi mire," *Kommunist,* February 1974, pp. 77-89. Shakhnazarov is deputy head of the Central Committee department responsible for relations with the communist and workers' parties.

24. *Ibid.*

25. Sergiev, "Leninizm o sootnoshenii sil," p. 110.

26. Shakhnazarov, p. 88. A similar rejection of alleged Western notions of "equality of forces" (*ravnovesie sil*) or "balance of forces" (*balans sil*) — presumably meaning the traditional concepts concerning the "balance of power" in Europe — can be found in Sh. P. Sanakoev and N. I. Kapchenko, *Teoriia i praktika vneshnei politiki sotsializma* (Moscow: "Mezhdunarodnye otnosheniia," 1973), p. 139.

27. Elliot R. Goodman, "Disparities in East-West Relations," *Survey,* Spring 1973, p. 89. He also wondered, if detente was truly the Soviet purpose in Europe, "then why the steady and unprecedented military build-up at the same time?" Similarly, in testimony before the Senate Foreign Relations Committee in July 1973, Leo Labedz quoted Soviet sources to the effect that "The strategic course of the U.S. policy is now changing before our very eyes from 'Pax Americana' — the Americanized formula of world domination — to a definite form of necessity for peaceful coexistence. But we must clearly understand that it is a forced change and that it is the actual power — social, economic and, ultimately, military power of the Soviet Union and other socialist countries — that compels the American ruling circles to make an agonizing reappraisal." And then Labedz said it was not surprising that when Mr. Brezhnev was faced with a direct question during his Washington visit — how he reconciled the Soviet military buildup with his "peace policy" — he "laughed it all off as being an aberration of intelligence services of NATO," Leo Labedz, "The Politics of Survival," *Survey,* Spring 1980, p. 45.

28. One of the first Western scholars to notice this was Peer Lange, *Zur Aufwertung der aussenpolitischen Rolle der sowjetischen Militärmacht,* Stiftung Wissenschaft und Politik, Ebenhausen/Munich, Research Paper SWP-AZ 2134, April 1977; also Lange's *Zur politischen Nutzung militärischer Macht: Der sowjetische Denkansatz,* Bundesinstitut für ostwissenschaftliche und internationale Studien, Berichte, October 1978.

29. Sergiev, "Leninizm o sootnoshenii sil," p. 107.

30. *Ibid.,* p. 104.

31. [Colonel] S. Tiushkevich, "Sootnoshenie sil vo mire i faktory predotvrashcheniia voiny," *Kommunist Vooruzhennykh Sil,* May 1974, p. 16. As this journal (Communist in the Armed Forces) is primarily meant for indoctrination in the armed forces, it is not surprising that its emphasis on military power as an important component in the "correlation of forces" is more obvious than that of other journals.

32. Milovan Djilas, *Conversations with Stalin* (New York: Harcourt Brace and World, 1962), p. 114.

33. Stalin's letter to the Yugoslav Central Committee, 1948, quoted by Malcolm Mackintosh, *Strategy and Tactics of Soviet Foreign Policy* (London: Oxford University Press, 1962), p. 15. Similarly, Roy Medvedev reflected that if it had not been for the United States, "Not only Eastern Europe but also Western Europe would have been liberated by the Red Army. The face of Europe today would be quite different." Roy Medvedev, *Let History Judge: The Origins and Consequences of Stalinism* (New York: Knopf, 1971), pp. 469-70.

34. For details of these probes see Ken Booth, *The Military Instrument in Soviet*

Foreign Policy, 1917-1972 (London: Royal United Services Institute for Defence Studies, 1973), pp. 38-40.

35. As quoted by A. Lavrent'eva, "Stroiteli novogo mira," *V mire knig,* No. 9 (1970), p. 4. This article reviews a biography of Boris Vannikov, People's Commissar of Munitions, who, by the nature of this position, was charged with primary responsibility for the Soviet nuclear weapons program. The book being reviewed (G. Ustinov's *Narodnyi komissar*), however, does not seem ever to have been published. My attention was drawn to Lavrent'eva's article by David Holloway, *Entering the Nuclear Arms Race: The Soviet Decision to Build the Atomic Bomb, 1939-45,* International Security Studies Program, The Wilson Center, Washington, D.C., Working Paper No. 9, 1979, p. 41.

36. Djilas, *Conversations with Stalin,* p. 182.

37. This is argued in more detail in Hannes Adomeit, *Soviet Risk-Taking and Crisis Behavior: A Theoretical and Empirical Analysis* (London: George Allen & Unwin, 1982). For the military aspects of the use of military power for political purposes by Stalin in the postwar period see esp. pp. 133-44.

38. Khrushchev's "Secret Speech" at the XX CPSU Congress in February 1956.

39. The changes which this doctrine underwent as a result of the Berlin crisis and the Korean war have been examined by Judson Mitchell, "The Revised 'Two Camps' Doctrine in Soviet Foreign Policy," *Orbis,* Spring 1972, pp. 21-34.

40. Raymond L. Garthoff, *Soviet Strategy in the Nuclear Age* (New York: Praeger, 1958), p. 62.

41. *Pravda,* 25 September 1946.

42. This, however, is still being denied by Soviet spokesmen. The use of nuclear weapons against Japan was, they assert, of marginal military importance, since the war was decided by the Soviet invasion of Manchuria. Hence, the primary rationale of Hiroshima and Nagasaki was to exert pressure on the Soviet Union. See, for instance, G. A. Trofimenko, *Strategiia global'noi voiny* (Moscow: "Mezhdunarodnye otnosheniia," 1968), p. 46; see also Grechko's remarks at the 30th anniversary of the formal Japanese surrender, *Pravda,* 3 September 1975 and the TASS interview by the retired wartime commander of the Soviet Air Force, Marshal Alexander Novikov, who asserted that "the atomic bombing of Hiroshima and Nagasaki was unjustified from the military point of view," as quoted in *International Herald Tribune,* 5 September 1975.

43. The account of Soviet military reorganization and force deployments draws on Phillip A. Karber, "The Central European Arms Race: 1948-1980," a paper prepared for the Conference on Arms Control, Stiftung Wissenschaft und Politik, Ebenhausen (Munich), 11-13 June 1980. See also Adomeit, *Soviet Risk-Taking,* p. 140.

44. This account of the "nuclearization" of the Soviet theater forces draws on Thomas W. Wolfe, *Soviet Power and Europe, 1945-1970* (Baltimore: Johns Hopkins, 1970), pp. 173-78, and Karber, "The Central European Arms Race," pp. 33-43.

45. Karber, "The Central European Arms Race," pp. 33-43.

46. [Colonel] Ye. Kosorukov and [Lieutenant Colonel] V. Matsulenko, in *Voennyi vestnik,* July 1955, p. 92.

47. [Major] N. Kopov, in *Voennyi vestnik,* March 1955, p. 77, as quoted by Garthoff, *Soviet Strategy in the Nuclear Age,* p. 110.

48. *Ibid.,* p. 111.

49. Marshal Rotmistrov, Commander of the Tank Forces Academy, *Kasnaia zvezda,* 25 April 1964.

50. *Pravda,* 2 December 1958.

51. *Ibid.,* 28 January 1959 (italics mine).

52. *Ibid.,* 15 January 1960.

53. *Ibid.*, 2 March 1960. Before claiming superiority in narrow military terms Khrushchev, at the XXI CPSU Congress, had asserted more generally that "the preponderance of forces (*pereves sil*) is now on the side of the peaceloving countries, and not on the side of the imperialist states." Khrushchev's arms production and capability claims, and their utilization for foreign-policy purposes, have been thoroughly analyzed by Arnold L. Horelick and Myron Rush, *Strategic Power and Soviet Foreign Policy* (Chicago: University of Chicago Press, 1965).

54. *Pravda*, 15 January 1960.

55. Khrushchev in a speech of 8 July 1961 to the graduates of the Soviet military academies — *Pravda*, 9 July 1961.

56. *Khrushchev Remembers: The Last Testament,* transl. and ed. by Strobe Talbott, with a foreword by Edward Crankshaw and an introduction by Jerrold L. Schecter (London: Deutsch, 1974), p. 53. Khrushchev continued: "Of course, we tried to derive maximum advantage from the fact that we were the first to launch our rockets into space. We wanted to exert pressure on American militarists — and also influence the minds of more reasonable politicians." In contrast to that, the confidence of the editors of *Voennaia strategiia*, that even the most obvious misrepresentation of fact will receive a fair hearing and fall on fruitful ground in the West, apparently is unlimited. They write: "The Soviet Union has had intercontinental rockets since 1956. It is difficult to overestimate the strategic importance of these rockets. They can reach any point on the globe carrying atomic or thermonuclear warheads of essentially unlimited destructive power. *However, the Soviet government did not utilize this advantage to solve any problems of foreign policy.* On the contrary, . . ." (*Voennaia strategiia*, p. 64; italics mine).

57. *Pravda*, 12 August 1961.

58. Khrushchev in talks with the British ambassador, Sir Frank Roberts, as reported in *Washington Post*, 12 July 1961.

59. *Pravda*, 8 August 1961.

60. *Ibid.*, 12 August 1961.

61. *Khrushchev Remembers*, p. 569.

62. This is a phrase used by Khrushchev (*ibid.*, p. 509), and the same metaphor occurs frequently in *The Penkovsky Papers*, introduction and commentary by Frank Gibney, foreword by Edward Crankshaw, transl. by P. Deriabin (London: Collins, 1965).

63. *Krasnaia zvezda*, 4 February 1965.

64. *Ibid.*

65. Some of the exceptions, i.e., some of the areas where increases took place, are U.S. strategic warheads, NATO anti-tank weapons, and NATO anti-aircraft systems.

66. U.S. Department of Defense, Report FY 1980, p. 34. *The Military Balance, 1978-79* (an annual publication of the International Institute for Strategic Studies, London), pp. 4 and 8, used a figure of 3.64 million men for the Soviet armed forces, excluding "some 750,000 uniformed civilians"; addition of these two figures produces the 4.4 million men in Defense Secretary Brown's estimate. Some of the increase in Soviet manpower figures is due not to *de facto* increases but to U.S. reassessment of estimates in 1975.

67. The trends in Soviet manpower and the number of divisions according to *The Military Balance, 1978-79*, p. 112; see also John Erickson, "European Security: Soviet Preferences and Priorities," *Strategic Review*, Winter 1976, p. 40.

68. This has been the case despite the fact that the number of divisions deployed in the Military Districts facing China increased by 25 in the late 1960s and 1970s.

69. Phillip A. Karber, "How to Lose an Arms Race: The Competition in Conventional Forces Deployed in Central Europe, 1965-1980," paper published (in German)

as Chapter I in *Sowjetische Macht und westliche Verhandlungsstrategie im Wandel militärischer Kräfteverhältnisse,* Uwe Nerlich, ed., Series Internationale Politik und Sicherheit, Stiftung Wissenschaft und Politik (Baden-Baden: Nomos, 1982).

70. Karber, "How to Lose an Arms Race," pp. 8-14. Whereas the Warsaw Pact had a 50 percent advantage in total weapons in 1965, it had increased this lead over NATO to about 100 percent by 1980. For every new weapon added by NATO the Warsaw Pact, in the same period, added 4.4 weapons (*ibid.,* p. 12). Ruehl has compiled the following figures for Warsaw Pact weapons increases at division level for the period 1965-1979 (TD = Tank Division; MRD = Motor Rifle Division). *Tanks,* 25% (TD), 66% (MRD); *infantry fighting vehicles,* 200% (TD), 80% (MRD); *artillery,* 80% (TD), 78% (MRD); *multiple rocket launchers* (tubes) from 192 to 720 systems (TD); *anti-tank weapons,* 70% (TD for 1975-79), 82% (MRD, same period); *air defense systems,* 20% (TD for 1975-79), 20% (MRD); *load-carrying trucks* (lift), 90% (TD), 460% (MRD). See Lothar Ruehl, *MBFR: Lessons and Problems,* Adelphi Paper No. 176 (London: International Institute for Strategic Studies, 1982), p. 5.

71. The figures are derived from *NATO and the Warsaw Pact: Force Comparisons,* 2nd Impression (Brussels, 1982), pp. 24-32.

72. *Ibid.* and various issues of *The Military Balance* up to and including 1981-82.

73. Aggregate military airlift capacity has more than doubled since the mid-1960s.

74. Such types include the helicopter and aircraft carriers of the *Moskva* and *Kiev* class, surface ships of the *Kara, Kresta II,* and *Krivak* class, the large combat ship *Berezina,* the ocean-going amphibious landing ship *Ivan Rogov,* the nuclear-powered "strike" cruiser *Kirov,* and the even larger *Sovremmenyi.*

75. The total tonnage of the Soviet commercial navy has increased sixfold since 1960.

76. Jurgen Rohwer, "Admiral Gorshkov and the Influence of History Upon Sea Power," *U.S. Naval Institute Proceedings* (May 1981), p. 172.

77. James M. McConnell, "Die Marine der UdSSR: Struktur und Einsatzplanung," *Marine-Rundschau,* No. 10 (1980), p. 606. For the development of the previous emphasis to combat U.S. nuclear-armed strategic submarines see Michael McGwire, "The Rationale for the Development of Soviet Seapower," *U.S. Naval Institute Proceedings,* May 1980, pp. 155-83.

78. Since 1964 a Soviet naval squadron (*eskadra*) has been operating in the Mediterranean, and another squadron in the Indian Ocean since 1969.

79. Sh. P. Sanakoev, *Mirovaia sistema sotsializma* (Moscow: "Mezhdunarodnye otnosheniia," 1968), p. 204 (italics mine). Sanakoev, at the time when the book was published, was Deputy Chief Editor of the foreign affairs journal *Mezhdunarodnaia zhizn'.*

80. A. A. Grechko, *Problemy istorii KPSS,* May 1974 (italics mine). The quotation continues: "The Soviet state with its foreign policy consistently opposes the export of counterrevolution and the policy of oppression, supports national-liberation movements, and resolutely resists imperialist aggression, in whichever far corner of our globe it may take place." At the time this was written Grechko was Defense Minister of the USSR and a full member of the Politburo.

81. *Voennaia sila i mezhdunarodnye otnosheniia,* V. M. Kulish, ed., p. 136 (italics mine).

82. *Ibid.* (italics mine).

83. This is the line consistently taken by Admiral Gorshkov, here quoted from *Morsboi sbornik,* No. 2 (1972), p. 32.

84. V. M. Kulish, "Detente, International Relations and Military Might," *Coexistence* (Glasgow), XIV, 2 (1977), p. 190 (italics mine).

85. All these quotations from Brezhnev in an "interview" (replies to questions put it writing) with the West German newspaper *Vorwärts,* a weekly publication of the Social Democratic Party, printed in *Pravda,* May 1, 1978. Publication of the interview was timed to coincide with the beginning of Brezhnev's visit to West Germany and given considerable prominence in *Pravda* (page 1, seven full columns).

86. This is a point noted by David Holloway, "Military Power and Political Purpose in Soviet Policy," *Daedalus,* Fall 1980, pp. 23-24.

87. "In certain situations, the fact of a Soviet military presence in a region where a conflict is developing or is already taking place can have a limiting (*sderzhivaiushchee*) influence on the imperialists or local reaction" (A. M. Dudin and Yu. N. Listvinov in *Voennaia sila i mezhdunarodnye otnosheniia,* Kulish, ed., p. 136). In this context the authors were explicitly referring to the presence of the Soviet *eskadra* in the Mediterranean.

88. Brezhnev at the XXVI Party Congress, *Pravda,* 24 February 1981. This theme was expressed as early as 1972 by General A. Yepishev, the Head of the Military Political Administration of the Soviet Armed Forces: "It must be realized that socialism's military might objectively assists the successful development of the revolutionary liberation movements and that it *hinders the exportation of imperialist counterrevolution.* In this lies one of the most important manifestations of the external function of the armed forces of a socialist state." ("Istoricheskaia missiia armiia," *Kommunist,* May 1972, p. 66, italics mine). See also note 80 above.

89. Robert Legvold, "Political Utility of Military Power: The Soviet Perspective," paper published (in German) as Chapter III in *Sowjetische Macht,* Nerlich, ed., (see note 69 above), pp. 32-36; the term "discontinuity" occurs in previous drafts of the paper and in oral presentations by the author.

90. Concerning the problem of whether doctrine is formulated by the political leadership alone or in conjunction with military leaders, see p. 71 of this supporting paper.

91. This is argued in more detail by Hannes Adomeit and Robert Boardman, *Foreign Policy Making in Communist Countries* (Farnborough, Engl.: Saxon House, Teakfield, 1979), pp. 25-31. Congruence of views by political and military leaders is stressed by William E. Odom, "The Party Connection," *Problems of Communism,* September-October 1973, pp. 12-26. It is, despite the points 1 to 4 made in the text, highly problematic to speak of "militarism" in the USSR. "Militarism" according to most definitions means that the political point of view is *subordinated to the military viewpoint,* and the position of the military establishment superior to that of the civilian leadership. These conditions, as argued, do not apply in the Soviet case. This is not made clear by Richard Pipes, "Militarism and the Soviet State," *Daedalus,* Fall 1980, pp. 1-12; see, however, the much more differentiated analysis by David Holloway, "War, Militarism and the Soviet State," *Alternatives: A Journal of World Policy,* 4 (1980), pp. 59-94.

92. Holloway, "Military Power" (note 86 above), p. 20.

93. Legvold writes that "Anyone who believes the Soviet Union is driven to add to its military power by political ambition must doubt the utility of arms control" ("Political Utility of Military Power," note 89 above, p. 40). This is, perhaps, expressed too strongly. It would probably be more correct to say that one must doubt the utility of arms control negotiations in Europe if they were to be continued in the same way as they have been conducted previously. One must doubt it in particular if such negotiations are meant to solve Western defense problems. Another point is worth making in this context. If the USSR were to succeed in codifying with the help of European arms control agreements its historically grown preponderance in conventional and intermediate-range nuclear weapons it could live with a SALT agreement that codifies parity. To that extent, the plea

made by A. Arbatov, son of the head of the Institute for the Study of the USA and Canada at the Academy of Sciences of the USSR, for "stability" (yes — *stabil'nost'* !) in the military strategic sphere may express the thinking of the Soviet political leadership. See A. Arbatov, *Bezopasnost' v iadernyi vek i politika Vashingtona* (Moscow: Politizdat, 1980), p. 272.

94. Among these are the Soviet Committee for European Security and Cooperation, founded in 1972 (leading members: A. P. Shitikov of the Supreme Soviet, D. Polianov of *Izvestiia,* D. F. Krasikov of *Za rubezhom,* and L. Samiatin of the Central Committee); the Scientific Council for Research in Problems of Peace and Disarmament, founded in 1976 (chairman: N. N. Inozemtsev, since deceased; other leading members: G. Arbatov, O. N. Bykov, M. A. Markov, E. M. Primakov, and D. M. Gvishiani); and the Central Committee Department for International Information, established in 1978 (head: L. Zamiatin; first deputy: previously V. Falin, demoted by Andropov).

Soviet Operational Concepts in the 1980s

by
Christopher N. Donnelly

Mr. Donnelly is the Director of the Soviet Studies Research Centre at the Royal Military Academy Sandhurst, United Kingdom.

The "Soviet Threat" is not an easy thing to describe in a balanced and objective fashion. The very word "threat" is emotive and subjective. First, its use presupposes that a conclusion as to the nature of Soviet power and its relationship to the West has already been made, and that further discussion will merely add detail to that conclusion. Secondly, there is the constant danger that the analyst will: (1) either overplay "the threat" in order to produce a "bogey man" for political or military psychological purposes; or that, (2) in attempting to display his "balance" and "objectivity" and to avoid being associated with a Western military or "bourgeois" outlook, he will conclude that the Soviet forces are purely self-defensive and present no "threat" at all.

In an attempt to avoid the pitfalls of these two approaches, and also to avoid the third and most seductive pitfall — to describe Soviet strengths and capabilities without any reference to intentions — this paper will try to approach the subject from the standpoint of Soviet reasoning and the Russian outlook.

WAR AND THE USSR: THE POLITICAL PERSPECTIVE

"War," said Karl Marx in 1855, "puts nations to the test. Just as mummies fall to pieces the moment that they are exposed to the air, so war

Notes are at the end of the paper.

pronounces its sentence of death on those social institutions which have become ossified." [1]

There can be few social organizations as ossified as the Communist Party of the Soviet Union (CPSU), and the Soviet leaders in the Kremlin must know this only too well. If a war were to occur which were to shake the fabric of Soviet society, then there would be a high possibility that Soviet power would be destroyed and the CPSU swept away. At the present time, there can be no doubt that a strategic nuclear exchange with the U.S. would accomplish this. Despite current Civil Defence efforts in the USSR, and however many Soviet citizens survived, a strategic nuclear war would so destroy the existing fabric of control that the Soviet Communist system as we know it would collapse. Even a limited exchange of strategic weapons — if such a war is thinkable — with, for example, the U.K. or China, would present to the Politburo an unacceptable risk of total social collapse. This would be especially true if the U.S. were to escape such a limited exchange. Consequently a strategic nuclear war is the kind of war the Soviet Union wishes to avoid at virtually all costs.

Soviet doctrine on war, however, leans as heavily on Lenin as it does on Marx, and emphasizes the importance of Lenin's appraisal, after von Clausewitz, that war is a tool of policy — war is nothing other than the continuation of policy by violent means. If the policies of war are the violent continuation of the policies of peace, logically then, the policies of peace, for Lenin, were only the non-violent continuation of the policies of war. War and peace, to a Communist leader, are only two alternative tools to achieve the all-important objective of policy. To that same Communist leader, the *all*-important policy is and remains to hasten the establishment of Communism (of his own particular brand) throughout the world. No ideological or pseudo-intellectual argument, however well-meaning, must be allowed to obscure this essential point. Equally vital is to understand that to a true Communist, the triumph of Communism is inevitable, and can only be hastened or delayed, not prevented.

War, then, is a tool to be used to achieve the basic aims of policy of the Communist-led state when and *only* when it is seen as the best tool for the task, and when its use does not risk precipitating a catastrophic (e.g., nuclear) setback.

Communists are, therefore, using war and armed force directly in an attempt to achieve their aims in several countries today — Afghanistan, Poland, Ethiopia, Indochina, to name but a few. War is not being used directly to communize *Europe* today because it is clearly *not* the best tool for the job in that part of the world at this moment. It can be argued, according to Lenin's thesis, that war *is* being used indirectly to this end through wars in third-world countries and (former) colonies, so as to deprive the capitalist world of cheap sources of raw materials. But this paper will focus on the subject of war *in Europe*.

The Politburo, therefore, is pursuing a policy of communizing Europe at the moment by peaceful means: subversion, espionage, political manoeuvring and pressures, economic activity — that is, anything which falls short of armed hostilities. It must always be remembered that peace, to a Marxist, has no connotations of goodwill whatsoever. Peace is merely "no war." "Peaceful coexistence" as defined by the USSR has no understanding either of goodwill or cooperation or convergence. It is a cold coexistence without war until the inevitable triumph of Communism occurs. Detente is seen as a reduction of international tension to make this triumph more certain by reducing the risk of a catastrophic war unleashed by capitalism in its death throes. Time after time the Soviet leaders have emphasized that detente means an increase in the class struggle, not a decrease.

In all this, Soviet military power has a most important role to play. The stronger that power grows relative to the power of the capitalist bloc, the more likely the world is to progress towards its ultimate Communist destiny in *peace*. The greater the *im*balance of power in socialism's favour, or as the Soviets put it, "the more the world correlation of forces tilts in favour of socialism," the less likely an Armageddon. So the first task of the Soviet forces in Eastern Europe (apart from that of policing the Warsaw Pact states) is simply to *be* there, and to be seen to be so big and strong that all the nations of Western Europe, starting with even the smallest, are gradually intimidated into accepting an even greater measure of Soviet influence in their affairs. In this way Europe will progress towards Communism in peace.

The first "threat," therefore, is not "war" at all, but rather it is "threat-of-war," and the danger is that we shall succumb to that threat and be gradually Sovietized without ever a shot being fired. It is most important to realize that the very existence of armed force is a most useful "tool," even though those forces may never be used in combat.

However, if history has any one lesson for the student of war, it is that wars break out unexpectedly, often even taking both parties relatively by surprise. The speed with which the popular mood in Britain changed between 1937 and 1939 from one of extreme pacifism to a preparedness to go to war is evidence of the rapidity with which radical changes in national outlook can occur. This was demonstrably true even in a democratic country with the horror of "a war to end all wars" still very alive in people's minds, with a vivid dread of poison gas and the bombing of cities very strong, and with no real vision of victory to tempt the population.

If war breaks out for any reason in Europe — and it is not the mission of this paper to dream up scenarios where that might happen — it will certainly be the task of the Soviet Armed Forces to win that war. The only way in which such a war could be *won,* as opposed to drawn, is by a massive offensive to shatter the military groupings and neutralize the political institutions of the enemy.

No war, however, can be considered as won if it escalates into a strategic nuclear holocaust. To be won, a war in Europe must be ended, and the victor must have achieved the aims of his policy, *before* that point is reached. That is, before the U.S. President (and perhaps also the President of France and the Prime Minister of Britain) orders the launching of his intercontinental ballistic missiles (ICBMs). This makes it essential, in Soviet eyes, for such a war to be won quickly, and for a military and political collapse of NATO in Europe to be encompassed before sufficient time has elapsed for the U.S. to commit itself to a strategic nuclear war.

However, such is the power of modern weaponry, both conventional and tactical nuclear, that, the Soviets maintain, if NATO can effectively deploy its forces before any such war starts (and particularly if NATO can make an early and effective use of tactical nuclear weapons to halt a Soviet offensive), a rapid victory is unlikely. *To be certain of a quick victory it is essential to achieve surprise, and to preempt NATO's deployment.* It is the realization of this essential need for both speed and surprise that to a large extent determines the shape, deployment and strategy of the Soviet Armed Forces in Europe, and is at present driving a Soviet redeployment and reshaping of their operational strategy.[2]

So if war is to be won at all, it must be started suddenly and won quickly. On this premise, the task of the CPSU, through the agencies of Soviet Military Doctrine and the Soviet Armed Forces, is to prepare for such a war (as well as for any other war they might need to fight). At this point one should emphasize the importance of Soviet Military Doctrine to the functioning of the whole Soviet system. Soviet Military Doctrine is far more than just a set of tactical regulations, as it is often dismissed in the West. Rather it is the logically codified accumulation of wisdom and experience of war fighting, modified by frequent experiment, academic and operational research, and debate. On the basis of this all-embracing Military Doctrine the CPSU integrates all military and civilian elements of the state, and tailors the armed forces more efficiently to fight the type of wars which policy may require. The Doctrine provides a *framework* on which reorganization can be accomplished more surely and with less disorganization; and it provides, in Soviet eyes, an essential foundation on which to base military modernization and debates on tactical and operational developments.

It must be stressed at this point that, although a quick and sudden war is clearly the Soviets' preferred option, they do recognise that their armed forces may be called upon to fight other types of campaign, even in Europe. A war could be nuclear from the outset, or could drag on for a long time. As well as having a largely ready force in Europe, the Soviet Union has an unparalleled reserve mobilization capacity, substantial war stocks, including many thousands of mothballed tanks and guns, and a significant Civil Defence programme. Although this paper is about the Soviets' preferred option for war in what they regard as the most important theatre, the other options that this military reserve permits must never be overlooked.

SOVIET STUDIES OF NATO PLANS

One of the principles embodied in Soviet Military Doctrine is that it demands that Soviet strategy, operations, and tactics be developed in the light of the strategy, operations, and tactics likely to be implemented by the opponent. Steps must be taken to minimise one's own failings and exploit those of the enemy. A study of NATO, therefore, is the essential first step which the Soviet strategist must take when making his plans.

As far as can be ascertained, the Soviet perception of NATO strategic weaknesses and strengths is as follows.

The weaknesses:

1. NATO is a coalition of states many of which have mutually opposed national interests, a good degree of mutual suspicion, and, in certain cases, active hostility towards one another.

2. The political-military structure of NATO and the organization of the decision-making process is likely to make for initial hesitancy and indecision in all but the most obvious and crucial crisis.

3. NATO lacks a real military doctrine and a standard concept of operations. The different member nations each plan to conduct their de-

fence according to national ideas. There is no real consciousness of the all-important operational scale.

4. The Atlantic Ocean separates the strongest partner from the most likely area of conflict.

5. NATO has little operational depth in the Central Region.

And following are the Soviet perceptions of NATO's strengths:

1. NATO has a massive military *potential,* far outweighing that of the Warsaw Pact.

2. The Western democracies of NATO have a remarkable degree of political resilience and are somewhat unpredictable in time of crisis.

3. NATO possesses a more advanced military technology than does the Warsaw Pact.

4. The strength and militarization of West Germany is an important factor in the Central Region.

5. The geo-strategic position of the U.K., and the position of the U.S. *may* make victory in the Central Region inconclusive, and make it difficult for the Soviets to bring a war to the necessary speedy conclusion.

Some member states have particular weaknesses and strengths in Soviet eyes. The U.S. and German armies are by far the strongest; other member nations get little attention in the Soviet press, other than assessments which might be of value to an operational commander.

At every level Soviet military planning reflects the intent to tailor their tactics and strategy to exploit NATO weaknesses and to minimize their own, while taking every possible measure to prevent NATO's profiting from her innate strengths and maximizing her potential. This Soviet objective could only be implemented by taking the initiative in military action — and this is yet one more reason to explain why Soviet Military Doctrine is wedded to the concept of the offensive as a basic principle.

MOVING TOWARDS THE OUTBREAK OF WAR

In the development of Soviet Military Doctrine as concerns the outbreak of war, three distinct phases can be perceived. Two of them must be successfully completed before the outbreak of hostilities if the war is to be a successful one. These first two phases can be entitled "The Preparatory Phase" and "The Crisis Phase." The third phase, that of hostilities, can be encompassed by the Soviet term "The Initial Period." In all phases it is a basic principle of Soviet policy to exploit NATO's weaknesses and prevent the development of NATO strengths. The three phases must not be viewed as independent; their interdependence must be appreciated.

The Preparatory Phase

The main task in this phase, which describes the period in which we are now living, is to minimize the extent of NATO preparations for and capacity to wage war, especially nuclear war. Efforts in this phase will be mainly of a political and economic nature.

For example, Soviet foreign policy will be designed to exacerbate rifts in the Western Alliance, particularly to drive wedges between the U.S., Germany, and the other member states. The Soviet Union is at present waging an intense campaign to dissuade NATO states from spending more on defence, and from allowing more nuclear weapons to be based on their territory. A similarly intense campaign is being waged against the manufacture of the enhanced radiation weapon.

All possible assistance will be given to any organization, even anti-Soviet ones, if it is considered that this will weaken the West's military potential or readiness. Campaign for Nuclear Disarmament, Green Peace, Grüne Welle and the like all receive some degree of Soviet support, stopping only at such over-obvious support as might prove counter-productive. That such organizations might not actually want Soviet support, and may even be anti-Soviet in attitude, is immaterial. The same applies to Communist influence in certain trade unions in Western countries. To accuse these organizations publicly of being "in the Soviet pay" or "extensions of Moscow's tentacles" is naive in the extreme, as it will alienate the average member who feels no loyalty to Moscow, and will only serve to strengthen the position of those who have gained positions of influence and who are intent on using their influence to a political end.

Fierce economic pressure can also be exerted during the Preparatory Phase in any area of the economy where the Soviet Union is particularly strong in comparison to individual member states of NATO.

To say that we are at present in the "Preparatory Phase" is *not* to say that we are headed inexorably towards war, or that the Soviet Union wants war with the West. It most assuredly does not. If this phase is truly successful, it will effect a gradual development of policy in Europe along lines which the Soviet Union would like, and the states of Europe should, therefore, be Sovietized gradually and without any dangerous and destabilizing war between East and West.

If the policy is *not* wholly successful, however, a crisis may arise in which the Soviet Union:

— feels that war is inevitable, or
— feels that war is the only way of achieving an *absolutely essential* objective of policy, and has exhausted all other alternatives, *and*
— is confident that the war can be won quickly and easily and without danger of escalation to global nuclear war, and
— considers that alternatives to initiating hostilities will be more dangerous and costly.

Only if these conditions are fulfilled will the Soviet Union willingly embark upon a full-scale war.

The Crisis Phase

If the war is to be won, some considerable degree of surprise is absolutely essential; but the likelihood of a true "bolt from the blue" seems most improbable, unless one believes that the leaders of the USSR actually want war and are plotting at this very moment to launch it on a fixed time scale. If one accepts, however, that they really do hold Leninist principles, and that their main aim is to achieve an objective of policy, then the following question must be answered: why go to war when there are less risky ways to achieve the said objective of policy?

If war occurs, it is almost bound to occur during a crisis of some sort, and the Soviet Union's concern will be to exploit that crisis so as to deter preparations in the West and conceal her own preparations.

Events in the Middle East (in 1973, for example) and elsewhere (e.g., Czechoslovakia in 1968, Poland in 1981) have shown that even in the most adverse circumstances surprise *is* possible. However, the surprise is unlikely to be complete, and some degree of NATO preparation and deployment is to be expected.

When it becomes apparent to the Soviets that war or military action is likely or inevitable, their first concern must be to control and manage the crisis so that war does not break out at a time and place which surprises *them*. Then more immediate steps must be taken to create favourable political and military circumstances for a successful campaign. The actual deployment and mobilization of NATO forces must be prevented, or at least hindered, and NATO efforts to pre-prepare positions must be thwarted by all possible means. These will include, of course, maximum political pressure of every type, active subversion and sabotage, and a massive campaign of deception. In this phase, too, the neutralization of NATO's nuclear weapons will be the prime target. At the same time, the forces of the Soviet Union and certain of the Warsaw Pact countries must be readied for war, but in a way which does not cause undue alarm in the West.

Preparations for war, of course, are bound to give indications to NATO analysts and so these "warning indicators," as NATO calls them, must be made ambiguous. Partial mobilization and reinforcement can become commonplace as repeated exercises (as was the case with Arab mobi- lization in the Yom Kippur War in 1973). Troop redeployment can be explained as being necessitated by internal economic or security reasons (as it was in Poland in 1981). A counter-mobilization by NATO could be labeled as "provocative" and rendered ludicrous by sudden, though tempo- rary, demobilization on the part of the Warsaw Pact. All in all, NATO's *warning time* may not equate to the *preparation time* NATO's com- manders will get. This latter *must,* if the USSR is going to start the war, be by definition very limited, so that NATO's defences are unlikely to be heavily fortified or well dug in in depth, and there will be no strong NATO operational reserve established.

During the last stage of the Crisis Phase (in what to the Soviets will be the pre-war days) crisis management becomes crucial to surprise. *Surprise will be lost if war is opened at the peak of the crisis.* Either a false "peak" must be engineered and the crisis "defused," so that the Soviet forces can attack when the guard is dropped, or the war must be started before the crisis reaches an alarming peak, when all others think they have time left to prepare.

An example of the first instance was the 1968 invasion of Czech- oslovakia. The crisis between the USSR and the Czech Party was defused by the placatory agreement at Cerna nad Tisou in July, when the USSR appeared to back down. All Europe breathed a sigh of relief, the U.S. President went off to Camp David, and, during the third week of August, with much of NATO on leave, the Soviet Army, with Polish and East German help, rolled into Czechoslovakia.

A good example of the second case — attacking before there was a recognizable crisis peak — is Jaruzelski's timing of the coup in Poland in 1981. In April of that year, in a joint Soviet and Polish exercise, a military communications system was established, independent of existing civilian or Warsaw Pact nets. It remained in being on a care-and-maintenance basis when the exercise ended. In July, when the biannual conscript rotation took place, those completing their two-year term were not released. As usually happens in summer, troops were deployed on harvesting duties and later in the year troops were deployed in cities and industrial areas to provide organized help and ensure law and order. In other words, over some nine months, Jaruzelski (1) set up a command and control system, (2) increased the size of his army at least for a time by 20 percent, (3) deployed it throughout the country. Yet these "warning indicators" failed to give Western analysts warning because there were other valid reasons for the actions. At the same time, Jaruzelski maintained an air of total political normality for deception purposes.

In timing his move to cope with the rapidly developing crisis in the Party, he had three choices. The first was to move over Christmas, but this was expected because people thought it to be the least likely time, and the memory of the Soviet invasion of Afghanistan two years previously was fresh in their minds. The second choice was to wait till after Christmas and attempt some false reconciliation with Solidarity. The third was to go *before* Christmas at a time when people expected the crisis to run on longer. He chose the third course, and achieved almost total surprise. Careful and clever orchestration of the actual coup completed his success.

HOSTILITIES: THE "INITIAL PERIOD" OF WAR

Marshal V. D. Sokolovskii, in the third (1968) edition of his author-itative work *Military Strategy,* stresses the great importance of achieving the main aims of a war in its initial period, without relying on additional mobilization. The "initial period" Sokolovskii defined as that length of time taken by the enemy to complete his mobilization. By then, the war's aims must, in the main, be achieved (i.e., NATO must be militarily and politically neutralized), and this must be accomplished by the Warsaw Pact forces in being at the start of the war. Freshly mobilized forces can be used to mop up, complete the destruction of the enemy, or impose a military occupation, but they will not be able to contribute to the achieving of the *main* aim.

When Sokolovskii wrote this work he was, of course, expecting the war to be a nuclear one. However, the many changes in Soviet strategy during the years since 1968 have by no means invalidated this concept, because NATO still plans on the use of nuclear weapons to halt the Soviet advance.

If NATO has a long period of preparation and deployment, then, the Soviets recognise, her forces will be so strong and well entrenched that a quick Soviet victory is unlikely.

Whatever the circumstances and however successful plans to achieve surprise are, some NATO troops will undoubtedly have time to deploy. In adverse circumstances, the Soviets recognise that they might under-estimate the number of troops that *have* deployed. If these troops can contain the Soviet forces in a cordon and prevent breakthrough, then NATO commanders may still be able to make effective use of their nuclear weapons if nuclear release is obtained in time. The Soviets accept that an early and effective use by NATO of tactical weapons will certainly cause disastrous disruption of their offensive.

This is of the utmost importance when considering the reasons for the current changes in Soviet operational doctrine.

In the light of the foregoing, the Soviet General Staff is clearly faced with the need to develop a strategic and operational plan which would (1) make it very difficult for NATO to implement its tactical nuclear option and (2) accomplish a rapid collapse of the NATO military and political system.

The strategy that must be adopted:

1. requires the achievement of surprise and assumes a NATO defence caught in some measure off balance;

2. will impose the maximum amount of shock on the defender in the first hours of the war;

3. must paralyse the enemy command and control systems and restrict his ability to react;

4. is designed to achieve a rapid rate of advance on several important axes deep into the enemy territory to shatter his defensive structure;

5. should reduce the risk posed by NATO tactical nuclear weapons (a) by destroying as many as possible during the conventional phase, (b) by adopting tactics which make it particularly difficult for the defender to use his nuclear weapons effectively, and (c) if NATO initiates tactical use, by destroying the remainder of NATO's nu-clear delivery systems in a massive "retaliatory" tactical strike, aimed primarily at those nuclear weapons.

Such a strategy offers, in Soviet eyes, the only real chance of victory should a war in Europe occur. The Soviet Armed Forces would have been guilty of a grave dereliction of duty had they not been actively seeking ways to implement such a strategy to cope with the eventuality of war.

The strategy adopted by the Soviet Union to deal with winning a war in Europe quickly must be seen *in toto*. There can be no *tactical* defeat of NATO. There can indeed be no certainty of military victory during the phase of hostilities if the Preparatory Phase and Crisis Phase have not succeeded in reducing NATO's capacity to react in time. It is inconceivable in present circumstances to envisage a gradual and predictable development into war, culminating in a declaration of war by the USSR, prior to an invasion of Europe.

In the closing hours of the crisis period, sabotage and subversive activities will be stepped up. Soviet special-purpose forces will become active, their main targets being nuclear delivery systems, air force and air defence installations, and command and communications facilities. This will really be the first act of hostilities, but this fact will not necessarily be obvious to the defenders. It will, of course, be accompanied by a coordinated campaign of deception and a political smokescreen which will continue even after the Soviet Ground Forces begin their offensive.

THE SOVIET OFFENSIVE AGAINST NATO

The Soviet aim in a full-scale war against NATO must be to surround, destroy, or otherwise neutralize NATO forces, and thereby bring about a collapse of the NATO political structure within a matter of days — during the "initial period." An invasion can stop at nothing less than the occupation of West Germany, the Low Countries, and the Baltic Littoral. It seems unlikely that the USSR would at this time willingly embark on an invasion of France or the United Kingdom.

The main theatre must be the Central Front. If victory is achieved there within the given time frame, then the flanks can be expected to take on a secondary significance. It is doubtful that the neutrality of Austria and Switzerland would be violated initially; thus the split would be maintained between NATO's Centre and Southern Tier.

Activities in the Southern Tier would likely be aimed at tying up the U.S. and NATO forces in that area and preventing any strategic relocation to the Central Front or counter-threat to the southern USSR.

The utility of the non-Soviet Warsaw Pact forces can be expected to depend to a large extent on the political circumstances prevailing. However, considerable elements of these forces can be expected to be used on secondary tasks, in second echelons or on minor axes, and for defense against NATO counter-attacks. The East German forces will provide the strongest support in the Central Region and on the Baltic coast: all six East German Army divisions and all the East German Navy and Air Force can be expected to be deployed in conjunction with Soviet forces. The Polish marine infantry and naval forces must be expected to be used in the first wave on the Baltic Littoral. Otherwise, perhaps one-third of the Polish Army could be deployed with Soviet forces from the Belorussian and Baltic Military Districts as a second strategic echelon. The location of the Czech forces makes it likely that they will provide a first wave to soak up the U.S. and German firepower in Southern Germany, to prevent those forces being diverted to the NATO Northern Army Group area. Hungarian forces would most probably be used to guard the flanks against NATO forces from Italy. In the Southern Tier, where the major operation will probably be to try to split NATO forces in the Eastern Mediterranean from Italy, Bulgarian troops can be expected to accompany Soviet troops in this task.

In all cases, it would be unwise to assume that the Warsaw Pact forces will not be loyal to the Soviet bloc. All evidence indicates that they *will* be, provided that:

1. Surprise is achieved by the Soviets. This will mean surprising not just NATO but also both Soviet and non-Soviet Warsaw Pact forces. If every Soviet soldier knows war is about to start, it will be no surprise to NATO. Given ample warning of possible war, the USSR's Eastern European allies might well discover ways of keeping out of the fighting, and their armies might have time to think twice about the cause for which they are dying. However, if the war starts suddenly and unexpectedly, then the non-Soviet Warsaw Pact armies will surely march to the Soviet drums.

2. The non-Soviet Warsaw Pact forces are deployed with national prejudices and enmities borne in mind. A Polish division will surely fight with greater enthusiasm against a West German division than against a British or American division. For an East German division the reverse might be true.

3. Western propaganda and psychological warfare can be prevented from affecting the non-Soviet Warsaw Pact forces.

4. The Soviet forces can be seen to be winning quickly and easily, and NATO fails to make early and effective use of nuclear weapons.

The strategic considerations having been made, the Soviet commander must now turn to operational considerations. Here, he must study the features of NATO's operational and strategic-operational defensive concepts so as to exploit them fully. His aim must be to defeat the NATO defense with an operational plan which achieves the strategic requirements listed above.

THE STRUCTURE OF THE OFFENSIVE

The Principles of Echeloning

For their concept of offensive operations, the Soviets rely a great deal on operational analysis based on detailed study of the lessons of the 1941-45 war against Germany and Japan.

As a result of their wartime experience, the Soviet Army has developed a concept of the offensive based on attacks in successive waves at each tactical or operational level so as to maintain the pressure on the defender while retaining a high degree of mobility and operational flexibility.

Each tactical level (i.e., battalion, regiment, division) or operational level (i.e., Army and Front) can, in theory, deploy in one, two, or three waves for attack. The commanders' choice will be determined by three considerations: (1) the depth and configuration of the enemy defence, (2) the extent of surprise gained and the consequent degree of preparedness of the enemy, and (3) the terrain.

In practice, the ground, i.e., the shape of the terrain and the space available for deployment, has proved the deciding factor at the divisional level and below, where attacks in two waves are most common. At the operational level, consideration of the enemy's defence came to have the greatest importance.

If operational or strategic surprise can be assumed, then the Front can afford to deploy its armies in one wave, maintaining a small (20 percent) uncommitted reserve. If the defences are well prepared, then the attack sectors must be narrowed and the Front must attack in depth, formed in two successive waves at both Army and Front level. When the defences to be breached are organized in one belt, the attacking forces will put the bulk of their combat formations into the first wave. Where the defence is organized in several successive belts, the attacking forces will attack in several waves, on a narrow frontage.

In the 1941-1945 war, the second or third wave at each tactical level was organized as either "second echelons," "reserves," or "mobile groups." A second echelon usually constitutes about 30 percent of the total force available. When a two-echelon structure was adopted, a reserve of 10 percent of the force or less was also usually maintained. Today as in 1945, a second echelon always operates to a prearranged plan or alternative plans, limiting it to set axes, objectives, and timing. Alternatively, when information as to the nature of the defence is insufficient to permit prior planning or the situation is fluid, instead of a second echelon, a substantial reserve of 30-35 percent could be maintained. The disadvantage of a reserve is that it usually takes longer to plan its action and to commit it to the battle.

Modern Soviet operational analysis establishes that second echelons are employed to build up pressure on the main axis so as to ensure the breakthrough of the enemy army's zone of defence. They are also used to: repel counter-attacks; cover flanks; create the external front of an encirclement; widen the breakthrough; or replace exhausted first echelons.

At the *operational* (Army and Front) level, the Soviets developed an alternative in World War II to the multiple "echelon" assault. This was the Mobile Group. This normally comprised the best equipped and therefore most manoeuvrable armored or mechanical formation (corps) in the Army.[3] Mobile Groups were formed either instead of or in addition to second echelons and had different tasks.

Mobile Groups were designed to *develop* the breakthrough by penetrating into the tactical and operational depth of the enemy; to break out into enemy routes of withdrawal and so complete the encirclement of the enemy; to destroy reserves moving up, pursue the defender withdrawing, and seize important lines and objectives in depth. In Soviet terms, they were primarily exploitation forces, whose use was designed to turn tactical success into operational success.

Postwar Developments in Strategy and Operational Art

Two very significant developments in the 1950s and 1960s did much to alter Soviet operational thinking. These were: (a) the deployment of battlefield nuclear weapons and the "tripwire response" strategy of NATO, and (b) the mass mechanization of the Soviet Army.

In a tactical nuclear war, the defence would be shattered by nuclear strike, and the breakthrough and exploitation would become mainly a problem in traffic management. Moreover, operational tasks could be fulfilled by tactical nuclear strike, and important targets could be neutralized or destroyed without the need to attack them with troops.

As a result of mass mechanization, all troops became "mobile" and even combined arms troops became capable of high speeds of advance, manoeuvre and exploitation. Thus the designation of tank formations as "Mobile Groups" came to be seen as rather anachronistic.

Consequently, the study of conventional operational art and strategy was somewhat neglected during the 1950s and development tended to be along the lines of tactics and nuclear strategy, for perfectly valid reasons.

However, NATO's gradual shift to a "Flexible Response" in the 1960s forced the Soviets to re-examine their own doctrine once again, in reaction to NATO plans, as NATO leaders state quite categorically that:

1. In the event of a Soviet attack, NATO will initially fight a conventional battle. A figure of "five" or "a few" days is usually quoted for this phase.
2. NATO will eventually resort to tactical nuclear weapons when conventional defence fails.
3. Initial nuclear use will be on a limited "demonstrational" scale.

Furthermore, during the 1970s, NATO has adopted a strategy of "Forward Defence" by which, in a period of tension or crisis, the bulk of her troops will take up defensive positions in a belt 20 to 40 kilometers wide, relatively close to the East-West German border, so as to meet the aggressor as soon as possible and give up as little territory as possible.

This, as is well known, puts the main defensive positions of NATO formations in many places a long way from their garrison areas, with consequently long deployment times. Furthermore, it makes only a shallow depth available for the covering force action essential to the identification of the main thrusts, and the zigzag path taken by the East-West German frontier brings that frontier very close indeed to the front and flanks of some of NATO's main defensive areas.

The national differences in NATO have resulted in dramatic differences in the operational concepts employed by different formations, and may well result in different states of readiness in the event of a crisis.

The Need for Change Perceived in Warsaw Pact Doctrine

In the Soviet view, invulnerability to NATO tactical nuclear strikes can only be obtained if the Soviet Forces can (1) maintain a high rate of advance and (2) prevent the establishment of clear lines dividing "our troops" from "their troops" from an early stage of the war.

The 1970s, therefore, have seen a return to the study of conventional tactics, operational art and strategy, with the added impetus of *finding some way to neutralize NATO's nuclear trump card*.

It would appear that experience with large Warsaw Pact exercises, coupled with some imaginative thinking, convinced many Soviet officers that their newly equipped and highly mobile units could find better ways to exploit the characteristics of their equipment.

Presuming that in a war with NATO a certain level of surprise would be achieved, it was reckoned both possible and highly desirable to get large-scale combat groups behind enemy lines very quickly. The effect of this would be to destabilize the whole of NATO's defensive structure at the moment that it was just setting itself up.

The Soviet concept of the forward detachment was an accepted means of doing this on a *tactical* scale. It involved pushing a battalion-sized combined arms group well ahead of an advancing division, to avoid contact with the enemy, slip through gaps in his defence, and penetrate into tactical depths to perform a mission such as seizing a vital piece of ground, conducting reconnaissance or a raid, or cutting off a retreating enemy force. It had been widely practised in the 19th century by the Russian cavalry. What was needed in the 1970s was a method of accomplishing such a manoevre on an *operational* scale.

It is not surprising that Soviet analysts turned to wartime experience for an answer, and of all the experience of the 1941-45 war, the experience of tank formations is seen as most relevant to modern conditions. This is because the development of mechanization has, in Soviet eyes, now succeeded in raising the level of mobility and protection of all arms to that enjoyed only by the tank troops in World War II. Tank formations were, therefore, most carefully studied. This trend was no doubt encouraged by the large number of senior positions within the Soviet ground forces occupied by tank generals — a factor not to be underestimated.

As tank formations were the most common subject of study, and also the most common component of Mobile Groups, it is hardly surprising that awareness of the concept of the Mobile Group as a valuable means of raising the tempo of the advance and developing success into the operational depth should grow throughout the last decade. The similarities between the intended NATO defence today and the style of defence adopted by the Germans in both the initial and latter stages of the war serve to make the study of the Mobile Group in World War II even more appropriate.

Many contemporary Soviet strategists are at pains to point out that however much the mobility and protection of all arms formations are raised, there can be no doubt that tank formations still remain more manoeuvrable. Tactical considerations, especially the widespread deployment of lightweight anti-tank weapons, have necessitated the inclusion of some infantry with tank formations and units nowadays; but this has only affected the issue to a slight degree and does not alter the principles.

Interest in the role, composition, and utility of the Mobile Group has been reflected in the Soviet press, particularly since 1974, and it is on this modern Soviet and related Warsaw Pact operational analysis that this paper is based. Soviet interest has been steady and at a high level, with exceptional bursts of attention in 1976 and 1979.

On the one hand, it can certainly be said that the activities of the wartime Mobile Groups are providing examples for operational analysis which are applicable to *all* modern mechanized formations. On the other hand, what all contributors to discussions in the Warsaw Pact press emphasize nowadays when referring to the concept of the Mobile Group is that a formation with a relatively higher speed and greater inherent flexibility than other formations presents the best means of achieving a rapid penetration into the operational depths of a modern defence of the style proposed by NATO. When that defence, if hastily established, possesses little in the way of operational reserves and no provision for a strong second operational line of defences, the premium on a rapid breach and rapid advance into the depths becomes immediately obvious. Such an advance at an early stage (day 1 or 2) of the battle would not only cause NATO serious problems of control, but would make the use of nuclear weapons very difficult, and would pose a serious threat to the security of NATO's nuclear weapons themselves.

On the basis of this reasoning, the Soviet analysts perceived the value of a change in doctrine, and have persuaded the General Staff to implement such a change.

The Development of Soviet Operational Doctrine in the 1980s

By its very nature, Soviet Military Doctrine[4] is a creature which has developed gradually over the years, and which has very strong roots in history. Even revolutionizing changes, such as that brought about by the introduction of nuclear weapons onto the battlefield, leave a great deal unchanged. In the main, the doctrine is evolutionary, and it leans heavily on historical operational analysis for the evaluation and re-evaluation of principles and of operational models on which Soviet military specialists rely so much when attempting to direct and develop that evolution down the most appropriate paths. The changes which have occurred in Soviet operational doctrine during the last two or three years and which continue to occur must be viewed in that light.

To quote General Krupchenko writing in 1981 (emphasis added):

> Modern conditions have introduced new factors into the equation of how to develop success: with complete mechanization, armour, and new weapons, all troops have become mobile. Consequently great possibilities have emerged for developing an *operation at high speed and engaging in manoeuvre with tank and combined-arms armies.*
>
> *In this connection there have been qualitative changes in the structure of action in the whole depth of the enemy defence.* There are far greater opportunities nowadays than in the past, especially on account of the great depths to which rockets, long-range artillery, aircraft and desants can be used. Even so, examples from the last war have in no way lost their relevance in theory or in practice. Rather they encourage ideas and suggest solutions to the *modern problem of how to get major forces in the offensive deep into the operational depths of the defence, so as to achieve decisive aims at high speed.* [5]

General Krupchenko was discussing the wartime concept of the "Mobile Group" in one of a series of articles on that concept, designed to examine and establish its validity on the modern battlefield. Rather more specific reference to the concept was made in an article by Major Wojciech Michalak in a Polish military journal in February 1982. He wrote as follows:

> The most characteristic features of modern warfare are:
> (a) conflict taking place over a wide front or on selected axes;
> (b) the high level of mobility of forces;
> (c) the availability of a constant supply of fresh forces;
> (d) the availability of a large quantity of nuclear weapons;
> (e) the capacity to exert pressure on the whole depth of an enemy's operational formation.
>
> Therefore, the success of an offensive operation will largely depend on depriving the enemy of the above mentioned capabilities and, above all, *on the elimination of nuclear missiles during the conventional phase of the battle.*

This situation makes it necessary to seek new methods of employing forces so as to break up the cohesion of the enemy formation over its whole depth. This might be accomplished, for example, by destroying objectives or elements of the grouping which are essential to the viability and combat fitness of the enemy forces. *Based on the analysis of experience of the last war, these requirements have led to the reappearance on the modern battlefield of detachments engaged in raiding activities and also of Operational Marching Groups.* [Major Michalak later used the more familiar term Operational Manoeuvre Groups.] The latter derive their origin from the so-called high-speed groups formed from armoured troops and widely used by the Soviet Army during World War II.

The feature common to the operational activities of both marching groups and raiding detachments is that they operate detached from their own main forces to penetrate deep into the enemy rear to operate for a limited period. Consequently they perform missions at a comfortable distance from the main forces, although in close coordination with them and always to their advantage. *These troops are intended mainly for destroying groupings of nuclear missiles, command posts, radio electronic warfare equipment and anti-aircraft defence weapons.* They are also used, *inter alia,* to prevent the withdrawal of enemy troops; to hinder the advance of his reserves from the depth; to paralyse his system of logistics; to capture major important areas and objectives; and to hold these till the approach of the main forces.[6]

On the same theme, Colonels Lachiewicz and Rajmanski wrote in the same Polish journal in June 1981: "The aim of deploying an army's Operational Manoeuvre Group (OMG) is to switch the focus of the fighting into the depths or rear of the enemy formation, to destroy important objectives which cannot be destroyed by other means, to achieve chaos and disorganization, and to limit the freedom of manoeuvre and the effectiveness of the enemy action . . ."[7]

The logic, therefore, is clear. *In active defence, NATO had found an effective answer to Warsaw Pact operational strategy. Therefore that operational strategy has had to be changed.*

A new operational strategy has had to be developed which will ensure the rapid and total collapse of a NATO defence and hence ensure a quick end to the war. This concept, developed from the "Mobile Groups" of the last war, envisages the penetration of flexible and highly manoeuvrable formations (divisions) into the enemy defenses very early during the battle, as "Operational Manoeuvre Groups."

It is neither an easy nor a quick task, especially in peacetime, to change the operational concept of an entire army. Consequently, it is obvious that we are seeing not a sudden or precipitous development in Soviet doctrine. It would appear equally true, from a perusal of the Warsaw Pact military press, that, whilst moves towards the implementation of a more flexible operational strategy were initiated probably as early as 1976, there was not then, and still is not, any detailed blueprint for this change. Resolution of the detail and amendment of the very principles themselves must be expected only as the basic ideas are implemented — through tactics and operational manoeuvres tried out in exercises; reorganizations and re-reorganizations commenced on the ground; alternative mixes of forces and weapons systems experimented with.

Many of the details of change and the amendments of minor principles have long been apparent in the Soviet army and have been taken as evidence of major changes. However, it is only as the new concept of operations has now come to maturity, and the weight of minor change reached major proportions that it has been possible, for this author at any rate, to perceive the "big picture," that is, the form of the restructuring of Soviet operational strategy in Europe and the reasons for it.

The restructuring of the Soviet forces and the rewriting of their operational plans is well under way, and there can be no doubt that, should war break out in Europe in the near future, the Soviet operation will be based on these new concepts and not those of the last decade. But, as indicated above, not all the details of these concepts are yet established and much theoretical and practical research is yet to be done to perfect the concepts, because they affect virtually every branch of tactics on the battlefield.

Consequently, it is worthwhile to look at the Soviet research and to list what the Soviet analysts say will be the characteristics of the new Operational Manoeuvre Group (OMG), as established by its wartime predecessor, the Mobile Group.

The Historical Framework and the Development of the Modern Operational Manoeuvre Group

1. The Mobile Group (and the OMG) is not so much a "thing" or an "organization," as a *concept,* i.e., a way of employing an existing force so as to (a) better exploit the vulnerabilities of the enemy, and (b) better exploit the capabilities of the friendly formation. Mobile Groups conferred genuine flexibility on the operational commanders and were employed on a wide variety of tasks. Their boundaries were the boundaries of the *operation* and not of the tactical formation through whose area they might be committed.

2. Mobile Groups were the most successful means of exploitation so as to turn tactical success into operational success, and achieve a high rate of advance to great depth. It is for this reason above all else that the concept has been revived in the OMG.

3. Mobile Groups were most important in achieving the continuity of the offensive and avoiding disastrous "operational pauses" — lulls in the operation which would give the enemy time to recover, or, in modern terms, to use his nuclear weapons effectively.

4. Mobile Groups were rarely employed in isolation in an operation: usually several were employed, and this would be the case today with OMGs.

5. There was always a great degree of flexibility in reorganization, echeloning, and grouping of forces involved in Mobile Groups, and Army Commanders had a lot of freedom to exercise choice of options. In modern terms, this freedom of choice between options and greater degree of flexibility may well be found at a lower level than in the past.

6. Formations and units comprising Mobile Groups were often reinforced or tailored to enable them to meet specific requirements: e.g., considerable engineering assets were added when obstacle crossing was important. The ideal basis for a Mobile Group was a tank corps or a mechanized (all arms) corps. In modern terms, this would equate to a tank or motor rifle division in size.

7. As the war progressed, the proliferation of anti-tank weapons made it essential to make tank formations operating as or in Mobile Groups more self-contained. Integral infantry and artillery and logistic elements became the norm. This can be seen reflected in the current reorganization and re-equipment in the Group of Soviet Forces–Germany.

8. Strong forward detachments — usually from the first echelon of the forces in the Mobile Group — were always deployed, and were most important to assuring the speed of advance. Their primary function was to reconnoitre the enemy and to preempt his deployment into prepared positions or into towns and villages. The importance of this is even more heavily emphasized today.

9. The committal of Mobile Groups was the most crucial moment of the battle, and the choice of that moment was crucial to the success of the Mobile Groups. Committal was invariably on two axes. It was essential that there be little opposition on committal, either by remaining defence or from counter-attack by land or air. Surprise was crucial and deception always practised. Massive air and artillery support was always provided

(50-70 percent of the Front's aviation; 18-20 guns per tank or infantry battalion in the Group), and this remains true for today's OMG.

10. Mobile Groups often operated in conjunction with air assault forces and partisans. The modern OMG would rely more heavily on operations in conjunction with air or heliborne assault, because greater means now exist to put troops deep in the enemy rear.

11. Mobile Groups often detached units to raid, and sometimes the whole Group had a raiding function. In the modern OMG, this function is more important still. Particular targets of raids are likely to be nuclear weapons, headquarters and electronic installations, reserves, and supply depots.

12. Mobile Groups *very* frequently engaged in encounter battles, either with withdrawing forces or with advancing enemy reserves which they "attracted" by virtue of the threat they posed to the stability of the defence. These encounter battles varied in scale from those of the Group's forward detachment (rapid battalion or brigade actions), to encounter battles up to three days long involving an entire army, with 500 tanks and 1,500 guns plus aircraft engaged on each side. Encounter battles were fought both by day and by night, often a long way forward of the advancing combined arms formation, and at up to 350 kilometers beyond the initial forward edge of the battle area. They were very demanding of commanders' skills but their successful outcome often had a great bearing on the overall success of the operation. This is perhaps one of the least appreciated problems that the OMG will present to the NATO commander, particularly in those armies, such as the British, which are not well equipped for encounter battles.

The whole concept of the OMG appears well founded in view of NATO's present defensive posture, and in view of the numerous historical examples of the defeat of a defensive concept because of the psychological inability on the part of the defenders to accept the need to yield ground, particularly home ground.

The applicability of the above principles governing the deployment of Mobile Groups to the modern Operational Manoeuvre Groups is well supported in the East European military press. The stress on the fact that the committal of this group was *the most important* and tense moment of the battle indicates just what an important role this new concept plays in the revised Soviet strategy for the 1980s.

There will be one difference of particular note between the role of the Mobile Group and that of the Operational Manoeuvre Group. That is, as the 1980s progress, the OMG will come to play a role relatively much more important in the overall operational plan of the Warsaw Pact than the Mobile Group played in the operations of the Red Army in World War II.

This is due to: (1) the decreased scale of modern operations in terms of overall numbers of men; (2) the increased importance of speed and a high rate of advance; (3) the certainty of strategic disaster in the event of operational failure; and (4) the particular nature of NATO defence.

Let us remind ourselves that the OMG concept provides the all-important link between strategy and tactics. It is a means to an end, the end being the rapid collapse of NATO and the limiting of the war to the battlefield, and the means being a *surprise* attack on a *broad front* with several axes. The concept of the operation will be to insert on *each* axis, as an OMG, a *strong division* behind the NATO main belt of defence *on the first or second day of the offensive*.

In addition it may prove feasible to deploy the best part of a tank army on this task as a *Frontal OMG*.

The control of these OMGs will at all times be subject to a centralized overall plan. They will *not* be operating independently, but on tasks set by the Commander-in-Chief. However, they will have considerable latitude as to *how* to implement the plans they are given.

Once they have achieved penetration, the OMGs will either act as a consolidated force to assault or seize major targets or objectives, or may break up as tactical raids to hit such small but operationally important targets as headquarters or nuclear weapons. The OMG may operate alone, or in concert with other OMGs. By definition the OMG (and its constituent raiding groups and forward detachments) will be three-dimensional, that is, the large *air element* will be an *essential* part of the organization.

The Effect of the OMG on the Nuclear Battle

As long as NATO retains normal (i.e., not enhanced radiation) nuclear weapons, with their high collateral damage, long dwell time, and with the political inhibitions about their use, NATO will only be able to use them effectively (1) if the attacking forces can be slowed down, and (2) if friendly and enemy troops can be kept apart. It will be extremely difficult for NATO to consider the use of normal nuclear weapons on the first or second day of the attack, well inside Western Germany, against Soviet forces in close contact with NATO troops.

Furthermore, if the offensive is in one operational echelon, NATO's plans for interdiction (with nuclear and conventional forces) against a *second* operational echelon will be in vain. There may well be no such second echelon within East Germany for several days.

If, as seems likely, it does take NATO several days to obtain nuclear release, by that time special-purpose forces, air strikes, OMGs, raids, sabotage and the like will, the Soviets hope, have eroded considerably the nuclear stocks and weapons available, and may also have seriously damaged the command and control system essential to their effective use.

A great deal of effort has gone into making the Soviet forces tactically well able to survive on a nuclear battlefield. This applies as much to logistic elements as to teeth arms. NATO, on the other hand, puts most of its nuclear, biological and chemical effort into preparing to survive a chemical rather than a nuclear war, which *may* prove a serious disadvantage. This is not to minimize the need for NATO to be equipped and trained to fight in a chemical environment, nor to deny that NATO's possession of chemical weapons would be the greatest deterrent to a Soviet use of them. Rather it is to point out that chemical weapons are very much secondary in importance in Soviet eyes to nuclear weapons, and it is the ability to survive on a *nuclear* battlefield which the Soviets deem more important. Yet most NATO forces do far more to train for chemical than for nuclear conditions.

Points of Difference between the Mobile Groups and Operational Manoeuvre Groups, of Relevance to the Development of the Concept

As already mentioned, the OMG will have a more important operational role than the Mobile Group did in World War II. Below is a more specific comparison between the two, based on recent analysis in the Soviet press.

Composition

In the past, only tank formations were capable of filling the role of Mobile Group. Now, all arms formations are also capable and may well be appointed to act as OMGs. On balance, however, tank formations are still seen as better in most circumstances, although they require integral infantry and more artillery than they previously held to make for a better-balanced force. Ideally, any well-equipped formation should be capable of operating as an OMG, and the widespread reliance on battle drills even at divisional level will facilitate the introduction of this idea.

Tactics

The increased emphasis on raiding activities and forward detachments will be very demanding indeed of initiative and competence on the part of young officers. Although a great deal of progress has been made in improving the mental flexibility of the junior commander and increasing his overall competence and understanding of the battlefield, there is still a long way to go. Initiative is a very difficult concept for the Soviet military system to come to terms with. As a partial remedy, a lot of effort has recently been put into automating command and control procedures by the use of algorithms and drills and by the introduction of computers. A great deal of effort has also gone into the improving of command and control systems, especially communications.

Targets

The importance of destroying nuclear weapons (especially in the conventional phase), electronic equipment, and command and control elements constitutes the biggest difference here. Otherwise the principles of engaging targets remain virtually unchanged. What modern equipment confers, of course, is a greater ability to carry out these principles. This is perhaps nowhere more marked than in the field of Electronic Warfare. The advantages of having a *strong* force deep in the enemy's defensive zone is immediately obvious in terms of radio and radar locations of targets, jamming of radio relay communications, and the implementation of deception measures.

NATO's Defence

There are changes having to do with water obstacles and minor built-up areas. Lachiewicz and Rajmansky note that "Fighting on the approaches to a water obstacle, and its impact on . . . the success of the forced crossing has recently become especially important because *the enemy has come to rely on exploiting water obstacles as a means of establishing a permanent defence*" (emphasis added).[8] Water crossing, as a consequence, has become an even more important part of the OMG than it was of the Mobile Group. As for the minor built-up areas — villages, small towns, and strip development — their defence has become an important feature of the NATO defensive scheme. This has led to a reassessment of tactics for fighting in built-up areas by the Group of Soviet Forces–Germany and a big swing away from the city siege tactics of ten years ago to lightning attacks on villages as a basic drill.

Night

Special attention is being paid to operations at night as a means of reducing the advantages of modern weapons in the defence. This too has over the last year been a topic of special interest in the Warsaw Pact. According to Lachiewicz and Rajmansky, "At night it is more difficult to identify where the OMG is, and what its direction of march is, and it is not easy to organize counter-measures to destroy it. *Therefore it is considered that night provides favourable conditions for the penetration of the Army's OMG in the depth of the enemy grouping*" (emphasis added).[9]

Combat Support by Artillery

This was always of crucial importance to the successful committal of a Mobile Group, and this has not changed with the OMG. However, mobile armoured artillery on the enemy side, together with modern location techniques, has made it necessary to move away from lengthy rolling barrages to short (4-5 minutes) and heavy successive fire strikes as a means of neutralizing the enemy. *Remote mining (especially by multi-barrelled rocket launchers) poses, in Soviet eyes, one of the very greatest threats to the successful committal and operation of the OMG.* Any means of delivering the mines will be a particular target for Soviet artillery and aircraft. The style and volume of the new gunnery practices have necessitated changes in the command and control of artillery, and in the ammunition logistical supply system. The new artillery weapons, such as BM27, have made it possible to provide artillery support at far longer ranges than was the case in the past. The mechanization and armouring of artillery is clearly of great importance for the viability of artillery accompanying the OMG.

The Role of Air Power

This is of much greater importance nowadays, particularly in view of the fact that 50 percent of NATO's firepower (including, of course, nuclear firepower) is vested in the Air Forces.[10] Consequently, an air operation has become an integral part of a strategic operation, and the air element is the third dimension of the ground battle.

This requires air support to be much more closely integrated with Soviet lower formations than was the case previously, and it demands of the Soviet forces much *closer* support, greater versatility than previously, and consequently a different system of coordination and control.

The increased importance of air support has, the Russians stress, made the *weather* a more important consideration than ever before when planning operations by OMGs. This is not to say that OMGs cannot be committed in bad weather, but their use will certainly be riskier in bad weather if the defender possesses aircraft better equipped for poor visibility, and if the defender's meteorological services are more reliable at predicting changes in the weather.

Combat support by air, by way of recce, fire support, mine laying, smoke screen laying, desants, logistic supply and so on has been revolutionized by the tactical anti-aircraft missile. This has necessitated a complete reorganization of air forces and air defence and of the management of air space on a more rational basis. Army aviation has returned as the formation commander's integral air arm and this helicopter (perhaps, in future, fixed wing as well) support has come to be of positively crucial importance in the concept of the OMG. This is so to such an extent that there are numerous articles dealing solely with this aspect of the operational strategy. The Frontal and Theatre aviation will provide resources for the air operation, i.e., the air element of the strategic operation. Resource limitations may well dictate that the corridor of air superiority established for the conduct of the air operation must be coordinated with the air-cover corridors created to protect the OMGs. Of tactical interest is the great importance allotted to combatting NATO's combat helicopters. These, together with remotely delivered mines and the multi-barrelled rocket launchers, are said to present the greatest threat to the OMG, after the nuclear strike.

Link with Special-Purpose Forces

The increased need for a *rapid* collapse of the enemy, plus the easily defined nature of crucial targets, the destruction of which will put the whole of NATO's defensive framework at risk, has increased the value of clandestine "behind-the-lines" operations. This, coupled with improved means of inserting special forces — by air, helicopter, in disguise, etc. — has led to a significant increase in the role played by special purpose forces, especially for the reconnaissance and verification of targets to be engaged by air or long-range artillery.

Problems in Implementation of the OMG Concept

It is probably no exaggeration to say that this recent development of Soviet operational doctrine is the most significant to occur since the changes wrought by the advent of nuclear weapons. It is nothing less than a complete operational shake-up designed to produce an effective method of winning a war quickly and by conventional means alone if necessary. At the same time its applicability to the nuclear battlefield is evident and impressive. As might be expected, however, it has necessitated a serious re-think by the Russians on how to run their formations. This is especially true in terms of (1) philosophy of command and control, and (2) all arms cooperation and coordination.

At the tactical level it is forcing a reorganization of logistics, air defence tactics, artillery practices, and repair and maintenance methods, to name but a few areas of interest. The press discussion shows that solutions to the problems generated by the change in operational strategy are only just being attempted. A long time will pass before the Soviet Army can even identify all its problems in this, let alone answer them.

There can be no doubt, however, that the Soviets are now irrevocably committed to a significant amendment of their operational procedures. Developing the capability to deploy Operational Manoeuvre Groups will be evidence of the acquisition of a very great degree of operational flexibility. It will give the Warsaw Pact another *alternative* means, and it is clearly an attractive alternative — let us not forget that it envisages large Soviet formations operating behind NATO's main defensive belt by the end of the first day of the main battle. This will, if it is accomplished, present NATO with a problem *at precisely that level with which it is at present least well organized to cope — the operational level.* If NATO is to meet this challenge, an effort at the corresponding scale is required, because, as the Soviets point out, no matter how good the tactics are, if the operational plans are no good, you lose. The aim of deploying OMGs will be to try and make us lose very quickly.

It is well at this stage to point out that the Russians do not and never have subscribed to the doctrine of Mutually Assured Destruction as a sensible policy. To base a defensive posture on the concept that, if the enemy wipes out your country, you will seek revenge and wipe out his in retaliation is, to a Marxist, positively immoral. Far better to ensure by your actions that the enemy never gets a chance to hit you in the first place. The Soviets maintain that if they perceive the enemy making serious preparation to destroy them, they are perfectly entitled to react to that preparation and destroy the enemy before he can inflict his intended attack: indeed, it would be their duty to do so and madness not to. The limiting factor, of course, is the Soviet Union's actual ability to destroy the potential attacker and prevent his retaliatory second strike.

In simple terms, this is the law of the Wild West gunfighter. If the opponent was seen to start drawing his gun, intent was assumed and the gunfighter had the perfect right to draw his own gun and kill his opponent before the latter could complete his draw. In the Wild West this was considered self-defence. The limitation, of course, was provided by how quick each gunfighter was on the draw.

At the level of deployment in Europe, the same logic may well be applied. The ability to mobilize quickly and achieve surprise is the equivalent of the fast draw. It is by no means the only element making for ultimate victory (others being accuracy of shooting, the lethality and reliability of the revolver, the failing nerves of the opponent, etc.) but it *is* an essential one. To continue the metaphor even further, in a sane and balanced man, the possession of the ability to draw fast by no means made him seek opportunities to use his skill — he would be too well aware of the chance of error, miscalculation, or some other fatal failure. However, the very knowledge of his skill would make him more awesome to his enemies, and he would be likely to get his own way much more easily, without having to fight for it.

In Europe, it may, in a worst case, come to war. If it does, the Soviet Armed Forces, assisted by selected elements of the Warsaw Pact, will face the problem of achieving a complete military and political neutralization of NATO in a matter of days, while at the same time maintaining their own military viability and doing everything possible to prevent the escalation of the war to a nuclear holocaust. This is a tall order, particularly as NATO is committed to using tactical nuclear weapons if necessary, and has, over the last decades, succeeded in developing tactical concepts which might effectively halt a Warsaw Pact advance. The threat posed by NATO's tactical nuclear weapons is of particular weight as these are, in Soviet eyes, NATO's best means of bringing a Soviet offensive to a dead halt and reducing the Soviet Army to a shambles in a matter of hours, *providing that they are used effectively*. It is clearly the aim of this new Soviet concept that their effective use should be prevented.

Perhaps I can be allowed a postscript to this long paper. I have been discussing Soviet concepts, and have made little reference to Soviet problems and vulnerabilities. This is not because of any belief that the Soviets have no vulnerabilities or weaknesses. On the contrary, such a major revision of their plans is evidence that they saw a *great* weakness in their previous operational strategy. By its own admission, the Soviet Army is riddled with problems and has an abundance of vulnerabilities. Perhaps the most significant is their own vulnerability to "being surprised." It is not *simply* "window dressing" to begin each major exercise in the Warsaw Pact with a NATO attack. If the Soviet Union were poised to launch an offensive, and were preempted in this by a NATO spoiling attack, there is little doubt that, in their own eyes, the Soviets reckon that *they* stand a good chance of collapse. The impressive thing is that the Soviets, through the comprehensive framework of their military doctrine, are able to recognise many of their weaknesses and try to structure their military system to minimise these when they cannot be resolved.

For all its faults, the Soviet Army is large, well equipped, and reasonably competent. Its equipment is not significantly inferior to that of NATO except perhaps in the field of electronics, and we can no longer hide behind the slogan "quality vs. quantity."

The British Army of the Rhine (BAOR) and the Soviet Third Shock Army (3 SA) are roughly the same size in terms of manpower. Yet compared to the BAOR, 3 SA fields:

— 2½ times as many tanks;
— 6 times as many artillery weapons;
— 1½ times the quantity of infantry;
— 1½ times the logistic lift capacity;
— and has greater electronic warfare, anti-aircraft, and nuclear, biological and chemical decontamination means.

Moreover, because of the design and engineering features of Soviet equipment, it has been shown that the total cost of this equipment is only about 15 percent more in real terms than the equipment of the British Army of the Rhine.[11] When one adds the comparison of air force support to the ground forces there is a similar disparity.

Is it unreasonable to suggest that in trying to evolve new conventional means to deter a Soviet attack, we might try and learn from the Soviets how they get such value for the money?

NOTES

1. Marx-Engels "Sochineniya" (Moscow, 1953) Vol. 10, p. 535, quoted in P. H. Vigor, *The Soviet View of War, Peace and Neutrality* (London: R.K.P., 1975). Mr. Vigor's book is essential reading for all who wish to understand the Soviet approach to war.

2. The Soviet term "operational" denotes military activity *specifically at "Army" or "Front" (Army Group) scale*. In the light of their wartime experience, this level is considered the most important on the field of battle, and it is at this level that the Soviets attempt to achieve flexibility. Plans below this scale, i.e., at divisional level and downwards, are reckoned as "tactical," and above this scale, i.e., at theatre level, as "strategic."

3. A World War II Soviet tank corps was almost identical in size to a modern Soviet tank division.

4. To all intents and purposes, Warsaw Pact doctrine and Soviet Military Doctrine are identical. The USSR has imposed the framework of its doctrine on all the Warsaw Pact countries and the Warsaw Pact Staff is little more than an extension of the Soviet General Staff.

5. General Krupchenko, *Voenno-Istoricheskii Zhurnal* (Soviet Military Historical Journal), C. Donnelly, transl., July 1981, pp. 13 ff.

6. Major Wojciech Michalak, "Lotnictwo w Dzialaniach Rajdowo-Manewrowych Wojsk Ladowych" (Aviation in the Raid and Manoeuvre Operations of the Ground Forces), Z. Agar, transl., in *Przeglad Wojsk Lotniczych i Wojsk Obrony Powietrznej Kraju* (Soviet Air Force and Air Defence Review), Poland, February 1982.

7. Colonel Lachiewicz and Colonel Rajmanski, "Potrzeby Wojsk Ladowych w Zakresie Rozpoznania i Wsparcia Ogniowego Przez Smiglowce w Dzialaniach Nocnych" (Helicopter Recce and Fire Missions in Support of Land Operations at Night), Z. Agar, transl., in *Przeglad Wojsk Lotniczych i Wojsk Obrony Powietrznej Kraju* (Soviet Air Force and Air Defence Review), Poland, June 1981.

8. *Ibid.*

9. *Ibid.*

10. See General Zaitsev, *Voenny Vestnik,* February 1979, pp. 23 ff for a definitive statement of this.

11. See J. W. Kehoe and K. S. Brower, "U.S. and Soviet Weapon System Design Practices," *International Defense Review,* June 1982.

PART III

REQUIREMENTS FOR CONVENTIONAL DEFENSE

How can NATO best deter or defend against a Soviet conventional attack based on the doctrine discussed in Part II? Without seeking to match Soviet forces, NATO needs the capacity to exploit the vulnerabilities inherent in any Soviet offensive operations.

This Workshop analyzed the specific tasks NATO should be able to perform in order to do so. It had the benefit of supporting papers by George S. Blanchard, P. G. Griffith, and K.-Peter Stratmann. This Part reproduces the Report of the Workshop and the supporting paper by Stratmann.

WORKSHOP MEMBERS

General George S. Blanchard (Author)
General, United States Army (Ret.); Consultant. Formerly: Commander in Chief, United States Army Europe and Commander, Central Army Group (NATO).

Professor Harvey Brooks
Benjamin Peirce Professor of Technology and Public Policy, Harvard University. Formerly: Dean of Engineering and Applied Physics, Harvard University; Member, President's Science Advisory Committee and Naval Research Advisory Committee.

Lieutenant General Sir Robin Carnegie
Lieutenant General, Armour (Ret.); Director General of Military Training. Formerly: Chief of Staff British Army of the Rhine; Commander 3rd Division.

Major General Roderich Cescotti
Major General, GEAF (Ret.). Formerly: Commander, Allied Air Forces Baltic Approaches; Deputy Commander, Second Allied Tactical Air Force; Commander, Allied Air Defense Operations Center.

Mr. Daniel Gouré (Rapporteur)
Senior Associate, Jeffrey Cooper Associates Inc.; Consultant on Space Issues to the BDM Corporation; Ph.D. Candidate, Soviet Studies Department, Johns Hopkins University, School of Advanced International Studies.

Dr. Patrick G. Griffith (Author)
Lecturer in War Studies, Royal Military Academy Sandhurst; author of *Forward into Battle*; currently writing a book on conventional warfare and NATO's Central Front.

Lieutenant General Hans-Joachim Mack (SHAPE Observer)
Lieutenant General, German Army; Deputy Chief of Staff for Plans and Operations at SHAPE.

Air Vice-Marshal Paul R. Mallorie

Air Vice-Marshal, Royal Air Force (Ret.); Scientific Research Fellowship, NATO. Formerly: ACOS (Informations Systems), SHAPE.

General John W. Pauly

General, United States Air Force (Ret.). Formerly: Commander, Allied Air Forces Central Europe; Commander in Chief, United States Air Forces in Europe.

Mr. Stanley Resor

Debevoise & Plimpton. Formerly: Secretary of the Army; Ambassador to Mutual Balanced Force Reductions negotiations in Vienna.

General Franz-Joseph Schulze (Chairman)

General, German Army (Ret.). Formerly: Commander in Chief, Allied Forces Central Europe; Deputy Chief of Staff, Plans and Operations, Allied Command Europe.

Lieutenant General Charles J. Simmons

Lieutenant General, United States Army (Ret.); Consultant. Formerly: Commander 3rd Armored Division and Deputy Commander in Chief, United States Army Europe.

Dr. K.-Peter Stratmann (Author)

Staff Associate, Stiftung Wissenschaft und Politik, Ebenhausen.

Supporting Papers:

1. George S. Blanchard, *Present and Prospective Tasks for Conventional Forces and Required Capabilities for Meeting Threats and In Exacting Heavy Costs from Possible Invaders.*

2. P. G. Griffith, *Winning Operational Freedom of Action — The Key to Any Truly Conventional Option.*

3. K.-Peter Stratmann, *Prospective Tasks and Capabilities Required for NATO's Conventional Forces.*

Requirements for Conventional Defense

IMPROVING NATO'S CONVENTIONAL POSTURE

The continuing growth in Warsaw Pact military capabilities, nuclear as well as conventional, is raising concerns within NATO about its ability to deter aggression and, should war occur, to provide a stalwart defense. This has given impetus to a wide-ranging and intense public debate regarding how to improve the manner in which the Alliance organizes and conducts its defense. Many of the changes to NATO practices and procedures that have been proposed in this debate transcend the bounds of military reform and would require a new strategy and associated force posture. But the realities of NATO's geographic situation, national manpower policies, and ongoing budgetary constraints make it impractical to consider the development of a new strategy.

NATO's existing strategy of Flexible Response and Forward Defense is entirely adequate to meeting the challenge posed by the Warsaw Pact. NATO should not seek a new strategy, but greater security through improvements to its capabilities to implement current strategy. At present, the most serious deficiencies are in NATO's conventional posture and its ability to maintain a credible conventional deterrent. If conventional forces are able to perform the required defensive missions without early resort to nuclear weapons, NATO security is improved. Nonetheless, NATO defense will continue for the foreseeable future to rest on the close and indivisible linkage of conventional, theater nuclear, and strategic nuclear forces.

Forward Defense requires that NATO not seek to trade territory for time or forces. This, in turn, means that NATO must be prepared to stop the first Warsaw Pact echelons as far forward as possible. A successful forward defense in the Central Region requires the ability to defeat many elements of the Warsaw Pact threat, ground and air, virtually simultaneously. The defensive character of the Alliance implicitly grants to an enemy the advantage of determining the time, direction, and weight of an attack. Because of this and because of the growth in the Warsaw Pact's conventional capabilities in the Central Region the requirements for an adequate forward defense appear increasingly difficult to meet.

Essential to an improved NATO capability to deter attack is the capacity to survive an initial massive onslaught. The Warsaw Pact's doctrine calls for a short swift and intense campaign against NATO, probably with an attempt to deliver a surprise first blow; NATO forces must be prepared to move very rapidly from a peacetime or crisis posture to one of active hostilities. Moreover, NATO forces must expect to have to change to a war footing under conditions of violent combat. NATO forces must have the resiliency to survive this form of warfare from the first minutes of hostilities.

NATO forces must not merely survive but must retain the ability to perform their assigned missions under the extreme stresses of modern war. The nature of modern war, the systems used, the numbers employed, and the concurrence of air and ground combat suggests that the fighting will be extremely intense and very costly. Rates of ammunition expenditure, for example, are likely to be very high and may rapidly deplete available war stocks. If NATO combat elements survive but do not have the command, control, and communications or the combat support to carry out their missions, then they are for all intents useless. Because modern warfare is a highly complex affair and involves the integration of diverse capabilities, it is important that the "system" as a whole be able to function. Breakdowns anywhere within the overall system can potentially threaten the viability of other elements. Hence, it is insufficient to speak of deep-strike or counter-air warfare without recognizing that this involves the proper functioning of a complex system of many parts. NATO forces must be sufficiently sustainable to conduct extended combat operations against a numerically superior opponent over a protracted period of time.

Solutions to the twin concerns of survivability and sustainability are essential if NATO is to have the confidence in its ability to mount a secure defense against Warsaw Pact aggression. The image of a strong conventional defense will also enhance deterrence. If NATO forces have the capacity both to survive Warsaw Pact blows and to continue to perform essential missions, then there is a good chance that NATO can effectively deter, and if necessary, defend.

CORRECTING NATO'S DEFICIENCIES

NATO is currently studying a number of concepts for enhancing its conventional defenses. Many of them emphasize the need to extend the range of combat operations relevant to Forward Defense into the Warsaw Pact's rear areas. In general, these concepts include a mix of technological, operational, and tactical means of improving NATO's ability to fight in the event of war. The ability to sustain a forward defense should itself inhibit the Warsaw Pact's willingness to risk a war in Europe.

It is essential that any effort to improve NATO's conventional deterrence be realistic in terms of the political and resource constraints which face the Alliance. To suggest dramatic shifts in NATO policies and forces could be counter-productive if such changes cannot be sustained. NATO's deterrent posture could suffer as a result. Above all, success in enhancing NATO's conventional capabilities demands the clear delineation of priorities in order to avoid dissipation of the limited resources available for improvement over too many problem areas. The choice among competing alternatives must take account of their budgetary impact as well as their military effectiveness. In estimating the cost of a given increment of military capability, as much weight must be given to life cycle costs, including operations and maintenance costs, as is given to initial investment costs. Moreover, solutions must be assessed according to what other capabilities might be purchased for the same expenditure.

It is also essential to determine what can and must be done now to ensure an adequate NATO defense in a period of rapidly improving Warsaw Pact strengths. Too often in discussions of new systems, future possibilities are confused with current capabilities. Technologies only in the early developmental stages can appear to be real alternatives to existing technologies and systems. In its planning, NATO must be constantly alert to the danger of counting too heavily on technology in general and in particular on technologies which have not been fully proven in relation to realistic operational environments. NATO can make better use of the technologies already available to it to ameliorate virtually all of its critical deficiencies, often at minimal incremental cost.

Viewed in the aggregate, NATO's problem is one of buying the most critical capabilities by the most cost-effective means. Some of the solutions to existing capability gaps can be provided only by high and expensive technology. If there is to be any hope of introducing new equipment in the numbers needed, there will have to be no wasted investment anywhere. Indeed, NATO should examine carefully all those areas requiring improvements to see what level of technology could meet those requirements in order to conserve funds for the most critical high technology items.

In addition, NATO must not overlook the importance of enhancement measures which cut across established national service and service branch boundaries. It seems to be particularly promising to look for improvements at the level of tactics which make use of integrated multiple functions and system components, rather than limiting our focus to the potential of individual weapon systems.

Five functional categories can be identified in which conventional capabilities could significantly enhance NATO's deterrent: blunting the first-echelon attack, holding follow-on echelons at risk, attriting Warsaw Pact air power, disrupting Warsaw Pact command and control, and ensuring secure and reliable NATO command and control. Within this framework, there is a set of critical problems, the solutions to which would markedly improve NATO's conventional capabilities. Some solutions will affect more than one category. For example, improved target acquisition and data handling could be viewed as contributing to the blunting of the first-echelon attack, to holding the follow-on echelons at risk, to attriting Warsaw Pact airpower, and to disrupting Warsaw Pact command and control.

In addition to specific improvements and reforms in force posture and weapon systems, NATO needs to give greater attention to improving interoperability to ensure that, in particular, the eight corps and two Allied Tactical Air Forces of Allied Forces Central Europe can fight as one force, unhindered by the fact that the soldiers and airmen come from many nations.* To date, NATO has made definite but qualified progress in this area. A number of measures are required to enhance NATO's interoperability further:

Operational interoperability refers to the essential international military cooperation among the sovereign nations of the Alliance to ensure a smooth interface between those nations on the battlefield. It includes material interface in cases where standardization has not been achieved; doctrinal, tactical, procedural operations; and agreements which permit national units to defend side-by-side against an enemy which will search for unit boundaries down which to attack. Command, control, and communication interfaces and codified understandings are included to ensure rapid, comprehensible orders across national and service boundaries.

— increases in multinational exercises and day-to-day training;
— further development of Standard Operating Procedures for multinational operations;
— priority attention to interoperable, multinational command, control, and communications to include command relationship, command and control procedures, and command and control equipment.

CRITICAL ISSUES FOR IMPROVING NATO'S CONVENTIONAL POSTURE

The problems addressed below represent those to which NATO must give priority attention in its efforts to develop an enhanced conventional defense. Correcting these deficiencies will substantially improve the ability of the Alliance to mount a stalwart conventional defense. The recommended solutions are not restricted to so-called technological "fixes" but include changes to NATO's operational procedures, organization, and tactics as well.

Limiting the Likelihood and Impact of Surprise

None of the improvements to NATO forces and capabilities proposed here and in the myriad of other studies and reports on this subject will add to NATO's defense potential if the Alliance is caught by surprise. The growing Warsaw Pact capability to initiate a surprise attack without awaiting mobilization is a serious threat to any NATO defense. Even where the Pact chooses to mobilize and hence where strategic surprise therefore is less likely, the Warsaw Pact will likely attempt to gain tactical surprise by denying NATO clear warning as to the time, place, and weight of an offensive.

This places NATO in a difficult position.

First, the decision to alert and mobilize NATO forces is inherently one to be made by NATO's political authorities. It is doubtful that any intelligence capability will be able to provide timely unambiguous warning. All NATO's experience with predicting Warsaw Pact activities indicates this. Hence, political leaders must be prepared to act on ambiguous warning, in order to provide time both for alerting and deploying forces, and, most important, for the preparation of forward defenses.

Second, the growth of Warsaw Pact capabilities in artillery, airpower and ballistic missiles places the entire NATO area as well as Central Region forces at increased risk, particularly in the event of surprise attack.

Successful Warsaw Pact efforts to disrupt NATO's capabilities for command, control, communications, and information will also complicate recovery from surprise.

If NATO forces are properly forewarned and able to occupy and prepare forward defense positions they can expect to exact heavy costs from an invader. In the absence of surprise and faced with the threat of high losses, the Warsaw Pact, with an operation style based on a highly preprogrammed and structured offensive, may be deterred. At the least, reducing the likelihood of surprise will present the Warsaw Pact with uncertainties regarding the ultimate attainment of their objectives.

In order to reduce the likelihood of surprise, NATO needs an integrated system for theater information and target acquisition, with high accuracy and near real-time data presentation. Such a system should consist of long-range radar and electro-optical ground-target acquisition as well as communication, radar, and jammer intercept systems, and should operate under NATO command like the available airborne warning and surveillance force. Furthermore, intelligence-collection assets organic to those national forces that are assigned or earmarked for assignment to NATO should be put under the operational control of the NATO commanders. Such intelligence assets would then have a status like that of NATO's air defense forces. Only in this way can NATO commanders properly coordinate national reconnaissance efforts, collect and analyze the necessary intelligence upon which to base a political decision to initiate alert measures, and ensure realistic training of national and NATO staffs for their emergency functions.

Operational control of intelligence assets by NATO commanders in peacetime would eliminate the need for shifting the command and changing the operating procedures during transition from peace to war, or in crisis. It also would allow rapid reaction to any ambiguous activity on the other side and a regular oversight of Warsaw Pact exercises in the forward area, similar to the way in which the Warsaw Pact increases its intelligence-gathering activities during all NATO exercises.

Nations must be made to see the importance of sharing national intelligence and the need to develop the capabilities for rapid evaluation and dissemination of national intelligence. Current national methods for the protection of sensitive sources operate to the detriment of NATO as a whole.

An improved system of data handling is required in order to make the most effective use of all-source intelligence information. Such a system must be capable of rapidly transmitting the required data to relevant political leaders and military commands in order to provide both with the required warning.

Many steps can be taken to reduce the impact on NATO of surprise. Because NATO decision-makers must be prepared to respond to ambiguous warning, and in order not to make NATO responses vulnerable to manipulation by the Warsaw Pact, NATO requires, in the event of warning, response measures which are cheap, repetitive, reversible, and non-provocative.

Several potential improvements were delineated by K.-Peter Stratmann (see his supporting paper in this volume):

> Those force components and functions which are essential for an assured initial-defense capability must have a commensurate peacetime status; dependence on time-consuming mobilization and readiness measures should be kept minimal. In addition, NATO's alert system should envisage the prompt and simultaneous execution of groups of preparatory measures for these selected forces. If these measures were calibrated and organized into a flexible set of low-visibility readiness, alert, and movement exercises, political inhibitions against timely action in crisis could be dampened.

Finally, in the negotiations with the Warsaw Pact for Mutual Balanced Force Reductions, NATO has proposed a comprehensive set of associated confidence-building measures, including an annual quota of ground and air inspections and limitations on points of entry of forces into Central Europe. Implementation of such measures would increase advance warning of possible preparation by the Warsaw Pact for attack and should make it easier to obtain necessary NATO political decisions in the event of Warsaw Pact violations of an agreement. They would also enhance crisis stability by reducing the risk of miscalculation in a time of crisis.

Improving NATO's Capability for Target Acquisition and Data Handling

No improvement in NATO's firepower provides major dividends without a decided improvement in NATO's capability for target acquisition and near real-time data handling. A Warsaw Pact offensive in the Central Region would present the most target-rich environment in history. During breakthrough operations, in particular, there would exist transient high-density concentrations of valuable armor and mechanized combat formations the destruction of which would seriously impede the Warsaw

Pact's offensive. In order to disrupt the timing and momentum of Warsaw Pact operations, attrite the mass of Warsaw Pact combat units, and support NATO forward-deployed forces, NATO must rapidly concentrate its fire support on transient concentrations of high-value, often mobile, targets.

Currently, NATO treats surveillance and intelligence as one function and target acquisition as another. There is great emphasis on the collection of general intelligence data to provide an overall view of the battlefield but much less on the crucial function of target acquisition and evaluation. Surveillance is treated as somehow different from target acquisition. But the argument can be made that an adequate target-acquisition system would provide the most valuable information for a general picture and serve as an essential component of a surveillance and general intelligence capability. More important, if the overall reconnaissance effort can be redirected to focus on target acquisition rather than surveillance, a more efficient utilization of resources can be expected, and the development of future systems can be influenced to correspond more closely to NATO requirements for enhanced target acquisition. In fact, NATO should develop the means to integrate target-acquisition systems and capabilities to provide an all-source system.

In addition to collection systems, NATO must improve its target data handling. This involves both the evaluation of targeting data and its dissemination to users. Currently, one of NATO's major problems in this area is information overload. Fusion centers, which receive and process basic data, suffer from too much information from too many sources. In addition, the evaluation time for many kinds of information is entirely too slow to make the information useful to those who must act on it.

Additionally, NATO needs sufficient and secure and interoperable transmission capabilities to ensure adequate information flow. This involves, *inter alia,* appropriate down-links for airborne or spaceborne sensors, and also horizontal transmission links between processing centers and user units. It is important that NATO's handling system for this information be resistant to and protected against both electronic countermeasures and the electromagnetic effects of nuclear explosions.

A system which provides transmission of targeting data to the weapons controller in a form suitable for immediate use is preferable. To reduce information overload, it may be possible electronically to eliminate the mass of data needed only by weapons units and to pass only relevant information, in processed form, from these to command echelons.

Overall, NATO requires target-acquisition systems which can be used interchangeably anywhere on the Central Front, with data formats and communication links which are fully interoperable among military services and across the boundaries of national forces, and which encompass the entire electromagnetic spectrum, with high resolution, long range, and resistance to electronic countermeasures. In addition, consideration should be given to the acquisition of a simple drone which has a real-time down-link and can be procured in large numbers. Such a mix of systems might provide additional assurance against system degradation due, for example, to better-than-expected Warsaw Pact electronic or active air defenses.

Neutralizing Warsaw Pact Artillery

A growing threat to NATO forces is posed by the massive increase in Warsaw Pact artillery. NATO should recognize the implications of Warsaw Pact superiority in numbers and range of artillery for the current NATO practice of deploying forces in the covering force area, forward of the main defensive lines. In particular, NATO cannot afford to expose its ground units as covering forces to the huge Warsaw Pact artillery barrages which are expected at the start of the battle. Under these circumstances, and unless the Warsaw Pact artillery threat is neutralized, NATO may have to rethink its current approach to the defensive battle.

The task of neutralizing Warsaw Pact artillery requires: appropriate target-acquisition capability; weapons delivery systems and effective munitions; and measures to complicate Warsaw Pact targeting.

Target acquisition must begin prior to the outbreak of hostilities. The buildup of huge artillery concentrations opposite breakthrough areas takes time and should not go undetected. Even in the case of an unreinforced attack, NATO can expect a significant buildup of artillery.

Early counter-battery fire would not only reduce the danger posed to NATO units but also exercise a spoiling function on Warsaw Pact attacks. In order for counter-battery fire to have the maximum effect, it must be initiated at the very outbreak of hostilities. Likely areas for artillery ammunition storage and artillery command and control centers should be considered as additional targets for immediate destruction. A combination of delivery systems must be employed against Warsaw Pact artillery; NATO cannot rely solely on its presently outnumbered and outranged ground-based artillery assets. There is a definite need for adequate numbers of improved longer-range ground-based delivery systems such as the Multiple Launch Rocket System (MLRS) or Lance Follow-On in a conventional configuration. Such systems must be capable of placing a large volume of fire on the target within a very short time period. Regardless of the mode of delivery, area impact weapons would have a great potential in fulfillment of this mission. These munitions need not be designed for direct kill. Suppression of enemy fire could be sufficient.

NATO needs to examine ways to complicate Warsaw Pact targeting in addition to direct attacks on Warsaw Pact artillery, ammunition, and targeting facilities. A combination of passive and active means is available emphasizing concealment, mobility, and deception in the design and operation of NATO weapon systems and forces.

NATO will still have to rely heavily on airpower to neutralize Warsaw Pact artillery, and in general, to provide large volumes of ordnance with sufficient rapidity to defeat the Warsaw Pact's mass and momentum. Yet NATO airpower is increasingly vulnerable to both offensive air operations and to Soviet air defenses. NATO needs to look at ways to improve both the survivability of air assets and airfields, and the penetrativity of aircraft and air-delivery weapons.

Interdiction and Attack of Follow-On Forces

Successful interdiction of Warsaw Pact follow-on forces and lines of communications by means of deep strikes is considered essential to the success of the forward defense. NATO cannot allow Warsaw Pact follow-on forces unimpeded progress across Eastern and Central Europe. Nor can the pace of Warsaw Pact offensive operations be permitted to go unhindered. The Pact offensive is heavily dependent on high rates of advance and a precise timetable. Pact offensive operations are very vulnerable to NATO attacks intended to cause delay, disruption, and attrition of follow-on forces.

Warsaw Pact ground forces enjoy sizeable numerical superiority. To counter this advantage NATO must either increase its ready forces on a considerable scale or seek to delay, disrupt, and if possible destroy the follow-on force while containing Pact forces already committed in the close-in battle.

NATO's forward defense can be strengthened by deep attacks on critical fixed targets in the Warsaw Pact rear. Our analysis of the wider questions of deep attack on mobile follow-up echelons identified two possible discrete tasks: (1) delay and disruption, and (2) destruction, the latter demanding higher technology and higher financial expenditure.

The ability to delay, disrupt, and otherwise complicate the operation of follow-on echelons is critical to the success of NATO's defense. Follow-on forces cannot be allowed to develop offensive momentum or to choose freely the time, place, and weight of attack.

On the question of deep attack aimed at the destruction of follow-on forces as a contribution to the general attrition battle, the sole criterion should be where it can be done most effectively and cheaply. In answering this question many things need to be considered including target-acquisition capabilities, overall costs, the net benefit to forward defenses, and the Warsaw Pact's ability to offset the effects of deep strikes. NATO should not pursue the objective of deep strike at the expense of capabilities for defeating forward Pact forces. Given the rigid timetable of Pact offensive plans, delay and disruption may be highly effective in determining the outcome of the close-in battle.

Warsaw Pact forces are highly mechanized. The majority of them will be moving targets. Because these are generally more difficult to locate and engage than fixed targets, NATO's task will be to create choke points which will cause these mobile targets to be delayed and to pile up. This requires the ability to attack fixed targets such as river-crossing sites and defiles behind which, when interdicted, enemy columns will accumulate, thereby presenting very lucrative targets justifying the employment of manned aircraft. In addition, nothing would help more to disrupt the enemy's strict timetable than disruption of his command and control — a topic referred to below.

A variety of installations fall under the category of fixed targets for destruction. Ammunition and fuel depots; elements of the Warsaw Pact air defense system; elements of the Pact's command, control, communications, and intelligence (C^3I) infrastructure; and mobility and logistics choke points are all candidates for destruction. A careful pre-selection process should establish a set of targets whose destruction would, in fact, severely disrupt Warsaw Pact actions.

There are several points to be considered in planning for deep attack. Although the cost of the delivery systems might not increase automatically with the depth of the target, the cost of the acquisition systems and data links is likely to. In addition, the effect of delay/disruption/attrition close to the forward edge of the battle area might be harder for the Pact forces to rectify. On the other hand, attacks in greater depth allow further opportunities for subsequent attacks. In many cases distances to be covered are dictated by specific terrain features which offer particularly attractive choke points, for example, the crossing points along the Elbe, Saale and Moldau Rivers. Concentration on these choke points could permit simplification of the technology needed for target acquisition and data links, and hence a reduction of the cost.

Many delivery systems are candidates for the deep-strike mission, including cruise missiles, remotely-piloted vehicles, and ballistic missiles, as well as manned aircraft (particularly for attacking concentrations of mobile forces). For most of the types of targets discussed above, area-impact munitions would be the most effective means.

Deep strike is but one of a series of measures necessary for the improvement of NATO's conventional defense posture. It cannot be considered as an alternative to a sufficiency of conventional forces to oppose the first echelon of attack. The effectiveness of the deep-strike mission could be degraded by Warsaw Pact air defenses, electronic warfare capabilities, camouflage and deception measures, and capability for reconstruction and repair.

Attriting Warsaw Pact Airpower

Recent developments in Soviet airpower present NATO with a qualitatively new offensive air threat. Improvement in aircraft capabilities and changes in the Warsaw Pact's organization of its air assets provides an enhanced capability to perform close air support, independent air operations, and air superiority missions. Countering this threat and eroding Pact airpower involves two tasks: (1) counter-air operations and (2) enhanced air defense activity.

Counter-Air

NATO air assets are dangerously thin to meet the new air threat and at the same time perform established missions. This situation poses a serious danger to NATO forces, both ground and air. NATO airfields and air defense installations would be particularly at risk. It is, therefore, essential that NATO rapidly erode Warsaw Pact airpower before its own is severely degraded.

Direct attacks on Main Operating Bases (MOBs) offer the single most effective means of defeating Warsaw Pact airpower. Attacks on airfields would disrupt operations and destroy exposed aircraft. Such attacks should be initiated while the first waves of Warsaw Pact aircraft are still in the air and thus would require surviving, returning aircraft to divert from the MOBs to Dispersed Operating Bases (DOBs) with an attendant reduction in sortie rates.

The manner by which such attacks might be effective deserves further study. Both the criticality of timing to the airbase attack program, and the growth in Warsaw Pact air defenses, suggests that ballistic missiles be employed against Main Operating Bases, and manned aircraft against less well-defended Dispersed Operating Bases. Both should carry runway-cratering munitions and anti-personnel or delayed-action mines to slow repair.

Air Defense

One of the most urgently needed improvements to NATO's defensive capabilities is an enhanced air defense system. NATO's air defenses need most urgently improved management and interoperability in order to better exploit available firepower and enhance the survivability of the air defense system. Currently, NATO air defense across the Central Region lacks the requisite modern command, control, and communications (C^3) and management systems to permit the effective use of existing assets.

A priority item, therefore, is the inter-netting of C^3 and firing units to permit target data to be passed among national firing units, control and reporting centers (CRCs), and sector operations centers (SOCs). This capability must also be hardened against the expected electronic counter-measure threat. By inter-netting fire control centers, control and reporting centers, and sector operations centers, NATO can permit certain units to remain in a silent mode but still be operational. The linkage, however, must provide real-time data transmission in order to be useful.

A second priority item is the ultimate resolution of the airspace management problem and with it the issue of integration of both offensive and defensive air and ground defense systems. Currently, the problems caused by the lack of an adequate system for identifying friendly and hostile aircraft severely constrain NATO ground-based defenses. Concern for accidental destruction of NATO aircraft may result in a situation in which attacking Warsaw Pact aircraft are able to penetrate unopposed. In order to remedy this problem, a system is required which would provide positive identification so that NATO ground and air units could fire more freely.

NATO must also look to the requirement to develop defensive systems against the new family of Soviet tactical ballistic missiles with conventional capability now entering service. These systems pose a qualitatively new threat which cannot be countered by existing NATO air defense systems.

Countering Warsaw Pact Command, Control, and Communications

Because of the rigidity of the Soviet command structure there is particular value in developing the capability to disrupt the Warsaw Pact system of command, control, and communications (C^3). It is imperative that NATO develop the capability to conduct extensive counter-C^3 warfare to include a combination of physical destruction, electronic countermeasures and deception as an integral part of land/air operations. Disruption of Warsaw Pact C^3 should have the effects of:

- Denying enemy commanders the ability to command and control their forces effectively.
- Denying or degrading the enemy's ability to exploit, disrupt, or destroy friendly C^3 through an aggressive program to safeguard NATO command and control assets and communications links.
- Selectively dismembering enemy C^3 in an effort to reduce designated combat units to isolated islands, uncoordinated and ineffective.

Counter-C^3, and indeed the entire field of electronic warfare, is sadly discounted in NATO planning. Improved counter-C^3 appears particularly valuable in dealing with a number of emergent threats to NATO defenses. Priority targets for degradation of the Warsaw Pact command and control system are divisional and army headquarters, air defense centers, and artillery fire control centers. In addition, counter-C^3 operations may be particularly effective in combating the Operational Maneuver Groups, which will require close control and direction for cohesion and effectiveness.

In order to carry on counter-C^3 operations, NATO requires an integrated concept of them. This concept should lead to better use of existing assets and provide a guide for future development. Electronic warfare is only one element of counter-C^3 operations. In conjunction with other elements such as physical destruction and deception, counter-C^3 can substantially change the nature of the combat environment in Europe. Currently, NATO is more vulnerable than the Warsaw Pact to counter-C^3 operations because of the Pact's extensive capabilities in "radio electronic" warfare.

To be successful, the NATO electronic warfare concept must be a concerted effort, NATO-wide, involving all services. Currently, each nation and indeed virtually every service conducts a separate electronic warfare operation (generally lacking effectiveness) and there is a need for NATO-wide interoperability. As with NATO air defenses, inter-netting and centralized coordination can increase the effectiveness of electronic warfare capabilities.

Because of the dearth of realistic combat exercises and the difficulty of conducting such exercises in a peacetime civilian environment, the effectiveness of any system of electronic warfare is difficult to prove. Yet the criticality of C^3 to any modern military operation makes investment in counter-C^3 capabilities mandatory. The need for high security of electronic warfare measures has tended to isolate development and planning in this area from other aspects of counter-C^3, and thus to retard its integration with operational plans.

Ensuring Secure, Reliable and Interoperable Command and Control

NATO requires the adoption of a common concept of command which: (1) reduces dependence on communications by rigorous discipline on the passing of information; (2) maximizes delegation of authority; and (3) focuses on a command decision requirement in wartime. However, a concept which reduces the load on communications and increases delegated authority can only be developed by commanders themselves and will require training for headquarters staffs at every level. The additional capabilities for command in times of crisis and peace need not be so hardened for survivability, and some savings may be possible.

The concept must recognize that NATO's command and control system is an overlay on the existing command systems of national forces defending, for the most part, their national territories. NATO should make better use of national systems, but at the same time ensure their interoperability which is nowhere more important than in the field of command, control and communications. Where NATO systems are developed they must be interoperable between different national forces. NATO has a significant advantage in the capacity for initiative and decision down to the lowest level of the military forces. This capacity should be exploited to the full in the development of any concept of command.

A critical problem for all command and control systems is information overload and the press of demands for information from higher echelons.

In part, the solution to this problem depends on the improved utilization of data-processing capabilities, and in part on a better concept of command and control which does not overburden units with reporting requirements. This can be achieved if the system is built up in the light of the requirements of combat units for command directives, information, and support from superior headquarters. This approach should exploit the capacity for initiative at every level. The normal approach of analysis of command systems from the top down tends to lead to the development of a top-heavy system.

Secure and survivable command requires a recognition of the multiple threats to headquarters and their communications links. Improvement of the survivability of NATO command, control and communications systems is considered vital. A variety of means exist for accomplishing this, including concealment; reduced sizes and signatures of units; dispersion, redundancy, and hardening. Survivability requires a trend away from fixed and known sites into small, dispersed and possibly mobile cells at all command levels. The most urgent need is at the corps level and below.

Additional Requirements for Forward Defense

Two additional requirements which have not been adequately addressed in the foregoing appear to be particularly significant: (1) meeting the threat to NATO's rear area and (2) capitalizing on low technology for some currently available forces.

Meeting the Threat to the Rear Area

There has been considerable discussion of late regarding the concept of the Operational Maneuver Group (OMG) and Warsaw Pact plans for its use. The basic concern for NATO is that if the concept is successful, Pact units could rapidly move behind the main battle-area forces before NATO reinforcing formations are in a position to oppose them.

NATO should look to making use of a variety of means to deal with the Operational Maneuver Group and its supporting air and artillery. Recognizing that the OMG is most vulnerable when it is massing for attack, NATO target acquisition systems and artillery-air strike capabilities should be focused on finding, identifying and attacking massed OMG units. Similarly, electronic warfare systems should be targeted on the Operational Maneuver Group to disrupt its command and control capabilities. In addition, combat support and combat service support rear area units should be equipped and trained to counter the Operational Maneuver Group, and in particular to defend against Warsaw Pact breakthrough, mobile raids, and airborne/heliborne assaults.

Capitalizing on Low Technology for Some Currently Available Forces

Because technology changes rapidly and maintenance of an adequate defense is costly, NATO may well seek to use a high-low mix in its deployed capabilities to achieve enhanced defense at acceptable costs. Two examples of areas for investigation are NATO's electronic warfare support capability and tactical maneuverability.

The rapidly increasing demands on NATO's command, control, communications, and intelligence targeting, and on its information infrastructure pose a serious cost issue. As demands for better data in near real time grow, so too does the complexity and cost of relevant systems. NATO should look to ways of mixing high and low capability systems, where possible, to increase capabilities at an acceptable cost. The importance of the high-low mix was noted by Stratmann:

> . . . rapid progress of advanced technologies could allow for a high-low mix of interlocking systems and functions. Investment into improved electronic support components thus may enable NATO to opt for *larger quantities* of less sophisticated aircraft, weapons, and munitions. Only in this way could surge capabilities and endurance of Western air forces be enhanced.

Much of the terrain along the NATO-Warsaw Pact border consists of close or broken country. Although the Warsaw Pact may not use approaches in strength through this terrain, history is full of the dangers of leaving difficult, or supposedly impassable, approaches unguarded.

At present, NATO often takes on this task with armored forces or light forces delivered by helicopter or soft-skinned vehicles. The former use costly technology, are often not fully suited to this task, and are needed to concentrate in the maximum numbers possible for the crucial battle in the more open terrain. The latter suffer from the disadvantage that it may be particularly difficult to redeploy them, once they are in contact, to meet a changing situation.

Developing technology and weapons in the form of better and cheaper hand-held and man-portable anti-armor weapons, new means of rapidly emplacing obstacles, and simplified battlefield transportation with protection features optimized against indirect attack — all these offer the opportunity in re-equipment programs to produce less costly forces well-suited to this task, as well as to release resources for the critical battle on the more open approaches.

CONCLUSIONS

The Workshop's findings can be summarized as follows:

NATO faces a serious and growing conventional threat. In many areas improvements in Warsaw Pact technologies, forces and operational art and tactics have resulted in a fundamentally new threat. Furthermore, the character of the Pact's military posture and the requirements of NATO strategy confront the Alliance with the clear risk of strategic surprise. Continued growth in Warsaw Pact conventional capabilities, if not countered, could erode the conventional component of NATO's deterrent as well as the prospect for an effective conventional defense.

NATO current strategy is one of Flexible Response and Forward Defense. Meeting the conventional threat requires that NATO possess the capability to stop the first attacking echelons as far forward as possible and in so doing, defeat the elements of Warsaw Pact ground and air power. Because of the defensive character of the Alliance and the ongoing improvements in the Warsaw Pact's conventional strength, the adequacy of NATO's strategy has come under increased scrutiny, and so has its capability to implement that strategy successfully.

Critical to meeting NATO's conventional defense requirements is the availability of forces and means to underwrite NATO's present strategy. Currently, many capability gaps exist in NATO's conventional posture. Remedying these deficiencies does not mean investment only in technologies or weapons systems; in addition, changes in existing organizational, structural, planning, training, and support procedures can have a major impact on NATO's capabilities. One of the most important areas for NATO attention is improved interoperability, which requires changes in many of the aforementioned areas. As noted in the foregoing sections, improvements to NATO interoperability can have an effect across the whole spectrum of NATO operations.

The objective of this Workshop was to identify improvements to NATO's conventional capabilities that would result in an enhanced conventional defense regardless of the character, size or timing of a Warsaw Pact attack. Such enhancement would make a Warsaw Pact decision to attack less likely.

Priorities in Addressing NATO Conventional Force Improvements

Progress towards enhancing NATO's conventional capabilities must be on the basis of step-by-step implementation of corrective measures. In identifying the first steps, the determining factors should be the availability of tested, affordable technologies to perform missions which hold the greatest promise of the most immediate payoffs. Four areas are considered priority candidates for investment by NATO: target acquisition and data handling, counter-battery firepower, interdicting and attacking follow-on forces, and attrition of enemy airpower.

Target Acquisition and Data Handling

Adequate systems of target acquisition and data handling are necessary if NATO is to utilize present or improved firepower capabilities. The development of such systems should focus on improving the near real-time flow of information across boundaries separating the military services and national forces.

Several specific measures should be undertaken in pursuit of this objective. NATO should press ahead with development of a target-acquisition drone (a trilateral program of the U.S., Federal Republic of Germany, and Canada is currently underway). Additional, more capable sensor systems are required with sufficient range to support attacks well behind the forward edge of the battle. The down-link between target-acquisition capabilities and weapons controllers must be made secure and reliable. The existence of technologies with which to attain these objectives suggests that such improvements could be achieved within two years.

Counter-battery Firepower

The task of actively neutralizing Warsaw Pact artillery requires: adequate target-acquisition capability and effective weapons delivery systems and munitions. In particular, longer-range ground-based delivery systems are needed. Area impact weapons appear the most useful for this mission.

The present Multiple Launch Rocket System (MLRS) program provides NATO with a system capable of high-volume rapid counter-battery fire. Area impact munitions are available for the Multiple Launch Rocket System. Acquisition of additional capabilities for placing large volumes of fire on enemy artillery could be achieved within two years.

Interdicting and Attacking Follow-on Forces

In order to win the close-in battle, NATO needs to delay and disrupt Warsaw Pact follow-on forces and, potentially, to create better opportunities for their attrition as they mass behind destroyed or mined crossing sites. Many attractive choke points exist. In particular, NATO should take advantage of the natural barriers of the Elbe, Saale, Moldau, Oder and Neisse Rivers. Crossing points and bridging sites should be surveyed and targeted for destruction by medium-range systems. Direct strikes against follow-on forces massing behind these barriers can be undertaken by manned aircraft.

An improved Lance missile system could provide a means for performing the interdiction mission. Armed with conventional warheads, including area impact weapons and guided submunitions, and supported by an effective system for target acquisition and command and control, this weapon system could perform an interdiction function. The proposed Lance replacement, or Corps Support Weapon System, must have the capability for strikes against fixed targets and for area interdiction. Depending on the system selected for this mission, NATO could deploy an effective interdiction capability in two to four years.

Attrition of Enemy Pact Airpower

In order to degrade the effectiveness of Warsaw Pact airpower, NATO must be able to strike Main Operating Bases and Dispersed Operating Bases. Direct attacks against Main Operating Bases pose the single most effective means of destroying and disrupting Warsaw Pact airpower.

The optimal impact is achieved when attacks on Main Operating Bases are carried out while initial Warsaw Pact sorties are still in the air, forcing those aircraft to divert to less well-defended and capable Dispersed Operating Bases. In order to achieve this objective, NATO requires a quick reaction capability. Currently, the best means of attaining this capability is with ballistic missiles armed with runway-cratering munitions and anti-aircraft and anti-personnel mines. Because the technology in question is available and tested, acquisition of this capability could be achieved in four to five years.

Prospective Tasks and Capabilities Required for NATO's Conventional Forces

by
K.-Peter Stratmann

Dr. Stratmann is a Staff Associate at the Stiftung Wissenschaft und Politik in Ebenhausen, Federal Republic of Germany.

CONVENTIONAL FORCES AND NATO STRATEGY

The definition of the tasks and requirements for NATO's conventional forces is contingent upon Warsaw Pact capabilities and options and also upon NATO strategy. Criteria for sufficiency vary as a function of the role attributed to conventional defense within the overall strategic concept.[1] Those who favor a change of this concept because they regard a full-fledged conventional option as a prerequisite for credible deterrence need to apply a different yardstick. In order to prevail in a conventional war NATO might even have to give up its concept of Forward Defense and prepare for a protracted "defense in depth" on a continental and even global scale. In addition, NATO might require forces and doctrine for strategic counter-offensive operations into Eastern Europe to enforce war termination under conditions acceptable to the Western Alliance.

The original title of this contribution did not specify the objectives for NATO's conventional defense any further than requesting that it should meet threats and exact heavy costs from possible invaders. Possibly, this requirement can already be met by NATO's present conventional forces. Certainly it could be satisfied by force improvements within the structure of NATO's current strategy. If we interpret this requirement in less ambitious terms than a fully independent conventional defense capability, there may be no need to redefine basic tasks and priorities for NATO's

Notes are at the end of the paper.

conventional posture. Adaptation and force enhancements could proceed gradually. If, however, it is decided that NATO must be capable of prevailing solely with conventional forces against all kinds of conventional aggression, the tasks and priorities for Western forces will have to be changed significantly and the force requirements will increase dramatically.

A change of this kind could easily prove to be counter-productive and subvert West European willingness to strengthen NATO's conventional defense. It is beyond the scope of this paper to deal with such proposals for the "renewal" of Western strategy. But some general remarks seem to be warranted:

Investing scarce resources in a long-conventional-war posture (strategic reserves and transportation assets, wartime industrial production capacity, etc.) with a global perspective[2] (naval power projection capabilities, mobile central reserves in airpower and ground forces) may detract from keeping sufficient ready in-place forces in Europe. The latter are essential to prevent rapid defeat in the theater which probably could not be reversed by follow-on operations. There is little hope that NATO could replay the final phase of World War II and push back Warsaw Pact forces once they had occupied strategic positions in Western Europe. In addition to a substantial loss of forces, military infrastructure and operational space, NATO would have to cope with Soviet nuclear options. Even strictly selected uses could very effectively deny any attempts at major landing operations.

Strengthening NATO conventional forces in order to threaten the "Soviet empire" in Eastern Europe by means of (counter-) offensive operations[3] is not appealing from a European point of view. Unless one is ready to seriously erode the NATO consensus it is absolutely necessary to abide by its political character as a defensive regional alliance. Its charter is to deter and defend against Soviet military aggression in Western Europe. It must not threaten offensive action against Eastern Europe in order to deter or react to Soviet military moves elsewhere. A global Western strategy of "horizontal escalation" that boldly envisages initiation of war in Europe is a prescription for disaster. It would relegate the West European countries to the position of pawns in a superpower contest which is beyond their political control and which may put their very existence at risk. The buildup of conventional forces required for such a counter-offensive doctrine probably would increase the likelihood of military conflict in Europe. In case of war it may enhance Soviet incentives to employ nuclear weapons. This is particularly unsettling when considered along with the proclaimed erosion of America's nuclear protection of its European allies. NATO governments, of course, have to devise concepts and provide capabilities for dealing with out-of-treaty-area contingencies. But it would be folly to put NATO's military strategy for Europe in contradiction to the overriding political objective of keeping peace and stability in this region. In terms of security Europe has achieved a "status sui generis." An approach which looks at this region as just another theater of military operations misses this essential point.

Thus, in order not to arouse strong opposition against any force improvement programs or to strain political coherence and stability within the Alliance, NATO would be well advised to preserve its strategic concept of *Forward Defense*. Moreover, a true counter-offensive strategy, which would be more than a gamble, would require forces strong enough to overcome deeply echeloned Warsaw Pact defenses while simultaneously shielding NATO territory against counter-thrusts. Given current and foreseeable future economic and budgetary constraints for almost all Western countries such force goals must remain highly unrealistic.

The concept of Forward Defense has become the center of considerable controversy. It has become popular to deride it as defense that is Maginot style, passive, static, inflexible, and linear. This is of course an exaggeration. Since long before the advent of the "airland battle concept" NATO has espoused an offensive air doctrine which gave high priority to counter-air and interdiction operations. That respective Western capabilities have been reduced and, in part, negated, reflects profound changes in the offensive and defensive force balance but can hardly be explained by doctrinal flaws of the Forward Defense concept.

As for the ground battle, the Bundeswehr has always stressed the virtues of mobile defense. Probably, its commanders would wish to go beyond counter-attacks at the tactical level to counter-offensive operations at corps and army group levels. In this respect the Germans have been at variance with some of their allies whose attrition-and-fall-back-oriented defense concepts were much less flexible.

Actually, the real problem has been the conspicuous lack of operational reserves. There is a growing tendency to ignore this simple fact and to invoke — in the best tradition of bourgeois idealism — the importance of "innovative doctrine," which is, of course, much easier than to pay for additional divisions needed (among other things) for a "stalwart" Forward Defense posture. Just as doctrinal volition cannot solve the problem of effectively interdicting Soviet second- and third-echelon forces, strong rhetoric about the need to win at the campaign level and of not accepting the mere restoration of the status quo ante does not create a counteroffensive capability. Defending and restoring the integrity of NATO's territory in a major war is a rather ambitious goal. There is no need to indulge in fantasies that reach even beyond that.

Another school of thought which is critical of Forward Defense advocates a defense-in-depth concept. From an operational point of view such a change offers some advantages. However, it also creates difficult new problems. In addition to well-known German political objections to a strategy that would envisage major parts of her densely populated and highly industrialized territory as a battleground, important operational concerns must be considered.[4] Without the dependable inclusions of French territory such a strategy cannot be executed. Because of the shallow depth of West German territory, deep thrusts of Warsaw Pact forces would disrupt essential lines of communication and endanger vital components of NATO's military infrastructure. Furthermore, in order to be meaningful, i.e., to gain sufficient time to substantially attrite enemy forces and to canalize them for counter-attack, delaying operations require strong and highly effective NATO forces. Substantial losses would seem to be inevitable. Additional forces would be needed to establish a stable front somewhere (Weser-Lech line? On the Rhine?). Finally, strong strategic reserves would be required to drive Warsaw Pact forces back to where they started from.

NATO does not now have the active and reserve strength needed for such a strategy, nor the money for major relocations of military facilities. If, however, it could muster these resources, achieving a strong Forward Defense posture seems to be an easier and better solution. Given adequate force-to-space ratios and sufficient reserves, NATO would not be forced into an early first use of nuclear weapons. (At the same time, the threat of executing nuclear battlefield options would continue to impinge upon Warsaw Pact planning for breakthrough operations.) NATO could exploit the familiar advantages of a defender. The difficult problems of coordinating multinational forces and of organizing effective air ground support, ground-based fire support, and other support functions could be handled much more easily than in the fluid and confused environment of a mobile "defense in depth."

For the political and military reasons cited above, this paper is based upon the premise that efforts to define the future tasks for NATO's conventional forces and to improve force capabilities pertaining to these tasks will be determined on the basis of the strategic concept of Forward Defense.

SOME DIVERGENT PHILOSOPHIES: THE NECESSITY FOR CHOICE AND BALANCE

Before addressing the question of which specific tasks and capabilities of NATO's conventional forces should receive special attention, some more general issues must be discussed. Confronted with a situation of tight defense budgets and rapidly expanding demands, NATO governments may opt for distinct philosophies or "styles" for defense spending which correspond to divergent perspectives on security needs.

Governments may perceive an imminent danger of war in Europe or they may regard this possibility as remote and more or less hypothetical.

In the latter case they will feel free to structure and equip their forces according to political concerns. In order to enhance perceptions of deterrence and to reassure domestic constituencies in a peacetime or crisis-management setting they will emphasize the most visible and tangible components of NATO's military posture, namely numbers and sophisticated quality of major weapons systems as showpieces, number of major military formations, etc. Accordingly, less visible but expensive elements which are essential for real combat power will be given less attention.

But in the first perspective — an imminent danger of war in Europe — it is exactly those less visible components that ought to receive absolute priority, e.g., stocks of ammunition and spare parts, protective measures, command, control, and communications (C^3) capabilities, electronic warfare capabilities, and realistic training. NATO forces, of course, will in any case continue to live with substantial weaknesses and gaps, but it is up to NATO's political leaders to determine "the period of maximum danger" and to strike an appropriate balance between peacetime utilities and "war-fighting" capabilities.

Another case in point is the choice between policies of conservative incrementalism and vigorous selective innovation for research and development (R&D), procurement, force structuring, and doctrine.

Military bureaucracies are habitually attacked by outsiders for their alleged inertia. They are said to prepare always to fight the last war again, to have no sense for the revolutionary potential of specific new weapon technologies, and to distribute funds according to established patterns, thus missing the chance to promote promising developments that ought to be pushed. However, as military forces are expected to be ready to go to war at any time, hedging against risks and potential failures has become an instinctive trait of collective behavior. In order to ensure control in a complex and highly unpredictable combat environment, military men tend to rely upon doctrine, force structures, and equipment which are familiar to them. Modernization proceeds gradually. Demands for high-risk innovative strategies that could result in spectacular payoffs, but may also lead to dramatic failure, meet with skepticism and reluctance. In R&D and procurement policy there is an interest in avoiding over-reliance on single specific developments. Flexibility and redundancy are valued highly. Multiple designs are pursued, tested, and procured in order to be capable of coping with multiple scenarios and different combat environments.

Generally students of the bureaucratic politics of decision-making and academic intellectuals specializing in defense are quite unhappy with this state of affairs. They are attracted to intellectual solutions which look clean and simple and promise dramatic progress. Thus, they continually search for *dominant* strategies and tactics and they expect to develop them by *doctrinal* innovation which effectively exploits elements of *technological* superiority. Concepts are built around predicted specific "breakthroughs" in the development of weapon systems and/or around the discovery of enemy vulnerabilities which, if properly exploited by clever action, allegedly could disrupt the Warsaw Pact campaign plan and upset the overall force balance. Very often proponents of alternative defense concepts display a remarkable degree of single-mindedness and selectivity.[5] Usually their models are presented as prescriptions for the solution of NATO's overall defense problem, although they focus on rather limited sets of parameters. Time horizons are confused by assessing current NATO policy on the basis of predicted future weapons capabilities which, for example, may not be deployed before the mid-1990s. Taken out of their proper context and fielded against *present* Soviet forces, these technological extrapolations do seem to offer revolutionary opportunities. They look much less dramatic, however, when analyzed as components within the projected total threat environment of the 1990s, i.e., when due attention is given to improved future Warsaw Pact capabilities, countermeasures, and operational uncertainties.

Following the current debate on how to improve NATO's conventional capabilities, one cannot but feel confused. Which prophets should one listen to? Should one adopt the view that the principles of maneuver, mobility, and shockpower will determine the future of ground warfare, or that, on the contrary, static defense, employing highly effective immobilizing and destructive "smart" firepower will dominate the battlefield? Will we witness the demise of the tank because of the growing lethality of anti-tank capabilities or will more tanks be needed in order to preserve vital operational options in spite of high attrition? Will the manned aircraft be replaced by missiles, cruise missiles, and remotely piloted vehicles, or will we have to buy more of them and enhance their survivability and effectiveness by adding complex supporting systems? Are we heading for the "automated battlefield" where highly centralized staffs assisted by automated data processing directly "manage" the integrated airland battle from the "electronic hilltop"? Or do we have to enable our forces to fight when central command, control, communication, and intelligence (C^3I) systems will not function, and thus provide them with autonomous operational capabilities at the tactical level?

Each of these competing "images" of possible future environments, as well as the incompatible prescriptions derived from them, captures part of the complex reality of NATO's defense problem. Confronted with multiple and very different simultaneous challenges on a broad front, NATO decision-makers will not profit from academic theorizing which generates innovation by artificial selectivity and abstraction. Rather, they must adhere to a policy of mixed capabilities and strategies and try to reconcile competing demands within the constraints of insufficient budgets. The resulting process of "muddling through" is almost bound to look unimaginative and bureaucratic.

In contrast to widespread public expectations, in a short-term and medium-term time frame there is little reason for reckoning with dramatic changes in relative force capabilities in NATO's favor. Neither well-advertised concepts for more effective interdiction of Soviet second- and third-echelon forces nor more determined Western efforts to degrade the Pact's C^3 system can be regarded as panaceas. These are extremely ambitious objectives. Success will in any case remain partial. Furthermore, the exclusive focus on Soviet vulnerabilities in these areas diverts public attention from a sobering look at the extent to which the improvement of the Warsaw Pact's interdiction and counter-C^3 capabilities threatens to disrupt *NATO's* Forward Defense. The net balance of vulnerabilities does not seem to favor the Western Alliance. As Warsaw Pact forces in Europe have pursued a vigorous conventional arms buildup since the late 1960s which has resulted in a major quantitative increase and in broad-based qualitative improvements, it would be a miracle if NATO could devise an easy and cheap way to catch up and prevail in this race.

If one looks at the traditional tasks and missions for NATO's conventional defense, it is difficult to find any that could be downgraded or discarded. Across the board, gaps are waiting to be filled and deficiencies need to be corrected. Furthermore, in most of these areas active development programs which profit from parallel improvements in the technologies of sensors, communications, data processing, propulsion, munitions, and other technologies, offer the prospect of more effective solutions for many familiar problems. At the same time the mirroring trends on the Soviet side pose new challenges and require additional countervailing efforts. Without much thinking one may write down a lengthy list of important and urgent measures which NATO should and could take in order to strengthen its conventional defenses, including improvements in rear-area security, the provision of additional infantry troops, the dispersal, hardening, and defense of airfields, higher numbers of major weapon systems, larger stocks of modern munitions, more effective air defense suppression assets, more responsive and survivable C^3 systems, and so on.

Thus, Western defense analysts must address the problem of defining priorities. They will have to reach beyond numerous preceding attempts[6] to rationalize ongoing defense programs or to merely assess the theoretical military utility of various emerging technologies. The task of sorting out priorities should be approached from the top down rather than from the bottom up. The tasks and capabilities for NATO's conventional forces which deserve special attention must be selected in accordance with NATO's primary strategic needs and objectives. The analysis of the development of Warsaw Pact capabilities and doctrine must identify those options which are most threatening to NATO's forward conventional defense. Then those tasks for NATO forces which are most relevant to countering these Warsaw Pact options should be spelled out and assessed in an integrative fashion, i.e., reflecting their respective contributions to NATO's operational strategy. In this way individual tasks and the capabilities pertaining to them can be related and rated in view of higher-lever priorities. Technical and tactical issues, to which a bottom-up approach may attribute undue importance, can be kept in perspective.

PRIORITIES FOR NATO'S CONVENTIONAL FORCES

The rest of this paper will be on tasks and requirements for the conventional forces. The discussion will proceed under four headings:

— The Current Situation;
— The Emerging Threat to NATO's Initial Forward-Defense Capability;
— The Needs for NATO's Initial Defense against a Short-Warning Attack;
— Beyond Initial Defense.

For obvious reasons the analysis must remain incomplete, subjective, and tentative. Given the scope and complexity of the issues which have to be addressed it is inevitable that one adopt a shorthand style and draw upon research and analysis advanced by other authors or institutions. However, this form of presentation may suffice in order to structure and stimulate discussion.

The Current Situation

To date NATO's planning for conventional Forward Defense has been beset by problems of its *limited staying power*. Because of superior Warsaw Pact capabilities for mobilization and reinforcement, there is little hope that NATO could avert a rapid breakdown of its defense once Soviet second strategic echelon and strategic reserve forces engaged NATO's depleted main defense forces and committed reserves. Thus, the time span for a successful resistance against a major Pact offensive usually has been assessed in days rather than weeks. Pessimists even doubt that NATO could defeat and hold the second-echelon armies of the first strategic echelon. This more recent concern has been stimulated by comprehensive Soviet and non-Soviet force-improvement programs which have effected a substantial growth of combat power and of logistic sustainability for these forward-deployed armies.

Consequently, NATO is faced with a twofold challenge. First, attrition of its active first-line forces probably will proceed more rapidly than previously thought and the need for readily available reserves will rise accordingly. Secondly, NATO may have less time for mobilizing its reserves and for transporting U.S. reinforcements across the Atlantic and moving them up to their battle positions. The danger of a short-warning attack has become more plausible to the extent that Soviet first-echelon forces (as well as those selected high-readiness East German, Polish, and Czechoslovakian divisions which are integrated parts of this echelon) can now move to battle without time-consuming prior mobilization measures and reinforcements from the rear.

In addition, the enhanced effectiveness of Warsaw Pact ground-based air defenses, the modernization of air intercept and battle management capabilities, and the buildup of an effective offensive air potential with Frontal and Long Range Aviation have significantly changed the air situation to NATO's disadvantage. The drawdown of forward-deployed Western air assets will probably even run ahead of the attrition of NATO's ground forces.

Being aware of NATO's acute problems with regard to the sustainability of its conventional defense, Western governments have agreed on multiple initiatives — which, under the label of the Long Term Defense Program (LTDP) — aim at redressing the most glaring deficiencies. Some commitments by NATO nations, in particular the U.S., do look impressive, but in view of the worsening economic situation of the West and of the present climate in transatlantic political relations, major setbacks cannot be excluded.

Because of the prohibitively high aggregate costs of what should be done in addition to planned modernization programs — for example in the areas of reserve, pre-positioned equipment for transatlantic reinforcements, host-nation support, collocation and survivability measures for headquarters and other C^3 facilities, increasing ammunition stocks in line with higher estimated consumption rates, and the like — numerous analysts tend to favor an alternate approach. They would prefer NATO to build up conventional capabilities for the effective early interdiction of Warsaw Pact second and third echelons throughout the entire depth of the theater. By slowing down, and significantly weakening and disorganizing Pact follow-on echelons during the initial phase of the war, future pressure upon NATO's Forward Defense in the close-in battle could be reduced to more manageable proportions. Whether or not effective *deep* interdiction systems for conventional delivery are technically feasible, and to what extent such systems would be cost-effective on a mission basis and affordable in total numbers required, are open questions to date. They will be addressed in a subsequent section. It seems obvious, however, that in any respect a credible Western posture for deep attack would be a most welcome countervailing factor to the Pact's offensive echeloning concept.

It would strongly improve the currently weak staying power of NATO's Forward Defense.

Coping with Pact second and third echelons, though, no longer seems to be NATO's only and most menacing problem. An even greater challenge is posed by the forward elements of the *first operational echelon*. Operating in conjunction with Soviet tactical offensive air, they may under specific conditions preempt NATO's defense preparations and thus *prevent it from even organizing an effective initial Forward Defense*. In this case rapid penetrations, major disruptions, shock, and paralysis might ensue. Without meeting effective resistance, Pact first-echelon forces and their follow-on armies could be strong enough to achieve their intermediate strategic objectives. As NATO's overall strategy is predicated upon the capability of its combined forces to achieve the "initial success," i.e., effectively to stop and destroy the assaulting divisions and the following army reserves, developments on the Pact side which may put this crucial capability at risk deserve serious attention and determined action.

The Emerging Threat to NATO's Initial Forward-Defense Capability

According to experts' analyses, recently advanced and mutually corroborating,[7] NATO's long-held (and very controversial) worst-case scenario of surprise attack may become the most likely one for a Pact conventional attack in Central Europe. The internal Soviet debate on how to react to the prospect of much stronger Western anti-tank defenses in order to retain the offensive option seemingly has led to the conclusion that an attack might be warranted before NATO could complete its defense preparation. Renewed Soviet interest in the "mobile group" concept,[8] the concomitant restructuring and re-equipment of Soviet mechanized infantry regiments and tank regiments[9] (which have provided them with an independent tactical capability for deep thrusts and raids), the organization of highly mobile helicopter-supported assault units for tactical desants, and the development of the "air offensive concept" — all these are indications of an ominous trend in Soviet operational doctrine and of a determined effort to acquire a preemptive conventional attack option.

The extent to which the Soviets can and, in fact, do utilize advanced on-the-shelf technology for their offensive missions is especially alarming. Radar homing missiles could be employed to suppress NATO's ground-based air defense systems. TV and laser-guided bombs and stand-off weapons would effectively threaten a broad array of fixed interdiction targets. Runway-breaking munitions may enforce shutdowns of NATO's air bases. Area impact weapons (cluster bombs, mines and other sub-munitions, fuel air explosives) could enhance the effectiveness of air-ground support operations. These would aim at delaying and disrupting the transit of NATO forces to their defense positions, at denying forward key terrain to them, and at keeping them from organizing their defenses. Armed helicopters may deliver third-generation infrared guided "launch and leave" anti-tank guided missiles (ATGMs) against NATO armored vehicles. In short, Marshal Grechkov's (and more recently Marshal Ogarkov's) public admonishments that the most innovative sectors of research and industrial production should be placed in the service of the Soviet Armed Forces for qualitative enhancement have not gone un-heeded.

Maturing Soviet capabilities for short-warning offensive air and ground operations exacerbate specific structural weaknesses in NATO's defense posture. The process of filling up understrength divisions, moving them up to their assembly areas and defense positions, and readying them for combat is very time-consuming and — in some respects — extremely sensitive to enemy interference. Without straining one's imagination it is possible to devise scenarios in which neither the Dutch nor the Belgian forces would be very close to their assigned corps sectors when the fighting starts. Timely selective destruction of key fixed targets in the West German railway and road system by means of sabotage or air attack may keep them away even longer. Of course, on the basis of emergency defense plans, Allied divisions could move in. But, as there is only limited space for delaying operations, they would have to defend and successfully hold early, i.e., fight with overstretched frontages and without significant tactical reserves. Under these conditions disruptive breakthroughs could occur rapidly. Furthermore, the forces expended during this initial period would be critically needed to subsequently hold in the main defense against Pact follow-on echelons. Thus, even if one realistically discards the notion of a *total* surprise, precluding any military resistance, NATO's improvised emergency defense remains fragile. If it takes NATO about 96 hours to complete the defense preparations of its assigned and territorial in-place forces (not to mention external reinforcements), Soviet attacks against a weakly-prepared Western Forward Defense cannot be foreclosed.

The glaring deficiencies of NATO's air defense system (including troop air defense assets in numerous allied sectors as well as Hawk and

Nike missile belts) — the absence of point defense for critical structures and insufficient numbers of air interceptors — and the growing vulnerability of its main operating airbases add another dimension to this gloomy perspective. NATO's air staffs must worry about the survival of their forces in case of a surprise Warsaw Pact mass air attack. Self-defense becomes a new and demanding task. Temporary local control of the airspace over NATO territory by Pact air forces cannot be excluded. This would allow enemy attacks on NATO airbases and C^3I components as well as battlefield interdiction, shallow interdiction attacks, sealing off breakthrough areas, and close air support. In this way, precursory air attacks could compound NATO's problems of establishing a continuous forward defense line on the ground. Western troops would be exposed to harassment and destruction from the air. Dependable massive friendly air support, which in this situation would be desperately needed, may not be available.

Additional problems could degrade NATO's capacity for an organized reaction even further. Millions of fleeing West German civilians may clog roads and highways needed for military transports. German police forces and territorials who are supposed to direct and control these movements are likely to be overwhelmed by simultaneous competing demands. The time-consuming calling-up of reservists and the resulting personnel shortages may leave critical components of the energy supply and railway and road system unprotected.

Furthermore, the C^3 systems of NATO's forward defending forces, all important to cope with a dynamic and confused situation, will be a high-priority target for immediate coordinated physical and electronic attacks (concept of radio-electronic combat). Because the attacking Pact forces could initially operate on the basis of a pre-planned sequence of actions, the impact of an intense jamming environment probably would be less inhibiting for them than for the defender. NATO does not seem to be well prepared to meet this challenge. Electronic warfare and C^3 have been neglected for a long time.

In assessing the threat of a surprise attack one must avoid the fallacy of mixing different levels of analysis. Tactical opportunities for successfully initiating a war — even if they could predetermine the outcome of the campaign — must not be seen as a sufficient motivation for going to war in the first place. The fact that nuclear weapons are integrated into the forces and doctrines of both alliances implies very high risks for any major armed conflict in Central Europe. War would not be started just because of some perceived advantage of surprise but most likely over some preceding major political conflict. Thus, in any case, there would be a preceding crisis and warning. Attempts at managing the conflict short of war would be expected. Likewise alert and other precautionary measures would be taken.

Nevertheless, for two reasons the option of surprise cannot be discarded. First, unless they are faced with unambiguous warning of an impending attack, NATO governments and parliaments may postpone those dramatic (but time-sensitive) steps of mobilization and defense preparation which could in their view inadvertently escalate tension, thus endangering political crisis management, not to mention being highly disruptive and costly for the economy and civil life in general. Secondly, if NATO waited for definitive tactical warning the time available would be significantly shorter than the time span needed for mobilization, transit, and the preparation of defense positions. Even more effective technical means and methods for intelligence collection, assessment, and dissemination cannot solve this dilemma.

The Needs for NATO's Initial Defense against a Short-Warning Attack

The importance of many of the tasks and capabilities to be addressed here is not limited specifically to a surprise-attack scenario and to the *initial* phase of war. Since a separate discussion of these issues would entail repetition the focus will be shifted when appropriate.

For one thing, there needs to be *a strong focus on minimum essential emergency requirements*.

The least complicated and most effective solution to NATO's predicament will remain a planner's dream: having strong ready forces suitably deployed. NATO must, therefore, live with second-best solutions. It must, in any case, establish a system of forces capable of surviving and thwarting any initial conventional onslaught and of protecting the process of mobilization, forward deployment, and reception of reinforcements in the rear. Forward-stationed army formations must be ready and able to screen effectively and hold temporarily a continuous zone of defense close to the border and so shield the organization of the main defense positions from any decisive enemy interference. NATO air forces must be organized to survive on the ground, to promptly execute emergency missions in support of army operations and — in cooperation with ground-based air defense — to defend friendly airspace against the intrusion of offensive air.

For several reasons these tasks ought to be analyzed within a comprehensive integrative "systems" framework:

- Because of the relative weakness of NATO's covering forces, emergency air support will be indispensable. Operational plans and options have to be coordinated in advance (target selection, timing); procedures must be defined and exercised jointly. Moreover, an integrated approach is mandatory (1) to cope with problems of deconfliction, directing aircraft to target, and indentifying friend or foe (IFF), and (2) to fully exploit the synergism of ground-based and airborne systems for air defense suppression and for other measures of electronic warfare. (Example: the Israeli combined tactics against Syrian surface-to-air missiles in the Bekaa valley; also the "assault breaker" concept.)

- Military and political leaders must address the extent that forces should be earmarked for emergency operations (e.g., dedication of aircraft to specific automatic attack programs) and receive preferential treatment with regard to readiness, quality and quantity of equipment and weapons, peacetime deployment, etc.

- The problem of adapting rules of engagement, border crossing authority, etc., to the conditions of surprise attack and to the requirements for quick reaction will be politically even more contentious. The employment of forces held on a quick reaction alert status (QRA) in a warning-mode launch may require the pre-delegation of such authority to tactical commanders. This, however, could endanger political control and enhance preemptive pressures. Authority to emplace and activate demolition charges and mines is another point in case.

- As a result of a strong emphasis on surprise, NATO's emergency defense plans for forward-deployed divisions could lose their present provisional quality as a fall-back option for unlikely contingencies. This may spell the end of NATO's "layercake" multinational defense concept in its Northern Army Group command area and remove any leverage to press for sufficient readiness of Dutch and Belgian ground forces.

- Those force components and functions which are essential for an assured initial-defense capability must have a commensurate peacetime status; dependence on time-consuming mobilization and readiness measures should be kept minimal. In addition, NATO's alert system should envisage the prompt and simultaneous execution of groups of preparatory measures for these selected forces. If these measures were calibrated and organized into a flexible set of low-visibility readiness, alert, and movement exercises, political inhibitions against timely action in crisis could be dampened.

Next, in the initial phase of the land battle, NATO would need *strong covering forces* in a state of high readiness to preclude early deep thrusts by Warsaw Pact reinforced forward detachments, advanced tactical landings, and so forth. In addition, selected heavy brigades should be earmarked for counter-attack missions in case of quick enemy penetrations. They must be capable of fighting encounter battles, that is, of attacking spearheads and executing flanking maneuvers. Covering-force formations should embody:

- an effective organic air defense component against low-level air attack by enemy close-support aircraft and armed helicopters. Ideally, these short-range air defense artillery and missile systems should be tied into a comprehensive airspace warning, control, and communication system in order to facilitate target acquisition and identification. However, they should also be capable of autonomous operation.
- an effective organic "over the hill" all-weather reconnaissance and target acquisition/location capability.
- powerful organic artillery fire support with suitable systems and weapon loads for immobilizing and destroying groups of targets, primarily enemy artillery and armored vehicles within and beyond visual range. Multiple rocket launchers, because of their area-covering effects and unrivaled surge capability, seem to be primarily important.
- a strong combat engineer element with modern mining equipment.

Covering forces should have full combat mobility and armored protection. Their weapons must effect high rates of fire and have high "kill" probabilities at close combat distance against hard-skinned targets. Their combat vehicles should have anti-tank guided missiles (ATGMs) operable under protection of armor. Elevating platforms could be employed as sensor carriers and launchers, thus extending the line of sight and making effective use of the range of the ATGMs. Night vision devices are crucial.

Covering forces should be backed up by rear-based long-range artillery assets, on-call close air support and attack/anti-tank helicopters. As these components all perform the same general task, questions arise as to how to coordinate and delineate their missions as well as how funds ought to be allocated. If suitable longer-range rocket artillery systems could be procured which would provide flexible deep coverage across entire corps frontage they should probably receive priority. Helicopter assets then could be centrally committed by higher commands as highly mobile fire brigades. Close air support by fixed-wing aircraft would become less urgent and problems of communication between forward-air controllers and pilots, as well as identification of friend or foe, could be reduced.

Covering forces must be highly flexible and enjoy full mobility and vehicular protection, because time for thorough preparation of the battlefield forward area (barriers, obstacles, fortified positions) may be lacking in case of a short-warning attack. Enemy action must be expected at unspecified sections across the entire borderline, and forces in place would be insufficient to achieve the density and depth required for a more static mode of defense. However, covering forces are affected by a general problem of armored troops. Such forces have become too expensive and cannot be procured and maintained in the quantities required. There seems to be consensus that for specific tasks armored units will remain indispensable in the foreseeable future. Certainly, covering operations will be one of these tasks. But there is an ongoing debate concerning to what extent heavy forces could be replaced by lighter mobile forces, which are not suitable for counter-attack, or by infantry forces capable of guerrilla tactics or fighting from static positions. Such adaptations, indeed, are likely to happen. They will be promoted by budget squeezes and reinforced by technological trends. Progress in the development of "smart" anti-armor submunitions, self-activating and directing mines, fire-and-forget anti-tank guided missiles, and improvements in standoff target acquisition foretell significantly higher attrition rates for armored vehicles. Sensor limitations and possible countermeasures may qualify this trend but they cannot reverse it. Consequently, in the long term the employment of armored forces may become restricted to specific tasks, mainly to counter-attack missions. If possible, they will be kept in the rear in order to protect them from enemy "smart" fires.

At the same time these new weapons technology developments would allow new ways to cope effectively with the Warsaw Pact's armored threat. NATO could move to a mix of heterogeneously structured force elements, the equipment, tactics, and support of which could be tailored to specific tasks and to specific environments. NATO could renounce its current policy of optimizing performance at the level of weapon systems (or subsystems) and could try to achieve optimal tactical solutions within a more comprehensive context. Until these promising perspectives materialize, however, NATO's forward-defense posture will be characterized by its armored and mechanized brigades.

An important task for research is to indicate more specifically in which way and to what extent changes in deployed new weapon systems and supporting components could be exploited in order to effect changes at the level of force structure and operational doctrine. As for the problem of initial forward defense, it may be desirable to look into the possible utility of infantry forces for the defense of built-up and densely wooded areas, and into the development potential of fortified positions which could be prepared in peacetime. Local reservists may have a role to play when the fighting starts. Because of its shortage of operational reserves NATO should consider ways to pull back armored covering forces from first-line positions and replace them by lighter screening and delaying forces in sectors where major enemy thrusts are no longer expected.

A restructuring of NATO's ground forces, however, probably cannot mean a significant reduction of the number of its armored vehicles. These must be retained unless NATO is willing to leave any operational initiative on the ground to the Warsaw Pact during the entire duration of the conventional campaign. If the capabilities of Western forces were limited to the delaying and attriting function, NATO's objective of restoring the integrity of allied territory (not to mention the possible interests in acquiring "tokens" of Pact territory) would become unattainable. Thus, "restructuring" may amount to the need to provide additional forces and to pay for more refined "intelligent" munitions, expensive sensors, and new delivery systems.

This paper will now turn to *air operations*, that is, the questions of air defense, air superiority, and close air support and interdiction operations for the ground battle. Air tasks and requirements will be discussed first in connection with survival of NATO's air forces and second in connection with support of missions.

In order to survive and function in case of a possible surprise mass air attack against NATO airbases, the following tasks and capabilities deserve special attention:

• NATO's ground-based air defenses must be improved. This pertains to the defense gap against low-level penetration; to the limited mobility of present surface-to-air systems; to the vulnerability of associated radars to attack by anti-radiation missiles and to electronic countermeasures (ECM); to insufficient numbers, etc. However, even the deployment of Patriot missiles will not cure all of these deficiencies. Pact air forces could saturate and cut corridors through the missile belt.

• Therefore, ground-based defenses must be complemented by intercepting fighter aircraft. The potential for improvement inherent in such developments as the airborne warning and control system (AWACS) — in conjunction with all aspect air-to-air missiles, multiple target engagement capability, and look-down shoot-down capability — has been described extensively in the literature. There is no need to repeat it here.

• Of equal importance is the task of offensive counter-air operations, in order to slow down the sortie rates of Pact air forces and to destroy them on their bases. Unfortunately, this mission has become extremely difficult. If executed by means of manned aircraft, intolerably high losses must be expected. The dense and overlapping system of the Pact's ground-based air defense artillery and surface-to-air missiles threatens significant losses. In addition, Pact main operating air bases are heavily defended. For these reasons a recently advanced concept which proposes to attack these bases by means of conventionally-armed ballistic missiles (AXE) does look very attractive. Delivering runway cratering submunitions, these systems could effect at least temporary shutdowns of airbase operations. Returning Pact attack aircraft would have to be redirected to alternative airstrips, which would be less well protected and equipped for servicing and supporting functions. The missiles could be kept on quick reaction alert status in hardened shelters, and moved out and launched rapidly against the pre-programmed target set prior to the second wave of a Warsaw Pact air attack. From a technical point of view this concept is assessed as viable. Its problem lies with costs. The program must compete with other important programs which may appeal to a larger and more powerful military and political constituency. Critics will point out that AXE would be an inflexible component with only limited (though important) impact. It could *temporarily* close a *limited* number of airbases (runway repair, if prepared, would not take a long time). In order to exploit the secondary effects and to destroy enemy aircraft, follow-on counter-air attacks by means of manned aircraft would be needed. Furthermore, the utility of AXE would be limited to the European theater of war. Some further questions include: Who pays for it? Who will man the systems? Where are the systems going to be deployed? Is there a problem of discrimination with regard to nuclear-tipped Pershing missiles? Possible political repercussions must be analyzed carefully.

• The list of further important steps for enhancing survivability includes passive measures (shelters, hardening, added dispersal bases, rapid runway repair capabilities) improved terminal defenses, short take-off and landing capacity for aircraft. In operational terms the preparation for airborne alert, aerial refueling, quick dispersal, and pre-programmed emergency attack missions for quick reaction alert aircraft seem to be promising.

• Does NATO have to be concerned about a future *Soviet* ballistic missile threat against its airbases?

NATO offensive air missions in support of the land battle will be crucial for defensive success in the initial phase of a short-warning attack. In addition, they will have a significant and perhaps decisive impact on the fate of subsequent main defense operations. The obstacles and force limitations which currently constrain NATO's capabilities for these missions are well known. On the other hand, progress in a broad spectrum of advanced technologies has encouraged hopes that NATO could regain maneuver room for effective interdiction. In order to attain this objective NATO will have to solve two complex interrelated sets of tasks which can be organized under two headings: (1) Penetrating Warsaw Pact Air Defense, and (2) Closing the Reconnaissance and Target-Engagement Cycle.[10]

Penetrating Warsaw Pact Air Defense

As mentioned before, NATO aircraft on offensive missions will have to overcome a deep zone of overlapping and netted ground-based air defense systems. Because of the density and mobility of air defense artillery and surface-to-air missiles it is difficult to fly around them or to saturate the system. The acquisition of more capable and less vulnerable radars and of improved passive seekers will further complicate this problem. NATO aircraft on *deep* attack missions in addition must cope with high numbers of air superiority fighters. In order to minimize losses Western air forces have developed two concepts for penetration:

1. The "task force" concept envisages supporting large formations of fighter bombers by fighter escorts and by specialized aircraft for electronic warfare and air defense suppression. Powerful stand-off and escort jammers will degrade enemy warning, communications, and target-engagement capabilities. "Wild Weasel" aircraft will directly attack ground-based radars and air defense sites. Friendly airborne warning and control systems (AWACS) are expected to provide the information needed to select routes with minimum exposure to enemy defense. There are, however, some problems with this approach. The required ratio of supporting assets to fighter bombers is relatively high. And the sophisticated specialized electronic warfare and defense suppression aircraft are so expensive that only the U.S. Air Force can afford them. Furthermore, as these complex operations depend upon careful coordination of multiple functions they have to proceed on the basis of a pre-planned schedule. Thus, offensive air operations cannot be executed continuously and flexibly. In mid-term perspective the Soviets probably will operate their SUAWACS and will employ fighters armed with long-range self-homing air-to-air missiles. These developments could put the "task force" concept at risk unless NATO stays ahead in the dynamic electronic warfare struggle and manages to suppress or at least significantly degrade enemy target-engagement capabilities.

2. The alternative concept for penetration exploits the fact that Pact air defenses — like those of NATO — are ineffective to date against aircraft flying low and fast. But in order to use this window, high-performance aircraft are required. They must be designed and equipped for autonomous operation in all weather conditions and for target acquisition and weapons delivery at very low altitudes. This may actually preclude the delivery of those types of precision-guided munitions which require line-of-sight connection between aircraft and target (laser and/or TV guidance; electro-optical imaging) and high angles of attack. At present, area munitions dispensed in a free-fall mode are best adapted to this low-level mode of penetration. But their delivery requires the pilot to overfly the target which can significantly raise the probability of being hit, even in a single pass attack, if these targets — for example, army combat units or airbases — are prepared for effective self-defense. Therefore the development of stand-off-delivery capabilities deserves high priority. In addi-

tion to these limitations the following aspects must be considered: Costs for high-performance aircraft such as the Tornado aircraft are so significant that the number of systems procured must be lower than that of the preceding generation. This trend is inconsistent with the expectation that NATO air forces will have to absorb increased attrition. Furthermore, low-level penetration may become more difficult in the long-term future, if the Warsaw Pact builds up an airborne warning and control system that could provide ground-based defense systems with real-time flight path direction information and could vector air defense fighters with look-down shoot-down capabilities.

Given these concerns it is no wonder that Western analysts, journalists, and politicians are looking for alternatives to the manned aircraft for the task of supporting the land battle. Conventionally armed ballistic missiles, cruise missiles, remotely piloted vehicles, and drones have been considered as replacements.

Without attempting to do justice to a very complex debate, some tentative judgments can be proposed, as follows.

Generalized assertions should be received with skepticism. One has to carefully differentiate the assessments according to operational ranges, missions/functions, target categories, environmental factors (weather, visibility conditions, terrain features), possible enemy countermeasures, and so on.

Drones and remotely piloted vehicles (RPVs) can and should substitute for manned aircraft in a number of important tasks and functions. For example, they can assist in degrading or can directly destroy enemy ground-based air defense components and communication emitters. They are capable of surveillance, target identification, location, and designation, as well as of emplacing beacons for precise offset targeting, emplacing various types of intelligence collection sensors, establishing data bridges, etc. In short, these systems can fulfill a broad range of very important special functions in a high-threat environment. The potential utility of these capabilities has been neglected for a long time because the operational functions and tactics which they could serve have not received the attention they deserve.

The utility of drones and remotely piloted vehicles as armed weapon systems, however, has to be assessed with significant reservations. They are very cost-effective when they can operate against targets which are easy to acquire and "lock on to" and which can be neutralized with a relatively small warhead (e.g., certain types of electronically emitting targets). They are less than optimal systems if they have to deliver higher payloads (requiring bigger size and larger radar cross-sections), autonomously find and identify mobile targets without strong signatures in all-weather and day-and-night conditions, flexibly match weapons to target distribution, adapt to enemy countermeasures, or defend against enemy attacks. Remote command guidance can be a solution. But it depends upon suitable imaging sensors and jam-resistant broad band data transmission links. Thus, if rather sophisticated electronic equipment is required and vulnerability becomes significant, armed RPVs and drones, being "use and lose" systems, may be rather cost-ineffective.

Although the penetration capability of ballistic missiles is unrivaled, the practical utility of such conventionally-armed systems is very sensitive to ranges and payloads required as well as to the nature of the targets that have to be covered. Employment for "deep attack" over long distances will probably remain limited to selected *time-urgent* high-value *fixed* targets, which must be attacked promptly and with high damage expectancy. Because of the limitations on the effects of conventional weapons, accuracies must be very good. Terminal homing and mid-course correction capacity will be essential. Thus, total costs will be significant.

Ballistic missiles look more competitive when used over shorter distances. Multiple rocket launcher systems can cover a range band of up to 50 kilometers. Linked to stand-off airborne target-acquisition systems or guided by target-spotting RPVs or drones, these delivery systems could fire a variety of mines and other area munitions which are effective against most military targets. Accuracies over this short distance probably could be kept good enough without advanced guidance components. Propulsion systems could be simple and payloads could be significant. Therefore, systems could be procured in sufficient numbers to have an impact on shallow interdiction operations against enemy first-line divisions and their support elements. For employment beyond the 50-kilometer range band, the cost-effectiveness of ballistic missiles would decrease (look, for example, at the estimated costs per copy of the Patriot derivative missile which is envisaged as part of the "assault breaker" program). With few exceptions aircraft and cruise missiles will remain the delivery systems upon which NATO has to rely for battlefield interdiction and other deep-attack missions.

Various versions of conventionally armed cruise missiles can be employed for attacks against a broad spectrum of targets. Because their range-to-payload ratio is significantly better than that of ballistic missiles, they seem to be more suitable for deep attacks. Equipped with terrain-following guidance and pre-programmed terminal homing instructions — which seem to be within the current state of the art — they could destroy selected fixed critical components within larger target sets (micro targeting) throughout the entire depth of the theater of war. Of course, they could not effect deep interdiction in the sense of stopping and destroying Soviet third-echelon forces. Although high costs (and limited budgets) will, in effect, limit their use to relatively few important targets,[11] the resulting uncertainties for Warsaw Pact planners will contribute to deterrence. Furthermore, such options are important for political and psychological reasons. They can demonstrate the fact that the Pact hinterland would not remain unscathed even during the conventional phase of a war in Europe.

Relatively cheap shorter-range conventional cruise missiles[12] could be developed for attacks against fixed and mobile targets within a zone of up to about 150 kilometers. Effective employment against mobile targets would, of course, require real-time target acquisition and engagement capacities that do not yet exist. But most experts agree that airborne surveillance systems can and will be designed which, operating over friendly territory, could collect and process the information needed to assess the operational situation within the corps commander's area of responsibility and to identify and locate enemy target concentrations. Target coordinates could be rapidly and reliably transmitted to executing units by correlating them with a common reference grid.

Until these capabilities become operational cruise missiles could be employed for the destruction or neutralization of known fixed interdiction targets. In conjunction with tactical aircraft they could also be employed for follow-on-attacks against queuing army formations. As depicted in the U.S. Army "airland battle concept," careful intelligence preparation of the battlefield, predeveloped targeting options, as well as coordinated commitment of available reconnaissance and attack assets on line with operational priorities, could significantly influence the tactical situation.

Self-homing anti-tank submunitions with weather and visibility insensitive seekers could, of course, dramatically increase the effectiveness of cruise missiles (and of any other ballistic or air breathing delivery system). The need for manned aircraft in ground attack roles could be reduced substantially if submunitions — instead of being dispersed stochastically — can accurately home on enemy armored vehicles. (Of course, similar Soviet capabilities would — as mentioned before — put NATO's armored forces at risk.) At present, the development of autonomous seekers seems to be faced with difficult obstacles. In order to cope with relatively cheap and effective countermeasures (smoke, aerosols, flares, decoys) seekers must be given degrees of sophistication that would make munitions prohibitively expensive.

So, in a short-term and medium-term perspective, the manned aircraft and the pilot's initiative may remain indispensable for interdiction attacks against mobile targets. Employment of cruise missiles and/or ballistic missiles (at shorter ranges) against fixed targets will help create rich target concentrations which can be exploited by subsequent attacks.

Closing the Reconnaissance and Target-Engagement Cycle

As mentioned before the extent to which effective support of the land battle can be achieved is contingent upon the functioning of specific supporting systems and activities. The availability of information on the disposition of enemy forces is crucial for almost all combat tasks. Timely warning and intelligence is essential for defending against Warsaw Pact air attacks and for the penetration of the Pact's air defense. Various modes of electronic support operation will have to serve the same functions. Surveillance systems must generate targeting information. Positioning and guidance systems have to direct platforms and weapons to targets. The command and control apparatus has to process the flow of information according to the needs of decision-makers, disseminate command information, and provide executing units with all data required.

It is beyond the scope of this paper (as well as beyond the expertise of its author) to scrutinize NATO's problems and deficiencies in these respective areas and evaluate the potential of numerous technical developments which in most experts' view could change not just some specifics of NATO's defense but the total operational environment. Some developments, however, are worth mentioning here.

For instance, while NATO has been incapable of timely collection and use of information on the disposition of threat forces beyond visual range, new airborne systems could expand all-weather and day-and-night capabilities for identification and location of targets to the depth of the corps commander's area of influence. Stand-off electronic collectors probably will be capable of intercepting and locating most actively emitting systems on the ground (communication emitters, jammers, radars) over a distance of more than 100 kilometers. On-board signal processing will allow for near real-time transmission of situation reports and specific target information. Target coordinates could be distributed rapidly. Using a common reference grid (distance-measuring equipment with ground-based or air-borne emitters — in the future, the U.S. global positioning system) these targets could be attacked by aircraft or by stand-off missiles/remotely piloted vehicles with high accuracies. Airborne "Pave Mover" radars are designed to have target pattern identification and tracking capacity over a distance of about 170 kilometers and to spot military units and provide target data to ground-based and/or airborne attack units in near real time.

In conjunction with the development of ECM-resistant data links for high-density traffic the operation of such remote sensors (which would be complemented by airborne high resolution electro-optical imagery sensors) could alleviate NATO's current problems of target acquisition. If, in addition, NATO succeeded in establishing locally benign operational environments for interdiction attacks by effectively degrading Pact air defense and C^3I systems and by defeating the Pact's electronic warfare measures, Western tactics for this mission and the design of requisite delivery systems and munitions could perhaps be changed significantly. Required capabilities and costs for major weapon systems could be kept much lower if, for example, peripheral supporting systems provided flight data, warning, electronic countermeasures (ECM), distance-and-time-to-target information, weapon release/fusing signals, etc. Penetrating aircraft would no longer be constricted to difficult low-level operations. Airframes and avionics could be simplified. Weapon loads could be increased at the expense of agility. "Dumb" area weapons, under these conditions, could be employed more effectively. Very expensive autonomously homing munitions would not be needed if remote direct guidance could be provided without unacceptable risk to the platform.

In short, rapid progress of advanced technologies could allow for a high-low mix of interlocking systems and functions.[13] Investment into improved electronic support components thus may enable NATO to opt for *larger quantities* of less sophisticated aircraft, weapons and munitions. Only in this way could surge capabilities and endurance of Western air forces be enhanced. The procurement of such high-technology components for intelligence collections, data processing, communications, and electronic warfare operations, of course, would require higher defense expenditures. Furthermore, it cannot be reliably predicted to what extent the synergistic potential of these developments could, in fact, be fully exploited. Some programs must overcome high technical risks. Moreover, systems of such complexity will be vulnerable to failures, malfunctions and deliberate enemy countermeasures, because they depend upon the effective coordination of multiple sophisticated subsystems, interfaces and data links. This uncertainty pertains especially to the electronic warfare field. Knowledge about respective enemy (and friendly) plans and capabilities is sparse because of tight security. Thus, technical and tactical surprise cannot be excluded. In fact, both sides will make every effort to achieve and exploit it. Projections on the basis of hardware characteristics — to the extent to which they are known — can only be tentative because software parameters would have a major impact.

In which way should NATO prepare its forces for the potential breakdown or degradation of essential electronic combat support functions? Should Western planners design different types of platforms, on-board equipment and weapons, as well as alternative tactics for the execution of identical tasks in significantly different combat environments? One way to avoid total reliance upon the functioning of large-scale "enveloping" electronic systems may be to retain sufficient numbers of major weapon systems which are capable of autonomous operations even under adverse conditions. Such systems (examples are Tornado, F-15, or Gepard), however, are bound to be extremely complex and can only be afforded in relatively small numbers. Thus NATO seemingly has no choice but to move to integrated operational concepts, if it wants to keep interdiction as a viable option. However, in order to hedge against major breakdown, redundancy and flexibility must be built into the system's key components.

Some further problems:

Electronic warfare, intelligence collection and fusion, and C^3 generally ought to be organized and operated jointly on a cross-service and cross-national basis. Failures in developing and procuring interoperable C^3 systems even for the services within the same national military establishment indicate how much effort will be needed to overcome current compartmentalization. Without an adequate joint C^3 systems architecture, future enhanced capacities for intelligence collection, situation evaluation, and weapons control will not be used to their full effect. Rather than contributing to well-informed swift decisions, the continuous flood of all source intelligence data could swamp overworked staffs and lead to confusion and delay.

Insufficient sharing of electronic intelligence among NATO allies is another major problem. It is perfectly understandable that governments and military organizations are reluctant to pass on sensitive information which, if leaked to the opponent, would compromise sources and collection techniques and would enable Warsaw Pact forces to prepare effective countermeasures. On the other hand, without very close coordination of Allied electronic warfare measures, the inadvertent damage to friendly operations may outweigh by far their positive effects. Surprise in this case would be a double-edged sword.

In summing up this discussion on air operations, the following conclusions seem to deserve attention:

Although NATO air forces are facing multiple challenges and certainly cannot ignore air defense and air superiority missions, current service priorities ought to be reviewed. Missions in support of the land battle seem to be most important for NATO's overall strategy. This assessment must be reflected in a much closer conceptual and operational cooperation betwen air and ground forces. This cooperation, however, should not be limited to the enunciation of doctrinal concepts but should become a determining factor for the organization and funding of R&D and procurement programs. Delivery systems, weapons, and supporting systems which contribute specifically and essentially to this task deserve high ratings. Without effective interdiction NATO ground forces probably could not aspire to hold their forward defense during the initial phase of a short-warning attack. Air ground support is mandatory to slow down, disrupt, and weaken tactical follow-on formations and thus break the momentum of the initial attack. In subsequent stages of the battle, interdiction must continue to delay and destroy Warsaw Pact follow-on echelons in order to deny attempts to rapidly concentrate a locally superior force which would be strong enough to wear down and break through NATO's main defense and to exploit such penetrations.

As NATO's operations on the ground probably would have to remain defensive and reactive until sufficiently strong reinforcements and reserves could be moved up, these operations could not actively influence the battle on the operational level during the initial phase. Therefore, air interdiction attacks which can quickly effect concentrated fires seem to be the only means by which NATO can actively interfere with enemy operational plans. Their effects may require the readjustment of time schedules and the rerouting of forces on the Warsaw Pact side. In this situation attacks against enemy C^3 could have an impact. For concurring operational and technical reasons NATO ought to concentrate its efforts and resources on improving Western capabilities for *shallow and battlefield interdiction*. The weakening of the Pact's first-echelon armies (and of follow-on echelons which would replace them in their positions subsequently) within a zone up to 150 kilometers deep will have the most immediate stabilizing influence on the close-in battle. It can be achieved by NATO's present forces. It is favored by the density of reconnaissance coverage. Targets are concentrated. Times to target are short. Range-to-payload ratios are acceptable. In addition, the aforementioned developments in the areas of remote surveillance and target acquisition, navigation, and communication as well as stand-off weapon systems and "intelligent" munitions can be used synergistically to upgrade NATO's current battlefield interdiction capability significantly.

Beyond Initial Defense

It is very likely that budgetary constraints will limit major NATO force improvement programs to a few selected areas. Inter-service competition will be fierce because projected funds have already been committed well into the late 1980s to ratified programs in most NATO countries. In spite of this lack of flexibility, NATO must not be forced into having to choose between programs which can help to provide more "depth" to its defense on the ground and programs which will improve the capacity of its forces to "see and attack deep." To ensure the stability of its defense posture against current and future Warsaw Pact options, both capabilities must be strengthened simultaneously and in complementary fashion.

With respect to required "depth," a few additional forward-deployed active and ready reserve divisions would make an important difference. Force-to-space ratios would then allow NATO commanders to deploy stronger operational reserves and thus enhance defense resilience and operational flexibility. These positive effects could not be negated by a corresponding buildup of Pact first-echelon forces. In addition, NATO must strengthen its rear-based air-mobile "intervention" forces and assets. Armed helicopters as well as close air support and interdiction squadrons could be employed with rapidly shifting "Schwerpunkt" in emergencies or in support of friendly counter-attacks. Airborne infantry units could be landed to block emerging enemy penetrations. Such force components are essential with regard to initial defense requirements in a short-warning attack scenario. But they will be needed as well within the framework of main defense operations in the absence of sufficiently strong local operational reserves.

As for the later stages of the conventional ground battle, it would of course be very desirable if NATO countries could be induced to prepare for the mobilization of large and well-equipped reserve forces. But such hope does not seem to be very solidly grounded in today's political and economic reality. It would be more sensible to allocate scarce funds to programs that enhance the readiness and combat power of assigned active divisions and to the organization, equipment, and training of selected additional *ready reserve formations*.

NATO's interdiction capabilities must also be made commensurate with the requirements of endurance. Because an early destruction of Pact second- and third-echelon forces by means of deep conventional attacks cannot be achieved, these forces must be weakened as they move forward into the battlefield interdiction area. Therefore NATO must be prepared to *sustain such attacks effectively* for at least two weeks. Survivability, reinforcement, and reconstitution measures for the requisite forces (including stocks of munitions and spare parts as well as supporting systems for air defense suppression) must receive attention.

If NATO adopts a first-things-first approach, sorts its priorities in a consistent fashion, and concentrates its efforts on its important tasks, it can certainly cope with the threat of surprise attack. Its initial conventional defense capability could be assured. Consequently, the deterrent effect of its overall defense posture would remain high. Unless Warsaw Pact planners can reliably predict a rapid breakdown of NATO's coherent forward defense, they must face NATO's options for a selective use of nuclear weapons. In particular, a Pact "standing" conventional attack could turn into a military and political disaster, if tactical nuclear weapons were employed by NATO. A major conventional attack against a carefully prepared NATO defense, however, could well lead to an initial setback and to a temporary stalemate. In such a situation political repercussions in Eastern Europe which could degrade the Warsaw Pact's military capabilities seem to be possible. In view of such risks the initiation of a war in Europe will not become a suitable means of policy for the Soviet leadership.

To preclude strong preemptive pressures which could spark the outbreak of war in a crisis, Western governments would be well advised to retain the dominant "defensive" character of NATO's regional conventional and nuclear force posture. This certainly need not and must not foreclose active defense measures reaching into Warsaw Pact territory. However, such "offensive" operations, the importance of which has been repeatedly stressed in this paper, probably could be executed more freely if they were to be clearly recognized as reinforcing components for NATO's Forward *Defense* strategy on the ground.

NOTES

1. For this aspect see Daniel K. Malone's and Kenneth Hunt's contributions to the topic "Perceptions of Conventional Force Sufficiency" at the U.S. National Security Affairs Conference on "Equivalence, Sufficiency, and the International Balance," July 17-19, 1978. The proceedings of this conference were published by the National Defense University, Fort Lesley J. McNair, Washington, D.C., August 1978.

2. Report of the Secretary of Defense Caspar W. Weinberger to the U.S. Congress, Feb. 8, 1982, pp. I-14 to I-17; Robert W. Komer, "Maritime Strategy vs. Coalition Defense," *Foreign Affairs*, Summer 1982, pp. 1124-1144.

3. Samuel P. Huntington, "The Renewal of Strategy," in *The Strategic Imperative: New Policies for American Security*, Huntington, ed., Cambridge, Mass., 1982 (forthcoming).

4. Some of these concerns are addressed by John J. Mearsheimer, "Maneuver, Mobile Defense, and the NATO Central Front," *International Security*, Winter 1981/82, pp. 104-122; and T. N. Dupuy, "The Nondebate over How Army Should Fight," in *Army*, June 1982, pp. 34-45.

5. For some illustrations see R. Levine et al., *A Survey of NATO Defense Concepts*, The Rand Corporation, Santa Monica, CA, June 1982 (N-1871-AF).

6. Johan J. Holst and Uwe Nerlich, ed., *Beyond Nuclear Deterrence: New Aims, New Arms* (New York, 1977); The International Institute for Strategic Studies, *New Conventional Weapons and East-West Security* (Parts I, II), London, 1978 (Adelphi Papers 144 and 145).

7. Phillip A. Karber, "Die Konventionellen Kräfteverhältnisse in Europa 1965-1980," (How To Lose an Arms Race: The Competition in Conventional Forces Deployed in Central Europe 1965-1980), in *Sowjetische Macht und westliche Verhandlungsstrategie im Wandel militärischer Kräfteverhältnisse*, Uwe Nerlich, ed., (Baden-Baden: Nomos, 1982). See also C. N. Donnelly's contribution to the present book (in Part II, above).

8. See C. N. Donnelly's paper in this book.

9. For an instructive summary of these trends see Karber, op.cit., pp. 79-81.

10. For a concise analysis of the problems involved see Hubert Feigl and Fred Verweinen, *Neue rüstungstechnische Entwicklungen im Bereich der Luftkriegführung und ihre Auswirkungen auf den taktischen Einsatz*, Ebenhausen, September 1980 (SWP-S 282); Steven L. Canby, *The Alliance and Europe: Part IV, Military Doctrine and Technology*, International Institute for Strategic Studies, London, 1975 (Adelphi Paper 109), pp. 31-41.

11. For a list of possible targets see Erik Klippenberg, "New Weapons Technology and the Offence/Defence Balance," in *New Conventional Weapons and East-West Security* (note 6 above), Part II, p. 29.

12. An operational concept for the employment of air-launched tactical cruise missiles is outlined by Hubert Feigl et al., *Tactical Air Evolution for Interdiction Missions*, Stiftung Wissenschaft und Politik, Ebenhausen, September 1980.

13. This promising analytical approach is presented by Hubert Feigl and Fred Verweinen (note 10 above).

PART IV

CONTRIBUTIONS OF ADVANCED TECHNOLOGY

NATO could use various means to enhance its capacity for performing the critical defensive missions described in Part III. Our Study has focused especially on how advanced technologies and associated measures could improve NATO's conventional capacity and thereby reduce reliance on nuclear weapons for deterrence and defense.

This Workshop examined the potential of advanced technologies for this purpose and the question of how they might be used. Supporting papers were prepared by Donald R. Cotter and John Keegan. This Part contains the Workshop Report and the supporting paper by Cotter.

WORKSHOP MEMBERS

Group Captain David Bolton

Group Captain, Royal Air Force (Ret.); Director, Royal United Services Institute for Defence Studies. Formerly: Central Operations Staff, Ministry of Defence.

Mr. Donald R. Cotter (Author)

President, DRC/LTD (technical and policy consulting firm). Formerly: Assistant to the Secretary of Defense (Atomic Energy) and Chairman, Military Liaison Committee to the Department of Energy; Advisor, Senate Armed Services Committee; Director of Systems Planning at Sandia National Laboratory (Atomic Energy Commission).

Mr. Johan J. Holst*

Director, Norwegian Institute of International Affairs. Formerly: State Secretary for Foreign Affairs; State Secretary for Defense.

Brigadier Kenneth Hunt

Brigadier, (Ret.), Royal Artillery; Visiting Professor of International Relations, University of Surrey. Formerly: Director, British Atlantic Committee; Visiting Professor at Fletcher School of Law and Diplomacy; Deputy Director, International Institute of Strategic Studies.

Mr. John Keegan (Author)

Senior Lecturer, Department of War Studies and International Politics, Royal Military Academy Sandhurst; author of several books including *The Face of Battle* and *Six Armies in Normandy*.

Mr. Simon Lunn (Rapporteur)

Staff Member, President's Cabinet, European Parliament, Brussels.

*Has reservations regarding some of the recommendations.

Professor Laurence Martin (Chairman)

Vice-Chancellor, University of Newcastle-upon-Tyne. Formerly: Professor of War Studies, King's College, University of London; Wilson Professor, International Politics, University of Wales; Associate Professor School of Advanced Studies, Johns Hopkins University.

Ambassador Dr. Rolf F. Pauls

German Diplomatist. Formerly: Ambassador and Permanent Representative to NATO; Ambassador to the United States, China and Israel.

Major General John W. Seigle

Major General, U.S. Army (Ret.). Formerly: Assistant Deputy Chief of Staff for Operations and Plans, Joint Affairs, and Director of Strategy, Plans, and Policy, ODCSOPS, U.S. Army; Deputy Commanding General, Allied Land Forces, Southeastern Europe; Deputy Defense Advisor, U.S. Mission to NATO.

Air Vice Marshal Anthony G. Skingsley (SHAPE Observer)

Air Vice Marshal, Royal Air Force; Assistant Chief of Staff for Plans and Policy at SHAPE.

General Johannes Steinhoff

General of the German Air Force (Ret.). Formerly: Chief of Staff, German Air Force; Chairman of the NATO Military Committee.

Professor Carroll L. Wilson

Director, European Security Study (ESECS), Mitsui Professor Emeritus in Problems of Contemporary Technology, Massachusetts Institute of Technology. Formerly: Director of the Workshop on Alternative Energy Strategies (WAES) and World Coal Study (WOCOL); Wartime Executive Assistant to Director of Office for Scientific Research and Development; General Manager, U.S. Atomic Energy Commission.

Supporting Papers:

1. Donald R. Cotter, *Potential Future Roles for Conventional and Nuclear Forces in Defense of Western Europe*.

2. John Keegan, *Means for Strengthened Conventional Capability*.

Contributions of Advanced Technology

THE PROBLEM FOR NATO

Soviet forces in general, but particularly those in or near the Central Front, are undergoing an extensive modernization program and operational reorganization which are significantly increasing the threat to NATO. One of the Soviet improvements is the increased capability to threaten NATO rear areas through the deployment of new tactical aircraft with greater range and payload, through expanded specialized forces, and through a massive growth in helicopter forces. Another is the increasing capability to conduct mobile, high-speed combat operations through improved firepower support, and through a more balanced divisional structure that permits added flexibility and includes the concept of the Operational Maneuver Group (OMG), a high-speed special-purpose exploitation force. The Soviet improvements also include better air defenses and substantially upgraded theater nuclear capabilities.

These developments are particularly threatening in view of the character of current Soviet military strategy, notably the requirements for swiftly gaining air superiority and assuring that the ground forces of the Soviet Union and its Warsaw Pact neighbors can achieve high rates of advance while maintaining a constant forward flow of critical reinforcements at a predetermined rate. This strategy is intended to capitalize on deficiencies in NATO's posture, which is a defensive one. The cumulative effect of these trends is substantial progress of the Soviet armed forces towards achieving their objective of denying NATO reassurance as to the adequacy of its defenses and, should war occur, achieving their objective of a rapid victory.

The improvements in Soviet conventional and theater nuclear capabilities are intended to exploit the weaknesses of NATO's defensive strategy of Forward Defense. These weaknesses include: the inability to trade space for time; the maldeployment of some NATO forces and the need to mobilize reserves; the limitations on available manpower; the vulnerability of critical rear-area targets; and a reluctance to engage in a long war of attrition. The threat posed by a swift offensive conducted with surprise by forward-deployed Soviet and Warsaw Pact formations demands that NATO initiate efforts to counter its current vulnerabilities and enhance its fighting capabilities.

Because NATO's capability to defend conventionally against a Warsaw Pact offensive is increasingly in doubt, NATO is increasingly dependent for both deterrence and defense on early recourse to nuclear weapons. The pressing task for the Alliance is to improve deterrence against a Soviet attack by improving its conventional capabilities. It is necessary to find ways to defeat a Warsaw Pact offensive with non-nuclear systems.

The Workshop on Contributions of Advanced Technology takes the position that new technological developments in non-nuclear weapons appear to offer early potential for a great improvement in NATO's ability to resist Warsaw Pact aggression.

CHANGING ROLES FOR CONVENTIONAL AND NUCLEAR WEAPONS

The balance between conventional and nuclear capabilities in NATO strategy has been one founded not on choice but largely on necessity. Failing to provide a conventional deterrent of sufficient size to ensure deterrence of conventional aggression, NATO has always relied on close integration of tactical nuclear weapons with its conventional defenses. The ability to threaten an aggressor with escalation was (and still is) considered the optimum means of deterring all aggression. However, now that continued improvement in Soviet conventional forces has magnified the weaknesses in NATO's conventional posture, there is growing concern that these weaknesses may increase Soviet willingness to risk sudden conventional aggression. In the event of such an attack it is feared that NATO will have no recourse but to initiate early, large-scale use of theater nuclear weapons. The growth in Soviet theater nuclear forces makes the likelihood of nuclear retaliation a virtual certainty. Thus, while the nuclear threshold is lowered, the plausibility of a NATO nuclear option is being undermined.

Enhanced conventional deterrence can be achieved by improving capabilities to perform missions previously assigned to theater nuclear weapons. Specifically, advanced conventional weapons can be used to hold at risk large elements of the Warsaw Pact's conventional airpower and ground forces. Employment of these new capabilities could produce results in some instances similar in kind if not degree to those now achievable by theater nuclear weapons such as destruction of airfields, creation of obstacles, and destruction of mobile combat formations.

While enhancing deterrence by improving NATO's ability to strike critical targets deep in Warsaw Pact territory, the employment of advanced conventional systems also could increase significantly NATO's ability to conduct a stalwart conventional defense and seriously complicate Warsaw Pact offensive operations. Such systems would be, indeed must be, used from the initial moments of a conflict. The willingness to use such systems could, itself, constitute a deterrent to an attack.

Changes in NATO's conventional strategy will inevitably have implications for NATO's theater nuclear posture. It will provide the opportunity to effect a restructuring of NATO's theater nuclear forces. In particular, raising NATO's ability to conduct conventional defense could in due course allow NATO to de-emphasize theater nuclear weapons, and in particular, short-range battlefield nuclear systems. A capability to attack large, dense Warsaw Pact ground force concentrations threatening NATO's forward defenses remains indispensable, but a restructuring of the nuclear force should be possible, producing a smaller but more effective nuclear force. One may hope that this would also remove the particularly harmful public perception that NATO plans to fight a large-scale nuclear war on European territory.

But the possibility of a shift of emphasis to conventional capabilities should not be interpreted as a renunciation of the role of nuclear weapons in NATO strategy. Nuclear weapons will remain an essential component of NATO strategy in order to deter Soviet use of nuclear weapons, hold Soviet forces at risk, thereby ensuring their dispersal, and threaten retaliation against Soviet first use. The ultimate threat of the use of nuclear weapons will remain the basis of NATO's strategy of deterrence as long as the Soviets present a nuclear threat.

Thus the deployment of advanced conventional capabilities should not be viewed as detracting from the important and continuing role in NATO strategy for theater nuclear weapons. The new concept constitutes not a change in the elements which make up Flexible Response, but instead a reaffirmation of essential objectives for the two forces. NATO first use is likely only in response to the threat of a major loss of territory or imminent defeat in the land battle. An improved conventional defense would reduce the likelihood that these circumstances would occur. There is no inconsistency between current NATO strategy and the posture and missions suggested in this Workshop Report.

In today's political environment, the adoption of new concepts which allow a shift in the roles of NATO forces toward more emphasis on non-nuclear means of deterrence and defense will call for thorough and detailed explanation. A posture that emphasizes the defensive and reactive nature of the Alliance will be more easily explained and justified to public opinion.

De-emphasizing battlefield nuclear weapons is generally regarded as a constructive development, but the question remains as to what response the Alliance would make if the Warsaw Pact were to use battlefield nuclear weapons first. Although such use would pose a serious political and military predicament, the Alliance need not possess directly symmetrical capabilities. In a situation of Soviet first use, NATO would possess a range of options not restricted to replying exactly in kind.

NEW NON-NUCLEAR OPTIONS

Technological advances are now making available the means to perform certain missions with guided missiles having advanced conventional warheads. A force of guided ballistic missiles with the mission of damaging runways and suppressing airfield operations and interdicting choke points with simple, unguided area munitions, would free NATO's aircraft for more decisive and appropriate targets. A force of ground-launched and air-launched guided missiles could be used to launch attacks with self-guided munitions against mobile targets of second-echelon forces. Deployment of this force would additionally require the energetic pursuit of research and development on means for swift, highly accurate target acquisition and surveillance. A key part of this new potential lies in the advances made in modern precision-guided area weapons. Demonstrated technologies show that the effectiveness of these advanced non-nuclear munitions is approaching "equivalence" with the effectiveness of low-yield nuclear weapons on certain targets.

The proposed operational concept for an integrated non-nuclear forward defense involves three interrelated missions, as follows.

Counter-Air and Interdiction

The Warsaw Pact conventional threat is very dependent on offensive air operations using aircraft staging from Main Operating Bases (MOBs), on the passage of troops and all forms of forces through choke points, and on rapid forward deployment of second-echelon forces. NATO's only non-nuclear means of attacking air bases and choke points today is manned aircraft, and it is the weakness of NATO air power *vis-à-vis* the Warsaw Pact that is the prime reason for early recourse to nuclear weapons.

The counter-air and interdiction mission can be performed by using medium-range, conventionally armed ballistic missiles to suppress enemy Main Operating Bases (MOBs) and key choke points. Follow-on attacks would be with manned aircraft against grounded aircraft in Dispersed Operating Bases (DOBs) and against disrupted ground forces at the choke points. This would:

1. Assure NATO of air superiority during the first critical hours or days when NATO comes under massive air and ground attack. Warsaw Pact ground-attack aircraft at Main Operating Bases would be suppressed in a matter of hours. Suppression of Main Operating Bases would force surviving first-wave aircraft plus second-wave aircraft to deploy to the less well-protected Dispersed Operating Bases. These DOBs, at present lacking aircraft shelters and poorly defended, would then be brought under attack by NATO ground attack aircraft, armed with a variety of ground attack area munitions.

2. Delay and disrupt echeloned and follow-on forces by interdicting key logistic lines of communications (bridges, railheads, highway junctions, etc.). Large concentrations of ground units would be created as targets for attack by manned aircraft using a variety of munitions against concentrations of follow-on forces.

The performance of these closely integrated missions would deal with the most important requirements of Forward Defense: buying time without trading space; and allowing NATO to reinforce.

Attacking Forward-Deploying Ground Forces

NATO needs to engage forward-deploying mobile targets prior to their actually making contact with NATO ground forces. The forces to be engaged are, first, those forces in the immediate battlefield at a depth of 30 to 100 kilometers, and second, follow-on and reserve formations over ranges of 100 to 300 kilometers. This would be done by a combination of ground-launched missiles for the 30-100-km depth and air-launched stand-off missiles for the 100-300-km range. Targeting of mobile forces presents additional requirements for surveillance. This can be done with a combination of available sensors and techniques of information processing and targeting, now being demonstrated in various locations of the Allied Forces Central Europe Command.

A common missile can satisfy the air-launched and ground-launched requirements. About 5,000 of these missiles would be required for this mission alone. The surveillance/targeting requirements are well defined and must be provided for the eight ground corps and NATO air forces in Central Europe.

Attacking Enemy Ground Forces in Direct Contact

Whatever measures are taken to cope with the problem of attacking Warsaw Pact rear areas and second-echelon forces, the problem of stopping the initial Soviet armored thrust will remain. In view of Soviet force doctrine and current NATO/Warsaw Pact force ratios, the ability of NATO forces to hold with conventional means is questionable. This will result in a situation in which there will arise the problem of early use by NATO of nuclear weapons. It is important to look for ways to reduce a dependence on early use of battlefield nuclear systems.

NATO requires a non-nuclear alternative to short-range nuclear weapons to engage enemy armored units (companies, battalions, regiments) on NATO territory. One approach is by increased use of terminally guided weapons delivered by the Multiple Launch Rocket System. A salvo of twelve rounds of submunition-armed rockets can achieve a "kill" capability equivalent to a low-yield nuclear weapon (1 kiloton) at about one-fifth the cost of nuclear artillery shells.

ADVANTAGES OF THE USE OF ADVANCED NON-NUCLEAR TECHNOLOGIES

The advantages of using missiles with warheads containing individual submunitions to perform the missions identified above are that they possess the combination of timely availability, range, accuracy, and lethality to attack those targets critical to a Warsaw Pact offensive. The use of missiles would thus fill an important gap in NATO's existing capabilities in several ways: It would provide NATO with improved deep-attack conventional capability. It would preserve and make available additional NATO aircraft for attacking Soviet reinforcements. It would reduce dependence on early nuclear escalation as the prime element of NATO's existing strategy. The new concept would raise the nuclear threshold by improving NATO's ability to hold conventionally.

The great strength of the missile-with-submunitions concept is that in the case of the counter-air mission, the technology has been demonstrated and is potentially available now. Furthermore, because the targets for the counter-air and choke-points mission are fixed, little further investment in surveillance is necessary. Though the additional costs for new systems may appear high, they should be measured against the totality of the advantages and trade-offs that the concept offers. Implementing the concept would free existing aircraft for crucial missions, including attacks on the less well-defended Dispersed Operating Bases to which Warsaw Pact aircraft will be compelled to resort. By contributing to the degradation of Warsaw Pact air assets, it would also effectively perform an air defense role. Its cost should be judged in comparison to the acquisition of other major Alliance programs or weapon systems such as surface-to-air missiles (SAMs) or F-15 aircraft.

It should be acknowledged that this is not the only approach to solving NATO's conventional problems that is currently under study. For example, the ground-attack problem is being addressed through the Airland Battle concept. This concept is a portrayal of the advanced weapons, control measures, and tactics necessary to conduct successful operations in the next century across an extended battlefield in which all forces are held at risk by the threat of both advanced conventional and nuclear weapons.

The effective use of barriers has tactical advantages. The creation of large-scale barriers (mine fields, tank traps, obstacles) would hinder a crucial element of Soviet operations, the need for rapid advance. The consequence of this delay would be to increase the difficulty for the Soviet planner. By placing a greater reliance on barriers, NATO could enhance the effectiveness of existing conventional forces, thereby reducing the need for early use of nuclear weapons. A greater emphasis on barriers would assist mobile forward defense by releasing manpower for mobile reserves. Barrier defense would have the effect of slowing both the Soviet offensive and the pace of the war, giving time for reflection and negotiation.

On the other hand, though in a tactical sense greater use of barriers would provide some assistance to the conventional battle, this would not provide a quantum improvement in NATO's capability to deter. The gain in manpower would not be significant, the Pact would certainly develop plans that would circumvent barriers (helicopters, specialist forces), and any preparation that required activation during a crisis would be of dubious value (barrier plans exist now but there are misgivings over their implementation). The peacetime preparations of such initiatives might raise serious political difficulties that could make them unacceptable to the German population, because such preparations might dramatize the division of Germany and be a constant reminder that West Germany would be the potential battlefield.

It is impossible to define precisely how much the means to perform the 3 missions would cost, but a figure of 10 to 30 billion dollars over ten years has been estimated. Closely related to the question of cost is the issue of whether the systems will function. Some would question the wisdom of placing so much reliance on new systems. However, a considerable amount of the technology is tried, tested, and available now; and the rest is in a well-advanced stage of development.

As the Alliance will shortly suffer serious shortages in manpower, the manpower implications of the new concept are important. The costs shown involve incremental personnel increases for the first two missions (counter-air and interdiction, and attacking forward-deploying ground forces). The third mission requirements (attacking ground forces in direct contact) are assumed to be subsumed under the normal Table of Organization and Equipment for Multiple Launch Rocket Systems. About one-half of these people will be required for the operations of the *new* surveillance/targeting systems described for the attack of *mobile* forces. The remainder are in support of the air-launched and ground-launched missile systems.

Command, control, and communications (C^3) for the first mission are assumed to be the same for the *current* support of the counter-air mission. The C^3 functions for mobile-force attack are an integral part of the surveillance/targeting functions necessary to support the basic targeting requirements for the second mission.

ISSUES TO BE RESOLVED

In order to make deterrence credible the Alliance must have defenses that are relevant to the conflict and that will directly affect the Soviet Union's ability to fight a war. Given the structure and doctrine of Warsaw

Pact forces, this will inevitably mean having the capacity to project power against Warsaw Pact forces on their own territory.

It is important to point out, however, that any NATO posture would be defensive and reactive. The missile-with-submunitions concept proposed above would be implemented only as a response to a Soviet attack which had already begun; in this sense, the concept has the advantage of blocking Soviet offensive options without itself posing an offensive threat. Furthermore, however offensive certain specific aspects of NATO tactics may appear, the overall NATO posture remains defensive.

The single most important criterion in assessing the implications of suggested measures is whether they strengthen deterrence by eliminating critical NATO deficiencies without contributing to crisis instability. Developments which represent a move away from nuclear to conventional systems, and which stress the defensive nature of the Alliance, would appear to fulfill this criterion.

There are obvious difficulties with regard to Alliance participation. Assuming that the United States does not want to shoulder the entire responsibility and that the Federal Republic of Germany is unwilling to be placed in a singular position, the optimal solution would be a multinational project. The appropriate mechanism for such a project should be decided on a pragmatic basis, but taking account of the fact that the use of normal NATO processes would probably make a rapid decision somewhat difficult to achieve.

It would also be important to attempt to find ways of co-production in order to lessen the impact of a straight European purchase of American technology, and in this respect a high degree of commonality should be sought concerning the missiles and compatibility for the submunitions.

The technological approach is only one method of improving NATO's conventional capabilities; there are many other improvements that will compete for resources. In this sense it will be important to decide whether conventional improvements should be sought through incremental changes which make due allowance for financial and political constraints, or through a quantum jump — a conceptual breakthrough — with all that this implies for Alliance planning.

These new requirements must be met within national budgets and existing force plans, most of which are declared and fixed until 1985. But this will be a question of reassessing priorities, of measuring the potential advantages that this concept offers — in terms of making a real improvement to Alliance deterrence — against the potential offered by existing plans. In assessing the contributions of these new systems to NATO's conventional defense, their utility must of course be judged in comparison to other available or potential systems that perform the same missions.

There is a further consideration, namely the choice of missile and the relation of this choice to arms control. The proposal involves the introduction of large numbers of guided ballistic missiles, systems which are associated in the public mind with the nuclear task. It would therefore be preferable if a system could be chosen which was distinct from those currently performing a nuclear role, and which would not therefore complicate arms control negotiations. In this respect the Patriot system, though costing more, would appear to offer political advantages. A related question is the advantages and disadvantages of dual-capable systems; whereas they greatly complicate the arms control process, they also greatly complicate the enemy's task by increasing his uncertainty. Obviously, all these problems which could have significant implications for arms control negotiations should be given attention.

A final issue is whether priorities should be set among the three missions described above or whether they represent an integral and synergistic package that should be adopted or rejected as a whole. The question of emphasizing a single component is complicated by the fact that the initial operational capabilities for the respective missions occur in different time phases. Regardless of the time factor, the question of choosing individual missions or the total package must be determined by the priority accorded to the respective missions and also whether the rationale concerning the interdependent relationship among the missions is accepted. To the extent that the difficulties NATO would encounter in carrying out deep attacks against enemy airfields and other fixed points is a major deficiency, then the counter-air mission must be accorded top priority. Such a priority would be convenient because the subsystems for this mission are demonstrated and available. Despite the fact that some NATO nations have already committed themselves to acquiring counter-airfield capabilities, the acquisition of missiles for the improved counter-airfield mission could be regarded as a valuable complement to these assets, effectively freeing them for other tasks. The crucial factor is to reconcile priorities with existing resource allocation and to identify possible trade-offs.

CHEMICAL WEAPONS

The use by NATO of chemical weapons as a means of improving its conventional defense has been suggested. Views differ widely on the necessity for NATO to possess a credible offensive chemical capability. Many believe that acquisition of an effective chemical capability is necessary to deter the Soviet Union from using chemical weapons against NATO — and that not having this capability is likely to drive NATO to the use of nuclear weapons.

It is generally agreed that major asymmetries exist in the force structures of NATO and the Warsaw Pact in the area of chemical weapons. Though both sides possess defensive capabilities, the Soviets possess a clear advantage in defensive and a virtual monopoly of offensive chemical capabilities. The result is that NATO forces are at a distinct disadvantage because Soviet chemical capabilities compel NATO forces to wear protective clothing which has a serious degrading effect on human performance. This represents a very substantial handicap and one that may not be given adequate attention in normal force assessments. Those advocating an offensive chemical capability argue that it would compel Warsaw Pact forces to operate under the same handicap of protective clothing as NATO forces.

Arguments against the need for an offensive capability center on the questionable military value of chemical weapons and on the point that NATO strategy does not require symmetrical capabilities in every category or level of forces. According to this last view, the most effective Alliance response lies in a declaratory policy that the use of chemical weapons by the Soviet Union would be interpreted as a decisive change of warfare which could, therefore, initiate a nuclear response from NATO. The credibility of this position is doubtful as many would question whether the Alliance would be willing to respond with nuclear weapons to a localized chemical attack.

General agreement exists on two points: (1) that lacking a credible chemical offensive capability the Alliance has no option but to emphasize passive defense and rely on the threat of nuclear retaliation, and (2) that the possible acquisition of a chemical-weapons capability by NATO would be highly controversial and politically unacceptable.

CONCLUSIONS

In order to shore up its strategy of deterrence, the Alliance must acquire the capability to disrupt, delay and hold a Warsaw Pact offensive without recourse to nuclear weapons. This will require the deployment of conventional capabilities to carry out missions previously inadequately covered or covered only by nuclear weapons. Through the substitution of conventional for nuclear systems NATO will reduce its reliance on nuclear weapons and improve its capacity to defend conventionally.

This change of emphasis does not represent a change in the strategy of Flexible Response but rather an adjustment to the means of implementing this strategy. Despite the diminution in the role of nuclear weapons and the potential reduction in the size of NATO's nuclear posture, the nuclear component will remain an indispensable element of NATO's strategy.

The most critical and urgent deficiencies in NATO's capabilities, which have seriously undermined the credibility of its deterrent, lie in the difficulty of performing three related missions with conventional means — deep attack and interdiction of air bases and other fixed points in rear areas, attacking forward-deploying reinforcements, and countering first-echelon forces.

New technologies are available that provide the potential either now, or in the relatively near future, for NATO to perform all three missions with conventional means, notably through the deployment of greatly improved guided missiles equipped with sophisticated submunitions. The advantages that flow from this concept have a synergistic effect and would result in the severe degradation of the Warsaw Pact offensive capability — sufficient to close off any hope of a rapid and cheap victory in Europe. In effect, these new technologies offer NATO the potential to make a quantum jump in improving its deterrent posture. Furthermore, it should be noted that the technology to redress this situation is not limited to the Central Region, but is available for deployment on the flanks.

The extent to which the Alliance will take advantage of these new developments, either totally or partially, will depend on the development of a consensus concerning NATO's most critical priorities. Competition for resources is intense and national force plans well established. Nevertheless, the urgency of the situation and the magnitude of the proposed change would suggest that the development of such a consensus is essential.

The basic point is that the deployment of advanced conventional forces for the missions described, which today must be executed by nuclear forces, would constitute a considerable strengthening of NATO's strategy of deterrence without detracting from the essential missions of theater nuclear forces.

Potential Future Roles for Conventional and Nuclear Forces in Defense of Western Europe

by
Donald R. Cotter*

Mr. Cotter is the President of DRC/LTD, a technical and policy consulting firm in Arlington, Virginia.

The European Security Study is premised on the assumption that NATO's "military deterrents to Soviet aggression rely on conventional forces and threatened use of nuclear weapons." A further premise is that "conventional forces" for NATO "have been relatively neglected" but that a "number of technologies and tactics . . . may offer attractive potentials" for improvements in deterring Soviet aggression.[1]

There is an over-arching reason for improving NATO's deterrent capabilities. The past decade has seen that deterrent erode with the Soviet Union's remarkable buildup of quantitative and qualitative capabilities in strategic, theater nuclear, and conventional forces. It is now evident that the Soviets achieved superiority in all categories. The implication for NATO is that meaningful modernization and restructuring of its theater

*The author wishes to express his gratitude for the support of several individuals in the preparation of this paper: Dr. J. V. Braddock, the BDM Corporation, for his assistance in analyzing the Soviet threat and concepts of Soviet ground and air offensive operations and for illuminating the targeting and information-processing requirements. Dr. N. F. Wikner, BDM consultant, for his contributions in the synthesis of the technology of new non-nuclear weapons, surveillance, and target management. Miss Suzanne Rich and Mrs. Jane Mason for the preparation of manuscripts, tables, and figures used in this study.

Notes are at the end of the paper.

forces must take place in the interest of both deterrence and raising the nuclear threshold. Needed improvements in conventional forces could significantly move NATO away from considering the early use of nuclear weapons if deterrence fails.

The focus of this paper, therefore, is to examine possible changes in the deterrent roles of modern conventional and nuclear weapons and define potential future roles for them in the defense of Western Europe.

The primary NATO forces to be examined are those in the Central Region, i.e., those of West Germany and the Benelux countries and the U.K. and American elements (stationed and reserve capabilities) committed to the *forward* defense of Western Europe. This is not to imply that the NATO northern and southern flanks are of less importance but rather that the Central Region is crucial in any discussion of the conventional and nuclear issues which have received much recent attention on both sides of the Atlantic.

A concept for a forward defense of Western Europe will be described in this paper. The strategic concept of Forward Defense relies on non-nuclear technology advances which now are *available* for exploitation if a national and NATO decision is taken to pursue a *program* for upgrading conventional forces and restructuring conventional/nuclear roles for certain kinds of missions. The concept further relies on providing a quality nuclear "overwatch" force in support of upgraded conventional forces. This nuclear capability will be necessary to maintain a credible threat of nuclear force, and, as will be explained, is fundamental to achieving an affordable and enhanced conventional deterrent, and if need be, defense options.

Survivability of the proposed force capabilities, including the political and military elements of command and control, is also a critical requirement. This will mean restructuring traditional ways of achieving survivability, with more attention to designing for mobility, redundance, and dispersal, and with greater reliance on new communications technology. In the technology of communications, civilian capabilities today far exceed those of military systems which are now less survivable, more costly, and outmoded.[2]

But the overriding requirement for attempting to achieve new non-nuclear deterrent options rests on the ability to make these upgrades within *current* force levels and within essentially current budgets — granting a real growth of 3 to 5 percent in defense expenditures. This depends on buying the right materiel and not buying costly and largely irrelevant (and counter-productive) hardware which does not aid in non-nuclear total force effectiveness and survivability.

The expected improvements in pursuing the outlined concept could lead to improved conventional combat potential for NATO and new deterrent options at the conventional level. NATO could reduce dependence on early nuclear escalation as the prime element of its de facto strategy. Ultimately, one could look towards credible and sensible proposals for arms control negotiations with reductions in the facing nuclear forces.

DETERRING SOVIET OFFENSIVE OPERATIONS — HOW MUCH DO WE KNOW?

Over the years a clear picture of the numerical threat to NATO's Central Region has emerged from the unclassified literature analyzing Soviet writings, from various government publications, from Congressional hearings, and from stories in the press about the stalled negotiations between NATO and the Warsaw Pact on force reductions. Table 1 is a summary of force levels in the Central Region.

But in dealing with this threat we must also consider, in addition to the quantitative aspects, the dynamics of how Soviet ground and air offensive operations might unfold. Such operations have been studied in great detail and a useful document is *Soviet Army Operations,* published by the U.S. Army in April 1978. A generalized description of those operations and their "management" or command control will appear below. A detailed analysis of Soviet air and ground operations is given in the supporting paper by C. N. Donnelly in this volume. Such examinations are necessary to determine what vulnerabilities exist which NATO could exploit.[3]

Soviet Force Combat Potential

An analysis encompassing the overall Soviet combat potential must include much more than the quantitative "bean count" of Pact forces and equipment. Of equal — and often greater — importance are the qualitative aspects, such as the superior range and firing rate of Soviet conventional artillery and multiple rocket launchers, and also their long-range nuclear and chemical strike systems (SS-20, Backfire). Additionally, the "management" and organization aspects of Soviet Union/Warsaw Pact forces must be included. The Pact Front commander has authority for maneuver forces (armored and motorized rifle divisions), suppression forces (artillery, rockets, and frontal aviation), air defense, and logistical support. This is the essence of the Soviet "combined arms" force concept for conventional, nuclear, and chemical warfare.

The Soviet Front commander also has recourse to additional independent assets which he can subordinate to Army and Division commanders

Table 1

NATO AND WARSAW PACT FORCE LEVELS IN THE MUTUAL BALANCED FORCE REDUCTIONS AREA, 1980

| | Manpower | | Equipment | |
	Ground	Air	Tanks	Aircraft
NATO[1]				
United States	193,000	35,000	2,000	335
Britain	58,000	9,000	575	145
Canada	3,000	2,000	30	50
Belgium	62,000	19,000	300	145
Germany	341,000	110,000	3,000	509
Netherlands	75,000	18,000	500	160
Total	732,000	193,000	6,405	1,344
WARSAW PACT				
Soviet Union	475,000	60,000	9,250	1,300
Czechoslovakia	135,000	46,000	2,500	550
East Germany	105,000	36,000	1,550	375
Poland	220,000	62,000	2,900	850
Total	935,000[2]	204,000[2]	16,200	3,075

Source: The Military Balance 1979-1980 (London: International Institute for Strategic Studies, 1979), p. 110, taken from Jeffrey Record, *Force Reductions in Europe: Starting Over,* 1980.

1. Excludes French forces in Germany, since France refuses to participate in MBFR. French forces deployed in Germany number some 50,000 troops and 325 tanks. Supporting tactical aviation forces are retained inside France.

2. Warsaw Pact negotiators claim significantly lower manpower levels.

as required to achieve success. These include additional artillery, armored fighting vehicles, transportation and engineering units. Finally, the Front commander has available to him a complex of hardened and redundant systems of command, control, and communications intended to provide him with reliable "top-down" control of all of these force elements.

Organizationally, NATO has some self-inflicted wounds which the Soviets have exploited. The single Front commander of the Group of Soviet Forces, Germany, faces seven NATO corps, each with independent national forces and logistics. The NATO governments plan to assign all forces to the Supreme Allied Commander (SACEUR) in wartime, but how this might work under the duress of conflict is anyone's conjecture. (In peacetime SACEUR exercises operational control over air defense and some nuclear forces.)

The Pact's Front commander in peacetime controls, trains and exercises operational staffs and forces on a daily and integrated basis. In contrast, the NATO force of national corps and air elements is controlled, trained, and exercised infrequently and in a fragmentary way by small international staffs, which are merely planning staffs. The Alliance has perpetuated an asymmetry in true readiness and interoperability, a flaw which has undone even superior forces in past campaigns in this region.

In Soviet strategic writing the key element of Soviet strategy, in the event of an attack on NATO, is to seize NATO's continental territories, ports, and airfields in roughly two weeks. This time frame, short in comparison with NATO's present mobilization and reinforcement plans, would mean the defeat of NATO's forces-in-being before they could be reinforced.

Ground Operations

The Soviet concept of offensive ground operations calls for the establishment of multiple, phased axes of advance. Each axis is to achieve predetermined space-and-time objectives for divisions and armies in second and third echelons as well as forces in contact. In this way the attack is intended to keep pressure on the defensive forces in depth and to exhaust their capabilities over a relatively short time. To succeed, the Pact must "force" rates of advance with precise timing of massed suppressive fire (artillery and air) and inflict "massive blows" with echeloned motorized rifle and tank formations. Additional and simultaneous Soviet operations would include suppression/annihilation of NATO's headquarters, aircraft, nuclear storage sites, major logistic depots, communications, etc., by aircraft and missiles throughout the depth of the theater.

The concept rests on a survivable "top-down" command, control, and communications system, plus detailed pre-planning and timing of reinforcements. Precise tasking of combat maneuver and logistical support units is also required, thus limiting the flexibility of the lower-level field commanders.

The Soviets echelon their ground forces to lessen their vulnerability to nuclear attack (see Figure 1). This simplified diagram shows the echeloning tactics for the first-, second- and third-echelon armies, and their axes of advance. Reinforcement depends upon meeting rather precise timetables to achieve certain norms for local, but overwhelming, force ratios in selected breakthrough areas. As shown, the Front commander has authority to subordinate forces to those field armies achieving success. The whole operation is vulnerable to disruption and delay by successful NATO attacks on divisions and armies in second and reserve echelons. Thus NATO could exploit the inherent vulnerabilities in the Soviet/Pact offensive operational concept.

Air Operations

Soviet offensive air operations against NATO are the key to success of their ground force operations. The objective is to deny NATO air superiority both over the battle area and in NATO's rear areas. The Soviets echelon their air armies to achieve survivability against the threat of NATO's nuclear air defense. A series of quick *conventional* attacks, in waves, is anticipated. The objective is to destroy NATO's numerically inferior air forces before they can be reinforced. First waves will attempt to suppress NATO's air defense surface-to-air missile system. Second waves will attempt to suppress NATO Main Operating Bases for air interception and ground-attack aircraft, including bases for NATO nuclear-attack aircraft. Third waves, composed of medium bomber forces, have the objective of destroying reserve and secondary air bases, aircraft, logistic networks, communication, the command and control structure, and nuclear storage facilities and nuclear delivery systems.

Force Ratios and Engagement Rates

The minimum numerical superiority ratio sought by the Pact is about 3 to 1 in both ground and air operations. Doctrinally, however, the ratios to be achieved in local conflict situations are to be higher.

FIGURE 1. ILLUSTRATION OF SOVIET CONCEPT OF OFFENSIVE ECHELONED OPERATIONS

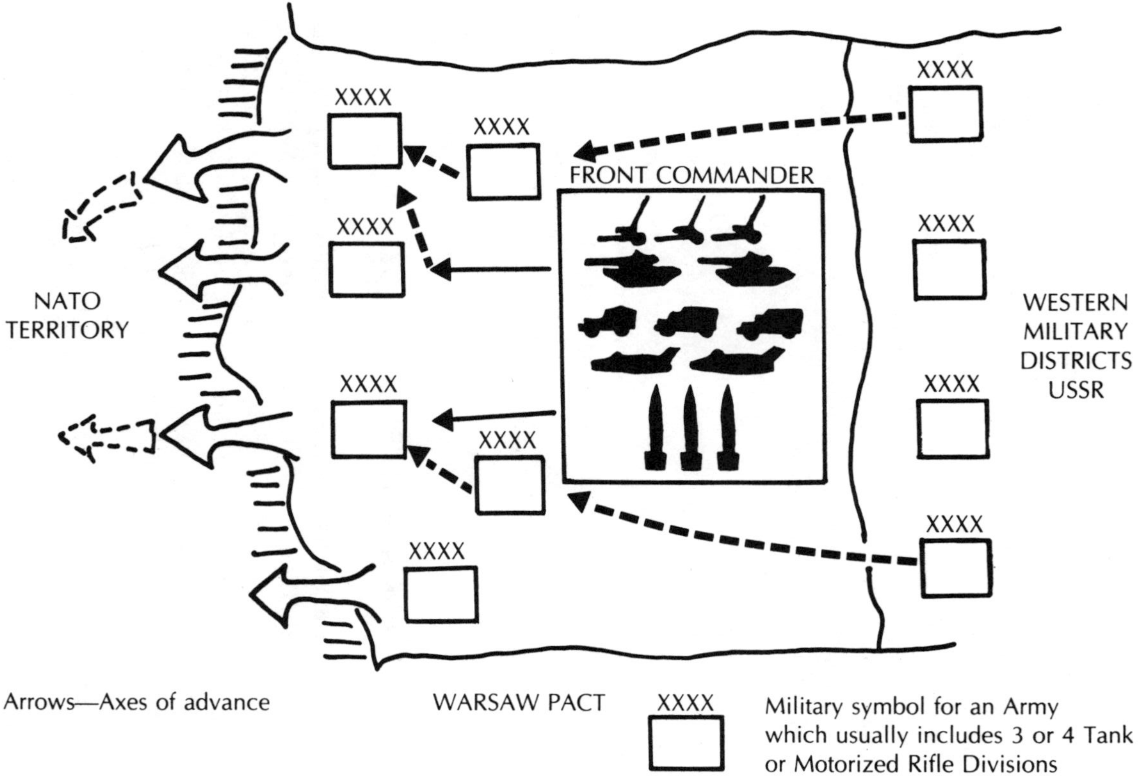

Soviet/Pact front-line ground forces, which would challenge NATO defenses on the inter-German border, are expected to present high force ratios on several (four to six) breakthrough fronts simultaneously. Armored fighting vehicle ratios of about 5 to 1, artillery ratios of about 6-1 to 8-1 and infantry fighting vehicle ratios of about 5 to 1 are to be expected in breakthrough operations. Manpower ratios would be about 4-1 to 5-1.

A NATO Corps commander would be presented with the task of holding off about 1,000 fighting vehicles on the first day of an attack. If successful in this, he must look forward to dealing with second-echelon divisions soon thereafter. The breakthrough ground defensive battle would be typically one of destroying a majority of 1,100 armored vehicles and 3,000 or so logistic support vehicles and 25 to 30 thousand troops. The task would be dominated by the engagement rate capabilities and force survivability of the defenders.

In the air battle, force ratios presented by the Soviet/Pact air offensive operation are expected to be similarly high. For example, of the 1,400 or so NATO aircraft readily available, about 500 in the Central Region are air defense aircraft. These have the mission of assuring air superiority over friendly forces and territory. These aircraft would be facing a penetrating force of about 1,500 fighter-bombers and 400 medium-bomber Soviet/Pact aircraft. Thus the force ratios in this case would be about 4 to 1, the same as in the Battle of Britain.

THE NEED FOR A NATO FORWARD DEFENSE

NATO is a defensive alliance and logically or illogically must bear the burden of aggression by the Soviet Union and Warsaw Pact before the Alliance can partially or fully function in terms of a military response. The NATO treaty has been interpreted to mean that an attack on any one NATO nation is considered an attack on all. Given this defensive stance, NATO must depend on a forward defense — one that does not conceptually allow large losses of territory.

A forward defense has political and psychological as well as military imperatives. If the Soviets could make multiple deep penetrations into West Germany, a loss of will could occur in the remainder of the Alliance. Full mobilization and putting forward a stalwart defense would be questionable. Politically, if NATO appeared to be trading space for time and allowing deep penetrations, it is possible that France would opt to defend her own borders rather than deploying her ground and air forces forward to counter Soviet/Pact incursions.

We have seen that the Soviet/Pact military deployments clearly support objectives which are offensive in nature. Soviet Military Doctrine indicates that their space-and-time objectives are such that quick occupation of Western European territory would result and that NATO would be defeated militarily before it could be fully mobilized and reinforced. Soviet forces depend on exploitation of breakthrough forces and air attack on NATO's rear areas which contain pre-positioned military equipment and its major deployments of nuclear weapons. They would also depend on Soviet sea power to gain control of ports in Belgium, Holland, and West Germany.

To implement a credible forward defense, NATO's defensive posture must include the ability to disrupt Soviet forces in Eastern Europe. This will help to delay their insertion and deny them the high force ratios necessary to maintain the breakthrough momentum.

In this requirement there are not only military imperatives but also political and psychological ones. The aggressors must bear the risk of considerable territorial damage, and they must be under the threat of attack to redress the aggression. NATO strike systems must be capable of inflicting damage at depths of 300 or 400 kilometers to assure that Soviet follow-on forces are not available for reinforcing in the direct battle area.

Today, under the Flexible Response strategy, NATO has a deficiency in conventional strike forces to accomplish this, and the missions are largely left to nuclear forces. An inability to underwrite the Forward Defense strategy with non-nuclear forces leads to a low nuclear threshold and the possibility of rapid escalation to nuclear strikes. Improved military capabilities must allow many options for the use of force by NATO. A defense based on the early and widespread use of nuclear weapons is neither feasible nor desirable. But a purely conventional defense now is neither politically, economically, nor militarily achievable.

It is interesting to look back at how NATO got into this "fix."

HOW DID NATO GET INTO THIS NUCLEAR "FIX"? — NEEDED CHANGES

If we look back to the genesis of NATO, it will be recalled that after World War II an attempt was made to define a conventional defense of

Western Europe. The so-called Lisbon goals, developed by the early military councils of NATO, envisioned a force about the size of the Normandy invasion, which was roughly 100 divisions and 10,000 aircraft. The Lisbon goals of about 96 divisions and 9,000 aircraft were clearly impossible to achieve in the environment of the early 1950s when Europe was struggling to recover from war. The compromise force which was later defined is essentially what we have today — that of 26 divisions (12 of which are Bundeswehr) and 1,400 aircraft for the Central Region.

In order to meet this shortfall in conventional forces, the United States proposed a nuclear posture based on equipping NATO forces — U.S. and non-U.S. — with "tactical" nuclear weapons. Initially a force of 15,000 weapons was proposed, including infantry weapons (Davey Crockett), short-range battlefield artillery and missiles, nuclear mines, and an inventory of aircraft gravity bombs. The notion in those days of massive U.S. nuclear superiority was that nuclear firepower could substitute for conventional forces and that nuclear weapons applied to the battlefield were merely an extension of conventional firepower.

Today, the nuclear-dependence legacy of the 1950s is still with us — weapon systems and a posture that leave NATO with serious shortcomings. We have a posture that is structured around large nuclear retaliatory attacks on the Warsaw Pact and Soviet forces.

It can be thought that this theater nuclear deterrent posture "worked," because there has never been any aggression against any NATO nation. But it quite probably "worked" because the U.S. underwrote these forces with its superior strategic massive retaliation capabilities. In the intervening years since the initial NATO deployments of nuclear weapons, little was done to modernize them, particularly in terms of survivability. In fact, a parallel can be drawn between this neglect and the neglect of NATO's conventional capabilities. Longer-range nuclear missiles were added in the form of Lance and Pershing in the 1970s and improvements were made in security features for some systems, but not much else was done. Perhaps the most disturbing part of this neglect has been that the survivability of NATO's nuclear forces has steadily declined to today's vulnerable situation at the very time when the Soviet Union determinedly upgraded its conventional and theater nuclear forces. A good portion of NATO's nuclear forces would not survive the type of conventional attack planned by the Soviets. The survivability of the remainder is questionable and might force NATO to early use if they were in danger of being destroyed.

So, as we look at the primary purpose of achieving deterrent options with new conventional capabilities, we must pay attention to modernization of nuclear forces as well, assuring them of greater survivability. This modernization includes the deployment of the planned intermediate nuclear force (INF). NATO could also alleviate some manpower problems by restructuring its nuclear forces, especially by reducing the large number of short-range weapon systems which, if resorted to, could only turn Western Europe into a nuclear battlefield. This is a politically and militarily unsound posture.

DETERRENT ROLES FOR FUTURE CONVENTIONAL FORCES

Key Technologies

New and effective deterrent roles for modern conventional forces can be achieved. The reason for this rests on certain available key technologies. These are in:

— advanced non-nuclear submunitions;
— accurate, long-range delivery by surface-to-surface or air-launched stand-off missiles;
— long-range surveillance and target acquisition and tracking;
— information processing and distribution techniques.

The key technology is in *modern precision-guided area weapons*. Demonstrated technologies show that the effectiveness of advanced non-nuclear munitions can approach "equivalence" to that of low-yield nuclear weapons on certain targets. These precision-guided weapons can be adapted to destroy *fixed* hard targets; the most important fixed targets are aircraft runways and taxiways, bridges, highway junctions, railheads, hardened command posts, and hardened storage facilities.

Area weapons with terminally guided submunitions and mines could be used to defeat *mobile* targets such as company-size tank formations. These weapons would be roughly equivalent to low-yield nuclear weapons in terms of the numbers of vehicles destroyed or disabled.

These capabilities would provide NATO with credible deterrence options at the conventional level and result in a raised nuclear threshold.

In examining the deterrent roles for modern conventional forces to be achieved as soon as possible — perhaps as early as three years from now — it is necessary to look at upgrading capabilities for certain *specific missions* rather than looking at upgrading conventional forces across the board.

The missions suggested in terms of priority for the forward defense of Western Europe are:

1. Counter-air.
2. Interdiction.*
3. Attack of echeloned and mobile follow-on ground forces.
4. Defeating massive armor attacks in the zone of contact.

This priority listing is also in the order of technical feasibility of accomplishment by advanced non-nuclear weapon systems. Feasibility is greatest in the first mission.

The four missions, with weapons and costs, are discussed in the pages that follow and then are concisely summarized in the Appendix to this paper.

The Crucial Counter-Air Mission

Without air superiority NATO has, realistically, only about 72 hours before the Soviet offensive air operations would cause loss of NATO airbases and reserve forces and destruction of NATO nuclear storage facilities and most of its nuclear retaliatory capability. The requirements for NATO counter-air operations are to:

— disrupt Pact air operations in their early phases;
— substantially reduce Pact attack sortie rates;
— complicate or deny Pact aircraft recovery and reinforcement operations.

The size of the problem is realized when one compares the NATO-Warsaw Pact combat aircraft inventories and considers the Soviet capabilities for executing its offensive air operation.

Of the roughly 4,600 Pact first-line aircraft deployed against NATO's Central and Northern Regions, about 1,600 are ground-attack fighter-bombers. NATO's defensive air interceptors number about 450. There are about 2,000 surface-to-air non-nuclear missiles (Nike-Hercules, Improved

---

*As the reader may have noticed, counter-air and interdiction are discussed under the same heading in the Workshop Report on Contributions of Advanced Technology. Thus the Workshop Report lists three major missions instead of four.

Hawk, Roland, Rapiers) plus about 5,000 anti-aircraft artillery pieces. There is little doubt that this NATO air defense capability could give a good account on the first day of an attack. But the massive preemptive air attack by the 1,500 to 2,000 modern Pact ground-attack and medium bomber aircraft would cut the sortie rate of the air interceptor force considerably. In addition, NATO's limited inventory of surface-to-air and air-to-air missiles would be exhausted in one to two days, by some estimates. (Procurement of more missiles would be possible but expensive; the major problem, however, is the unavailability of trained troops to man the launchers.) Thus, NATO would lose control of the air over its own territory by the second or third day. Consequently, it would lose its capability to provide air support to the defensive ground battle and to have enough surviving aircraft to perform other important missions such as interdiction and deep attack of Pact echeloned forces.

The loss of NATO's air capability and reserve forces and the incipient loss of its nuclear capabilities present a very unstable situation. This leads NATO to consider the early use of nuclear weapons against Pact Main Operating Bases (MOBs) supporting their offensive air campaign. The alternative to nuclear weapons, of course, would be to use NATO's dual-capable ground-attack aircraft equipped with non-nuclear weapons to attack Pact MOBs. There are several problems:

- There are too few all-weather, penetrating aircraft. NATO has about 500 of these aircraft which must penetrate a defensive force of about 4,000 interceptor aircraft, about 6,000 surface-to-air missile interceptors and about 10,000 anti-aircraft artillery pieces. (The 4,000 interceptor aircraft do not include those interceptor aircraft assigned to the Moscow Air Defense District.)
- There are no effective non-nuclear munitions which can successfully suppress MOBs or destroy aircraft in their *shelters*.
- The required number of attack *and* support sorties (about 1,000 per day) cannot be reliably generated.
- The attrition of these valuable penetrating aircraft against these heavily defended and hardened targets would be very high (25 to 50 percent by some estimates).

If the U.S. and NATO wish to find alternatives to the early use of nuclear weapons to perform the counter-air mission, we must look to other more reliable means of attack than initial attacks by manned aircraft against the relevant 30 to 40 Pact Main Operating Bases.

The Time-Urgent Interdiction Mission

If NATO is to maintain a forward defense and the integrity of its borders, it must simultaneously fight the direct fire battle against invading ground forces and prevent the echeloned Pact reinforcing units from arriving at the point of contact. NATO must disrupt and delay these reinforcements within a few hours or days by interdicting the main lines of communications (bridges, road junctions, railheads, etc.) supporting the reinforcing ground units. Failure to prevent the timely arrival of Pact forces will result in force ratios which will overwhelm the local defending forces.[4] There are about 100 targets which require interdiction.

Conventionally armed aircraft would suffer the same problems iterated above in attempting to deliver non-nuclear munitions against these heavily defended and tough targets. A lower attrition and more reliable non-nuclear method of execution must be found for accomplishing the interdiction mission.

Fortunately, there are several feasible methods of doing both the counter-air and interdiction missions with advanced precision-guided missiles armed with a selectable family of special "hard-target kill" unguided submunitions. Today, the only effective means of executing the counter-air and interdiction missions in the necessary time resides in NATO's Nuclear Quick Reaction Alert Forces, that is, dual capable aircraft and Pershing I missiles.

A Proposed NATO Concept of Operations for a Conventional Counter-Air and Interdiction Campaign

To understand how the Soviet/Pact offensive air operation against NATO can be countered, we must examine their concept of operations for vulnerabilities. As was described earlier, a Pact air attack against NATO main airbases (of which there are less than 25 in the Central Region), nuclear air defense missile sites, ports, and nuclear-weapon facilities would be a massive one. Doctrine calls for the attack to come in closely timed waves — echeloned for both nuclear survivability and control. The attacks are anticipated to be mounted from about 30 to 40 MOBs in East Germany, Poland, and Czechoslovakia. During the first wave, aircraft of the second and third waves will be moving up to the Main Operating Bases and Dispersed Operating Bases (DOBs) for refueling. Surviving aircraft from the first wave are to recover at MOBs and DOBs for re-sortie preparation. The timing is critical and the aircraft and forces on the bases will be vulnerable to attack. NATO can disrupt the operation, reduce sortie rates, and deny recovery and reinforcement if the MOBs are attacked while the Pact air operation is underway.

This would require an ability to assess that NATO is under a massive attack and have a quick-reaction force which could retaliate on the MOBs *while under attack, in all weather and night conditions.* The counter-attack must take place *within 15 or 30 minutes* to be successful in suppressing the MOB operation.

The proposed suppression method envisions repeated attacks by long-range ballistic missiles with hard-structure submunitions, accurately delivered. These could damage runways and taxiways thereby denying the use of these bases for a critical period of time — say two or three days. The Soviet/Pact air armies therefore would be locked out of these Main Operating Bases and would have to go to unhardened Dispersed Operating Bases where they would now come under attack by NATO ground-attack aircraft. The DOBs have few aircraft shelters and are not as heavily defended as the MOBs. The aircraft on the ground would be vulnerable to NATO ground-attack aircraft using low-level strafing attacks and saturation attacks delivering available mines and unguided area munitions (the Federal Republic of Germany's MW-1 dispenser, the British BP-755, the American Low Altitude Dispenser (LADS)/Combined Effects Munitions, etc.). DOB attack effectiveness could be maximized by using Airborne Warning And Control System (AWACS) aircraft information to inform the attackers as to which DOBs are occupied. Thus, Pact aircraft could be more efficiently destroyed on the ground.

A similar "one-two" missile-and-aircraft punch is proposed for the interdiction mission. Accurate guided missiles would be used to attack the "choke points," destroying bridges, railheads and road junctions in the first few hours after a Pact attack on NATO. This would be followed by manned aircraft attack of the ground forces which would accumulate behind the interdicted points. This would give the aircraft very large and vulnerable targets. And it would give NATO the option of containing the attack *on Pact territory.*

Under the proposal, those two critical and time-urgent missions, counter-air and interdiction, now expected to be executed primarily by nuclear forces, could be accomplished with non-nuclear forces. This change could be accomplished in the near future. An initial operational capability (IOC) could be achieved by 1986 if an early decision were made.

It should be emphasized that these critical targets, in fixed and well-known positions, would require no advances in target-acquisition capabilities. Further, the number of these critical targets is quite limited; there are about 30 to 40 MOBs and an equal number of DOBs in the high-threat area. About 100 interdiction points would need to be suppressed for a similar period of time.

It must be emphasized, too, that the missile force component for this concept is primarily a *suppression* force against MOB operations and the interdiction targets. The main destructive force would be manned aircraft using area munitions which are available but would need to be procured in large numbers. The suppression operation would likely need to be repeated over a period of days to suppress again those MOBs which have had their runways and taxiways repaired. Similarly, repeated attacks would be required against the interdiction points as repairs were made or as tactical bridging was installed.

Time is the essential element in dealing with these suppression missions. If the theater air-offensive operation cannot be defeated in two or three days, NATO will be defeated or be forced into an early use of nuclear weapons.

Being able to execute these *suppression* missions with conventional forces would relieve NATO of the necessity of early dependence on nuclear strikes to blunt the aggressive ground and air attacks. The missile systems would be designed to launch while under attack. Survivability would be achieved by basing the missiles in standard aircraft hangarettes, hardened against conventional and chemical attack. Alternatively, a mobile-basing capability could be provided for these missiles or for a Ground Launched Cruise Missile version.

A key benefit of this concept — attack of *fixed* hardened, defended MOBs and interdiction points by missiles and follow-up aircraft attacks on DOBs and choked-up ground forces — would be less attrition of NATO's valuable but limited penetrating ground-attack aircraft. They could be more usefully used to attack *mobile* ground forces and aircraft on the ground. This appears a more logical role for manned aircraft with their large and deadly firepower capabilities.

A *minimum* number of 900 suppression missiles would be needed for the counter-air and interdiction missions. The cost of these missiles, their basing, and the ten-year manning needs would be about $2.3 billion. These costs should be shared by NATO nations based on the prorated costs of maintaining today's counter-air and interdiction capabilities (roughly

30 percent for the U.S., 40 percent for the Federal Republic of Germany, etc.).

The Missions of Defeating Pact Mobile Ground Forces — Echeloned and in Contact

Whereas the first two missions involve fixed targets, these two missions involve mobile targets. To defeat mobile ground forces — echeloned, follow-on, and "in contact" — requires adoption of several advances in technology, primarily in methods of real-time surveillance, automated targeting, and information development. This must then be coupled to precision-guided delivery systems with *terminally guided* submunitions and new and clever mines. The targeting methods attempt to turn mobile targets into "fixed" targets by assessing past and present locations and predicting probable future locations. A description of a proposed capability for accomplishing these missions will now be discussed in the context of a notional concept for an integrated forward defense of NATO.

A NOTIONAL CONCEPT FOR AN INTEGRATED FORWARD DEFENSE OF NATO[5]

"Holding at Risk" and Defending Forward

The proposed concept of operations for a NATO forward defense requires that all Soviet power projection forces be "held at risk" by NATO nuclear or advanced conventional forces. "Hold at risk" means to:

1. continuously target enemy forces with operationally ready U.S./ Allied nuclear forces; and
2. maintain the ability to execute limited or major strikes quickly across the full range of echeloned forces, as well as on threatening military forces in the Soviet Union.

The concept is analogous to current U.S. strategic capabilities and planning, but it adds the task of targeting Soviet mobile forces.

For NATO's modernized *conventional* deterrent to be successful, NATO's defense must be able to accomplish the suppression of the Warsaw Pact's offensive air operations, interdiction of key targets supporting Soviet logistic operations, and the attrition of a large number of Soviet combat units at a high rate. For example, one Warsaw Pact breakthrough operation could feature 600 tanks, 500 armored fighting vehicles, about 50 batteries of artillery, almost 200 surface-to-air missiles (SAMs) and air-defense guns, and more than 3,000 trucks. As many as six major break-through efforts could be proceeding simultaneously.

The challenge to a NATO conventional response is thus heavy, but it is not insurmountable if appropriate modernization measures are under-taken. Also, existing assets, particularly NATO's tactical air forces, must be re-allocated. NATO's air forces in Central Europe would need to ex-ecute thousands of attack sorties per day. To achieve this, all NATO air bases would have to be kept operating at high efficiency — an extremely difficult assignment in face of the Pact's attack potential. This is why a conventional counter-air operation is vitally needed if early use of nuclear weapons is to be avoided.

The number of successful conventional air sorties required to cope with the described breakthrough operations, using today's weapons ("iron" bombs and low-rate-of-fire precision-guided munitions), are sub-stantially beyond NATO's current capabilities. Technologically advanced area munitions and better dispensers, however, could reduce these sortie requirements by a factor of 10 to 50.

For example, studies show that the target array for a single break-through, described above, would require NATO to execute the following *successful* attack sorties:

— 5,500 aircraft sorties expending 33,000 metric tons of unguided gravity bombs, or
— 600 sorties using anti-armor unguided submunitions (3,000 metric tons), or
— 50 to l00 sorties using terminally guided anti-armor submunitions (TGSM) (500 metric tons).

A metric ton of terminally guided anti-armor submunitions would have a "kill" effectiveness against company-sized units of armored vehicles roughly equivalent to a low-yield fission or enhanced radiation weapon.

Theater-Wide Information Development

Systems for surveillance, integrated operations planning, and targeting are essential to an integrated concept of operation for the new conventional forces. NATO's conventional forces will have to be improved and struc-tured so as to be capable of inflicting annihilating levels of damage on

Warsaw Pact first- and second-echeloned forces. (The Soviets define "annihilation" as 60 percent destruction of a given unit.) NATO theater nuclear forces, including those elements of U.S. strategic forces committed to the NATO Triad of strategic nuclear, theater nuclear and conventional forces, will be assigned the task of holding Soviet/Pact projection forces at risk, forcing their dispersion, imposing constraints on their command and control and on their mobility and massing, and increasing their susceptibility to non-nuclear attack.

The proposed concept of continually pre-planning, targeting, and exercising conventional forces is quite analogous to what is now conducted by the U.S./NATO Joint Strategic Targeting Planning Staff for strategic nuclear forces in the Single Integrated Operational Plan (SIOP) and SACEUR's Nuclear Operation Plan (NOP). In the application of this concept to NATO, the pre-planned targeting options would include most of the forces of the Warsaw Pact field armies, the nuclear and chemical-capable units of the ground and air armies, and the surface-to-surface rockets of the Soviet field armies opposite NATO.

A key part of the concept would be the perfection of a theater information system. One of the greatest deficiencies in NATO's posture today is lack of timely information on the past, present, and expected future status and location of Warsaw Pact forces. Yet, for NATO to be able to position and successfully engage numerically superior Soviet/Pact forces, such timely information is needed with respect to enemy forces in depth.

Again, the technological components of such a theater-wide surveillance system are available but need to be "wired together." The major components are the following:

- Electro-optical imagery and signal sensors and airborne motion-detection radar (and other sensors) with the ability to locate enemy units — which are either transmitting or moving — quickly and accurately.
- Low-cost digital data-processing systems and display systems permitting real-time processing of operationally significant information to be provided to commanders quickly.
- Grid systems allowing the integration of information and locations of both NATO forces and Soviet and Pact forces all referred to a common grid *to turn mobile warfare into positional warfare*.

Figure 2 displays a conceptual description of a peacetime multi-sensor system. This array would be costly and therefore limited in number. Operated largely as a peacetime system, it would have the main objectives of information gathering and tracking to avoid surprise and deception. In wartime, low-altitude penetrating systems would be required in addition. Larger numbers would be required for survivability reasons. Miniaturization of the available sensors is underway and could be fitted to "stealthy" drones having low observables. The information derived from wartime systems would be "fused" with other battle-management systems such as AWACS.

Not only would the implementation of a theater information system reap all the military benefits associated with improved and comprehensive intelligence — earlier warning of attack, timely mobilization and deployment of defending forces, and the conduct of the kinds of integrated operations and targeting that have been described above — but it would exert a deterrent effect in its own right. A military commander who knows that his forces are under constant and detailed surveillance will move those forces differently. He might reach for counter measures, but these will be costly and time-consuming at best. And these constraints would apply particularly to the Soviets, whose penchant for secrecy and surprise seem well-nigh obsessive.

The kind of comprehensive plan of integrated operations that has been outlined would require some restructuring of NATO planning staffs. Thus, conventional and nuclear-strike planning could be integrated and expanded at each division and corps. This planning function would serve as a strong "demand" function on the information system for information on the location and status of Soviet forces for targeting purposes. Information on the status of NATO forces would be needed as well, for purposes of mobilization and movement. As Soviet forces change their disposition, NATO could maneuver its forces correspondingly in order to defend effectively with conventional forces against the altered Soviet force formations.

New Conventional Munitions — Nuclear "Equivalence"

The new conventional attack systems proposed for deep attack envision a family of medium-range surface-to-surface (SSM) and stand-off air-to-surface missiles which could be targeted by the new theater information system. The missiles would be equipped with terminally guided submunitions (TGSM) which would seek out their targets. For shorter-range attacks, terminally guided submunitions could be fitted to mortars, such as the Multiple Launch Rocket System (MLRS).

FIGURE 2. PEACETIME SURVEILLANCE AND WARNING SYSTEM

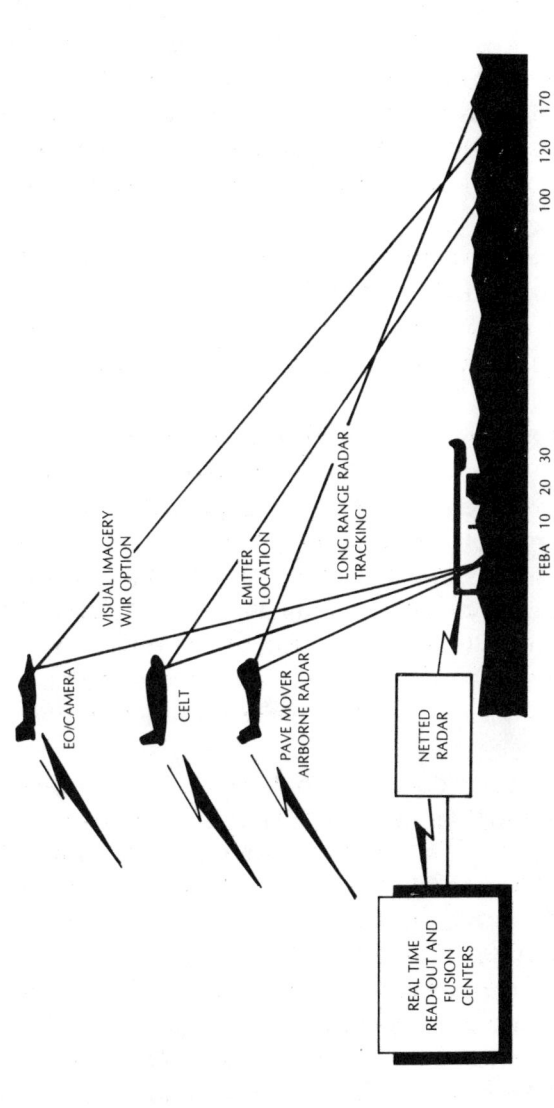

EO—Electro-Optical Imaging Camera provides real-time visual observations over hundreds of kilometers

CELT—A signal analyzer to develop precise locations of electronic emitters

Pave Mover Airborne Radar—A long range detection, classification and tracking radar which also provides guidance information to air or ground launched missiles

Netted Radar—A ground surveillance radar system which can detect people, vehicles and low flying aircraft at ranges of 10, 20, 30 km, respectively

FEBA—Forward Edge of the Battle Area

It is in this area that one can best understand the nuclear "equivalence" comparison that was referred to earlier. Two examples are provided.

The first example is an attack on an armored unit. The target in Figure 3 is 13 armored vehicles in a transit mode along a road. The attacking system is the Multiple Launch Rocket System equipped with terminally guided weapons known as Skeet. Two salvoes of six rockets each are fired and dispense 72 Skeet Delivery Vehicles (SDV) (Figure 4). Each Skeet Delivery Vehicle contains four terminally guided Skeet munitions, each of which has a search mode to detect the "hot spot" of vehicle engines and exhaust systems.

A composite of search patterns for the 288 warheads is shown in Figure 5. The elliptical pattern shows the search area of the munition's infrared sensor. The calculations show that all of the armored vehicles in this target array would be destroyed by this dense cluster of terminally homing weapons.

For a comparison to the effects of nuclear weapons, in Figure 6 we overlay the nuclear radiation kill radius of a 0.1 kiloton normal fission nuclear weapon. This effect, which could be generated by the current W-48 155 mm artillery shell, is about 400 meters in radius. Also superimposed is the nuclear radiation kill radius of a 1 kiloton enhanced radiation weapon — the so-called "Neutron Weapon" Artillery Shell — which has a kill radius of 730 meters. The numbers of vehicles killed is the same as for the Skeet attack. The difference would be that all tank crews would be immediately incapacitated by the radiation from the nuclear weapons.

Thus, battlefield nuclear deterrence options could be achieved by a conventional deterrence option in this example. It is anticipated that the described terminally guided submunitions could, in the future, have a revolutionary effect. They could have an impact on combined arms combat forces (which depend on large numbers of armored vehicles) as severe as the machine gun had on infantry forces in World War I.

The other example pertaining to "equivalence" is that of contrasting the number of weapons required to destroy 60 percent of a Soviet armored division, the Soviet criterion for "annihilation" (see Table 2). This target would contain about 400 armored vehicles, about 2,500 trucks, air defense vehicles and artillery tubes. If aircraft armed with conventional 250-kilogram unguided bombs were used, it would require 2,200 *successful* sorties to achieve the 60 percent destruction level. If available unguided submunitions were used on this target array, similar to those in the West

FIGURE 3.   TARGET—ARMOR CONVOY (13 TANKS)

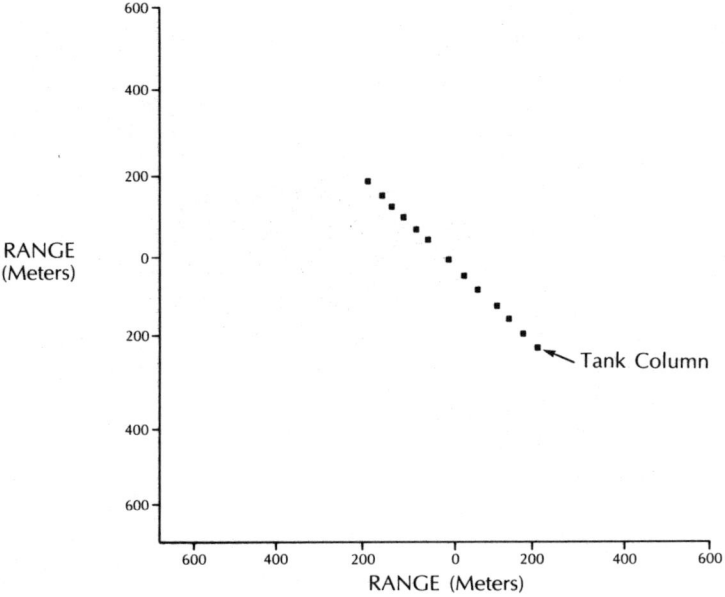

FIGURE 4.   TARGET ENGAGEMENT—34 KM RANGE

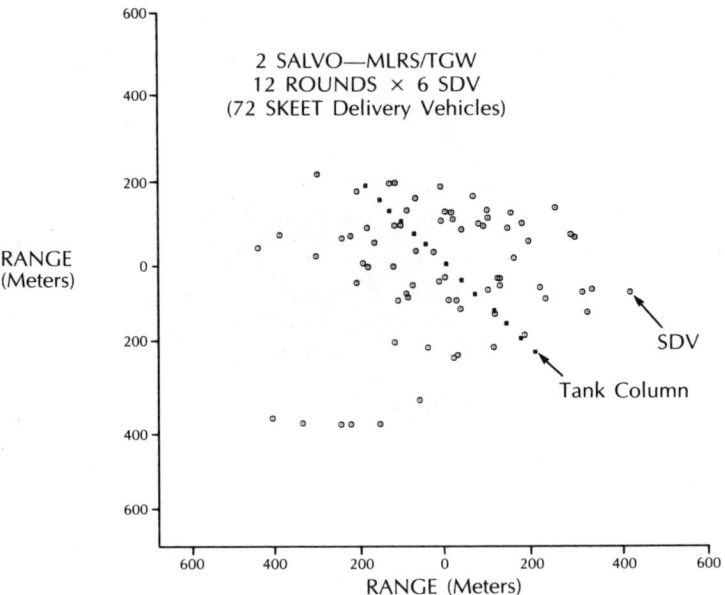

FIGURE 5. SKEET MUNITION SEARCH/ATTACK PATTERN

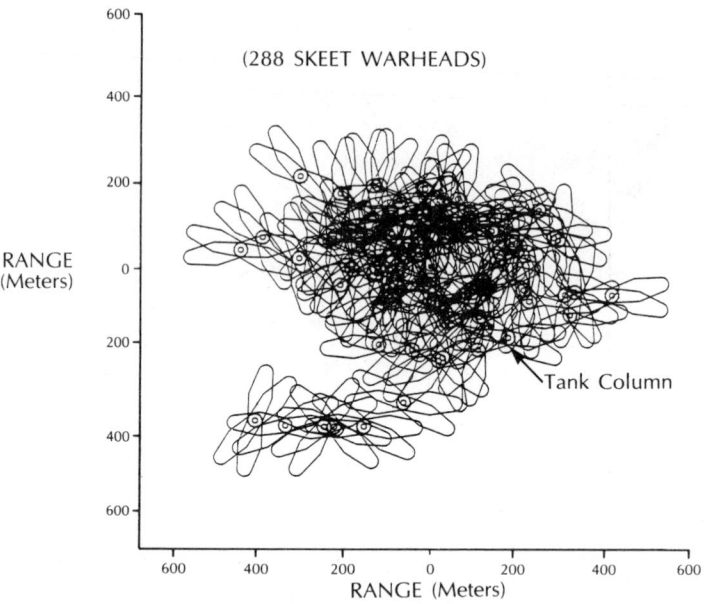

FIGURE 6. COMPARISON OF SKEET ATTACK WITH LOW YIELD NUCLEAR WEAPONS

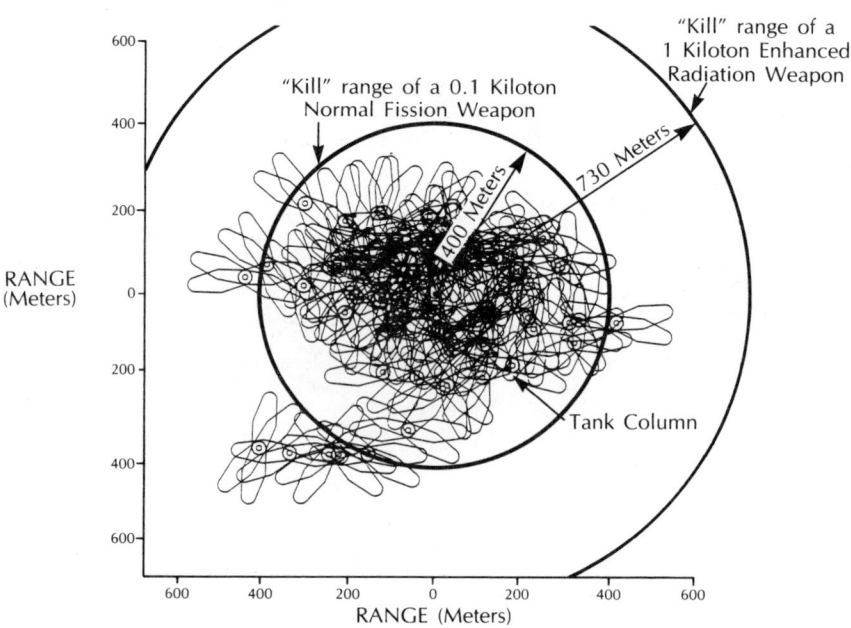

German MW-1/Tornado System, approximately 300 successful sorties would be required. If these aircraft were equipped with dispensers having terminally guided submunitions similar to the Skeet munitions described above, it would require only 50 to 60 successful sorties. On the basis of the current SACEUR collateral-damage constraints for nuclear weapons, it would require 20 to 25 nuclear attack sorties using 10-kiloton weapons to achieve "annihilation" levels.

Therefore, combining the advances in target acquisition, tracking and engagement with terminally guided submunitions, one can see that NATO could approach a credible conventional defense having nuclear "equivalence" for the mission of attacking mobile ground forces.

Further descriptions of the missile candidates for counter-air, interdiction, and deep attack of Pact ground forces will be covered later in this paper, along with estimates of their acquisition and operation costs.

Table 2

MISSION EFFECTIVENESS FOR AIRCRAFT WITH VARIOUS MUNITIONS

Successful Aircraft Sorties Required to Destroy 60% of a Soviet Armored Division (3,000 vehicles)			
5 Metric Ton Payload (Tornado/F-111)			
	Current 250 KG "Iron" Bombs	Unguided[1] Submunitions	Terminally Guided[2] Submunitions
Required Sorties	2,200	300	50-60[3]

1. FRG MW-1 Dispenser with KB-44 shaped charge and mines or USAF Low Altitude Dispensers (LADS) with combined effects bomblets and mines.
2. Skeet or TGSM systems
3. These sorties could be accomplished by aircraft carrying 2 air-to-surface missiles or a salvo of 2 surface-to-surface missiles per company sized target.

CHANGED ROLES FOR MODERNIZED NUCLEAR FORCES

In a discussion of moving from primary nuclear dependence for executing certain missions to a greater role for conventional forces, some raise the question as to what purposes, if any, nuclear forces should serve.

The "if any" question can be put to rest quickly. As long as the Soviets present *any* theater nuclear threat to NATO, it must have *at least* a deterrent-retaliatory capability to deter Soviet use of nuclear weapons. The question then is what force levels and posture would meet this minimal requirement? Next, what qualitative characteristics should such a force have?

An important principle, borne out by observing changes, over the years, in Soviet doctrinal patterns for survivable deployments, has been formulated:

The realistic threat of the use of nuclear weapons will enhance NATO's ability to defend with conventional forces.

The effect of battlefield nuclear weapons, and, more important, the medium-range aircraft weapons, on Soviet doctrine and tactics when those weapons were first introduced in the mid-1950s, has been remarkable. The Soviets went through great restructuring of their large conventional forces to achieve survivability for conventional operations. They adopted a concept of dispersal and echeloning of forces which, while giving higher levels of survivability, introduced vulnerabilities and complexities in their operations which were previously described.

An example of the doctrinal and tactical impact of the threat of NATO's early nuclear posture can be seen in Figure 7, showing the evolution of densities of Soviet ground forces over the years.[6] In the postwar era Soviet Fronts, Armies, and divisions were heavily massed. Division densities were about 5,000 troops in areas of about ten square kilometers — that is, about 500 per square kilometer.

When NATO forces were equipped with nuclear artillery and short-range rockets in the mid-1960s all deployment areas were increased. Division densities now became about ten troops per square kilometer. This was so even though Soviet division troop sizes grew by about 70 percent. As the Soviets improved their ground-force mobility with the advent of high-quality armored personnel carriers (BMP/BMD), self-propelled artillery and air defense systems, and new 10-ton trucks manufactured at the Kama truck plant with Western technology and assistance, they were able

FIGURE 7. EVOLUTION OF DENSITIES OF SOVIET GROUND FORCES

	FRONT		ARMY		DIVISION		DENSITY
	Width	Depth	Width	Depth	Width	Depth	TROOPS/KM²
1945	100 × 40 KM		20 × 10 KM		2-3 × 3 KM		
	80,000		23,000		5,000		500
				NATO NUCLEAR THREAT			
1960-1965	250 × 350 KM		75 × 100 KM		25 × 35 KM		
	150,000		44,000		8,500		10
			IMPROVED SOVIET MOBILITY				
NOW	165-230 × 180 KM		80 × 100 KM		20 × 30 KM		
	230,000		63,000		12,000		20

to increase the density of their now enlarged divisions to about 20 troops per square kilometer. The impact of NATO short-range systems on close-in Soviet forces over the years (at the Forward Edge of the Battle Area (FEBA)) can be seen in specific detail in Figure 8.

Lance deployments had the effect of further stretching division deployments into echeloned posture. For the future, more survivable medium-range missile systems should provide the hold-at-risk function to maintain this stretch-out for the more mobile and high fire-power Soviet divisions operating as Operational Maneuver Groups (OMG).

But the "advantage" of the short-range battlefield systems was a waning one. Their threat ran out in the mid-70s when the Soviets introduced rapid-fire long-range conventional artillery able to destroy NATO's 15-km-range nuclear-artillery capability.

Now, the political and military price NATO is paying for this large inventory of short-range weapons is onerous. The Europeans and others now seriously question the credibility of these forces as being able to defend Western Europe.[7]

Given such an inventory the perception is that NATO intends to fight with nuclear weapons on friendly territory. This is a militarily unsound posture. It is a politically disastrous posture.

Future nuclear forces should include longer-range strike systems in sufficient quantity to be able to threaten and hold at risk Soviet/Pact forces throughout the depth of their deployment. The main objective should be to threaten *Soviet* power projection and follow-on forces in Second and Third Front organizations deep in Pact territory and the Western Military Districts. In the near term, a portion of this missile force should have sufficient accuracy and effective low-yield warhead capabilities to threaten close-in forces 20 to 30 km from the battle area. These would cover the Pact second-echelon regiments and divisions.

Assuming NATO decides to field the types of advanced conventional weapon systems having the described nuclear "equivalence" capabilities, this deterrent role could shift to them.

CANDIDATE MODERN CONVENTIONAL WEAPON SYSTEMS AND COSTS

Counter-Air and Interdiction Operations

Under the postulated concept, the main objective for the counter-air mission is the suppression of those Main Operating Bases which support

FIGURE 8. EVOLUTION OF DENSITIES—SOVIET DIVISIONS UNDER NUCLEAR THREAT

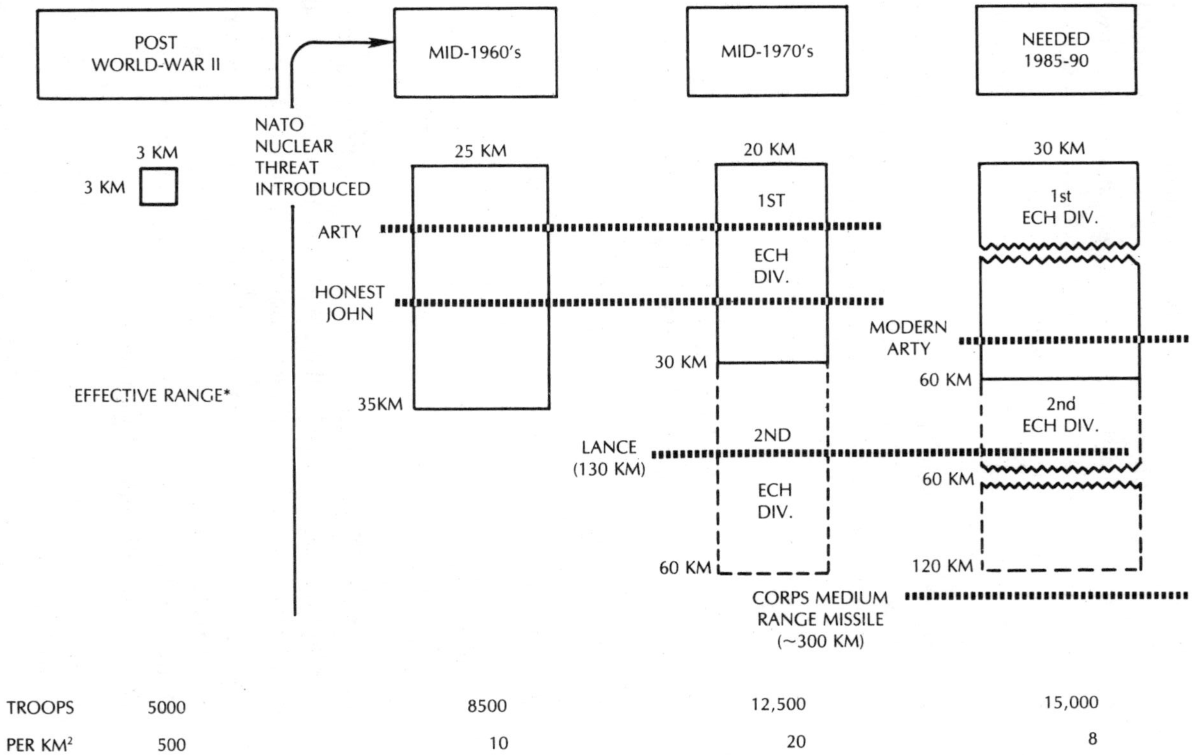

	POST WORLD-WAR II	MID-1960's	MID-1970's	NEEDED 1985-90
TROOPS	5000	8500	12,500	15,000
PER KM²	500	10	20	8

*NATO ARTILLERY AND SURFACE-TO-SURFACE MISSILES DEPLOYED ⅓ RANGE BEHIND FEBA

Pact offensive ground-attack operations. There are at least five options for executing this mission with non-nuclear forces.

1. Attack by manned aircraft. (This is a current option). It is estimated that four F-4 aircraft with runway attack munitions would be required per runway for this mission.[8] These attack aircraft would be accompanied by about 6 to 8 protective aircraft (MIGCAP, ECM, Defense Suppression, etc.). Attrition estimates for the attack aircraft run from 20 to 50 percent against those heavily defended Main Operating Bases.

2. Five cruise missiles of the Medium-Range Air-to-Surface Missiles (MRASM) type would be needed per runway, plus delivery aircraft or a similar number of Ground Launched Cruise Missiles.

Attack by ballistic missiles could be executed by one of three currently proposed methods:

3. CAM-40, a 40-inch solid rocket booster using the Pershing II single-or-double-stage rocket. (Based in West Germany the single-stage system could cover the high-threat 57 Main Operating Bases and 48 Dispersed Operating Bases; the two-stage system could pick up the remaining 16 Main Operating Bases and 20 Dispersed Operating Bases in Eastern Europe.) The CAM-40 would have a terminally guided "bus" filled with kinetic energy penetrators (KEP) fused to explode beneath the runway (see Figure 9). It is estimated that three CAM-40 missiles would be required per runway or taxiway.

4. BOSS/AXE. This is a large booster based on the Trident missile. A larger payload similar to the CAM-40 kinetic energy penetrators could be carried. One missile would be required per runway.

5. Total Air Base Attack System (TABAS). This is a very large multiple booster system carrying a 25-metric-ton kinetic energy penetrator payload which is estimated to take out an airbase including "bonus" kill of support facilities.

The cost estimate below (see Table 3) is based on CAM-40 since the components (booster, guidance, and penetrators) have been developed and tested. This same missile was costed for the interdiction mission. The second "punch" for the counter-air and interdiction mission would be accomplished by all-weather F-111 and Tornado aircraft with area mu-

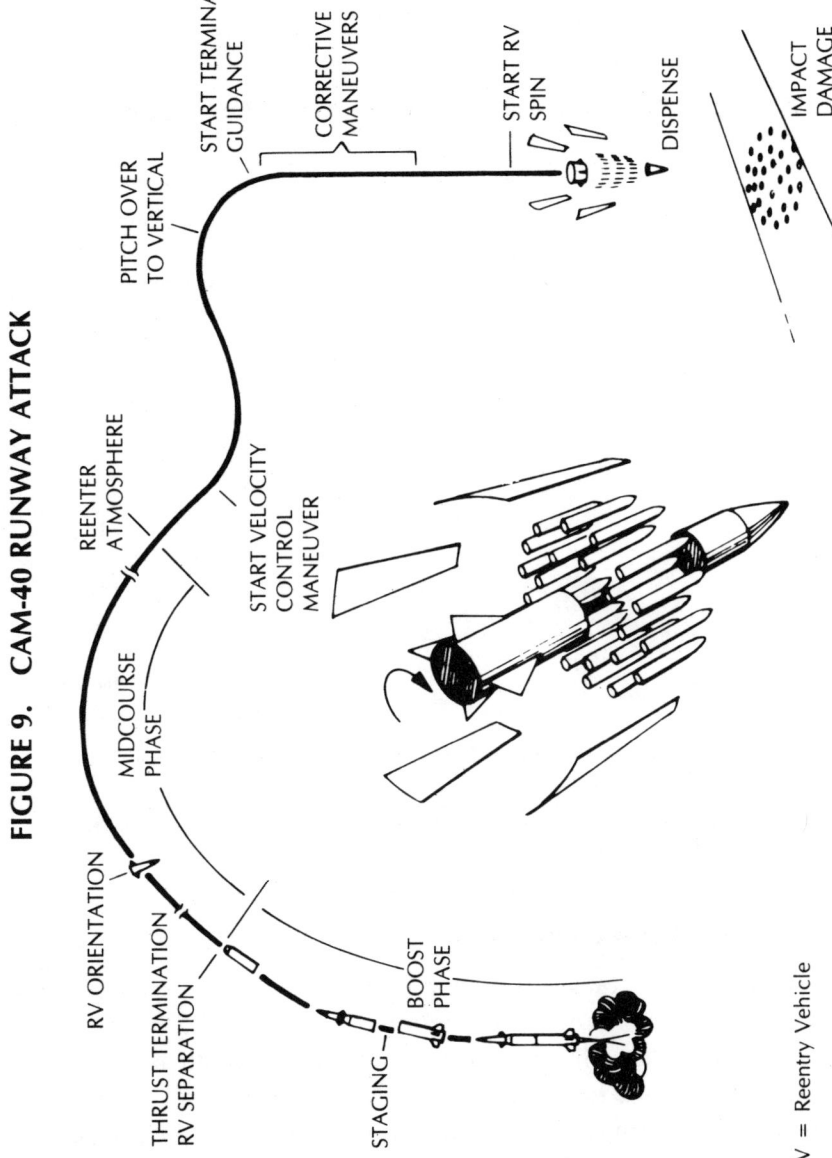

FIGURE 9. CAM-40 RUNWAY ATTACK

RV = Reentry Vehicle

nitions. These costs were not estimated since the majority of the costs have been sunk.

Table 3

COSTS — COUNTER-AIR AND INTERDICTION MISSIONS

Objectives:

- Close 30 Main Operating Air Bases for 3 Days (600 missiles)
- Interdict about 100 choke points (300 missiles)
- Base missiles in standard aircraft shelters

  — 8 missiles per shelter: 110 shelters total
  — Hardened against chemical/conventional attack

CAM-40

Missiles	$1.8 billion
Shelters	0.22 billion
People (10 years)	0.25 billion
Total	2.3 billion

These figures do not include the costs of Tornado/MW-1 or F-111/LADS with airfield-attack munitions.

Counter-Ground-Force Operations

Attack of mobile forces requires a large number of weapon systems having high engagement rates and terminally guided area weapons. In addition, real-time surveillance and targeting systems would be required to essentially turn mobile targets into "positional" targets.

NATO ground armies would require a capability in support of Corps operations. NATO air operations would include suppression of air defenses (mobile and fixed) plus deep attack on Soviet follow-on ground forces.

Several missile options can be pursued based on available booster systems (for example, the T-22/Lance and/or the T-16/Patriot/Assault Breaker). The costs were derived on the T-16/Assault Breaker/Skeet technology base simply because it has had considerable development and demonstration.

The costs for the described Army executed mission follow:

Table 4

CORPS SUPPORT WEAPON SYSTEM — CSWS

Objective:

- Destroy 2nd-echelon and follow-on regiments, divisions
    - 1 battalion per Corps; 18 launchers per battalion
    - 72 missiles on launchers; 72 immediate reloads
    - 360 missiles per Corps
    - 3,000 Corps Support Weapons Systems in Central Region

per Corps

Missiles (@ $600,000)	$0.22 billion
Vehicles, etc.	0.01 billion
People (10 year costs)	0.10 billion
Total	0.33 billion

Central Region (8 Corps)	2.64 billion
Surveillance/Targeting per Corps	0.15 billion
Surveillance/Targeting Total Central Region	1.20 billion

Costing on a Corps basis indicates the burden-sharing possibilities for NATO, i.e., two U.S. Corps, 25 percent; three German Corps, 35-40 percent; British Corps, 10 percent, etc.

The costs for Air Force executed missions follow:

Table 5

AIR FORCE MISSION COSTS — ATTACK OF DELAYED/DISRUPTED GROUND FORCES AND MOBILE AIR DEFENSE

CONVENTIONAL STAND-OFF WEAPON — CSW

Objective:

• Destroy air defense system and follow-on forces at choke points and enroute

— 30 Aircraft/Corps; 2 Sorties/Day
— 2,000 CSW in Central Europe

2,000 CSW	$1.2	billion
People (10 years)	0.30	billion
Equipment	0.005	billion
Total Central Region	1.51	billion
Surveillance/Targeting Costs	0.50	billion

Attack of Pact ground forces in direct contact (0-30 km) can be accomplished with one of several candidates. Ground-launched Corps Support missiles (CSWS) or air-delivered missiles with terminally guided submunitions could be used. However, NATO division and regimental level commanders would prefer weapon systems under their immediate control. Originally, nuclear battlefield short-range missiles and artillery shells were intended to be readily available to these commanders when, in the mid-1950s, these weapons were introduced as extensions of conventional firepower. This concept and these weapons, of course, are no longer considered suitable for the purpose of defeating massive armored attacks in localized battle situations. An attractive conventional alternative would be the provision of terminally guided submunitions to close-support weapons such as the Multiple Launch Rocket System (MLRS).

The example discussed earlier in connection with "nuclear equivalence" was the application of the Skeet munition to the Multiple Launch

Rocket System. This terminally guided weapon system would constitute an alternative option to nuclear artillery shells. The ongoing Multiple Launch Rocket System program could be modified to adapt Skeet to provide this option in an estimated five years. The additional cost for an inventory capable of one thousand engagements — i.e., 1,000 enemy armored companies — is estimated to be about $200 million (see Appendix to this paper).

Target acquisition and engagement could be generally satisfied by available sensors now in the field. However, more effective sensors and target-processing systems would be desirable. The proposed Theater Information System and Netted Ground Surveillance Radar System previously described (Figure 2) should be pursued for this mission.

Overall Central Region costs for missiles, basing, manpower, and surveillance and targeting systems are:

Table 6

COST SUMMARY — CENTRAL REGION

CAM-40	$2.30 billion
Corps Support Weapon Systems	2.64 billion
Conventional Stand-off Weapon	1.51 billion
Missile Total	6.45 billion
Surveillance/Targeting	1.70 billion
Multiple Launch Rocket System/Terminally Guided Weapons	.20 billion
Total	8.35 billion

The funds estimated to complete Research, Development, Test and Evaluation for the specified missions are:

CAM-40	$150 million
Conventional Stand-off Weapon	380 million
Corps Support Weapon Systems	420 million
Surveillance/Targeting	100 million
Total	1,050 million

Schedule and Further Development

Conservative estimates indicate that a *fixed target* conventional counter-air and interdiction system could be operational in NATO by 1986. This requires political will and a decision to substitute, for these missions, conventional capabilities for nuclear.

The *mobile target* capabilities could be developed by about 1988, since considerable development, testing, and evaluation and engineering for production of the terminally guided submunitions are required. The surveillance and targeting Theater Information System (TIS) could be operational in a survivable mode by 1986 as well.

An advanced development program on countermeasure resistance for terminally guided submunitions and other terminally guided weapons is crucially needed. More advanced infrared and millimeter-wave homing devices are needed. Passive homing systems, based on radiometry techniques appears feasible and should be pursued.

FORCE AND POLICY RESTRUCTURING

Feasibility of Conventional Deterrence — Consideration of Roles and Missions

A strong conventional defense of Western Europe is feasible. The foregoing discussion and cost estimates indicate that initially four major mission areas could be executed with non-nuclear forces. These capabilities could be available in this decade and at a *minimum* ten-year cost of less than $10 billion. Given these new capabilities, we should examine what force restructuring might be needed. The counter-air mission can be viewed as an element of the conventional air defense problem. However, NATO has a serious problem in availability of aircraft to perform the air defense mission (air superiority over NATO territory) *and* simultaneously to do the suppression of air bases. Further, ground-attack aircraft for deep strikes against follow-on Pact ground forces are in very short supply.

Thus, a restructuring of the conventional force capabilities should be based on providing surface-to-surface missiles with "smart" payloads which can perform the now *nuclear* counter-air and interdiction missions. There will be a "cultural" problem within NATO air forces to turn from aircraft to the missile mode of attack. But, these are Air Force missions and the counter-air role for missiles should be looked at as part of the overall superiority mission. The Luftwaffe presents an interesting opportunity since the Luftwaffe operates both aircraft and surface-to-surface Pershing missiles. They have the responsibility for supporting both missions and, in fact, have the infrastructure for a missile system such as the CAM-40 based as it is on Pershing technology. They also have responsibility for the air bases on which it is proposed that these counter-air missiles be based. Perhaps the Luftwaffe could undertake this mission for the entire Central Region.

No changes in roles are necessary for attack of ground forces since these missions currently fall within both Army and Air Force purview.

Nuclear Force Restructuring — Inventory and Levels

The most significant restructuring would come in NATO's nuclear forces. This would be a consequence of providing a wide range of conventional-force options aimed at raising the nuclear threshold. The major restructuring would come in the area of battlefield nuclear systems. These weapons should be de-emphasized. This is a political imperative since it is clear that Western Europe should not be perceived as being a nuclear battlefield by the very populace which NATO is dedicated to protect. Thus, we should look toward reducing the large inventory of nuclear artillery shells and substantial number of atomic demolition munitions (ADMs) now contemplated for barrier production. The ADMs suffer from the knowledge that their use is intended primarily on friendly soil. This has always been a political problem underscored by the fact that there are strong doubts that these weapons would ever be used. They add little to deterrence.

The fixed nuclear air defense system using Nike Hercules missiles will be phased out and a large number of warheads will ultimately be retired. The main problem with the Nike Hercules is that it lacks survivability under conventional attack and will be a prime target for Soviet conventional aircraft in the first hours of any aggression. However, this nuclear threat still imposes restrictions and constraints on the Soviet use of their air power, denying them the ability to run rapid attack waves or massed high-altitude attacks. Thus, a nuclear air defense system does have desirable "hold-at-risk" functions. A future air defense system based on Patriot should have a small percentage of the force equipped with nuclear warheads to provide a nuclear threat.

The current Gravity Bomb inventory should be replaced with modern bombs having enhanced security and safety features. (This process is already ongoing, according to recent Congressional testimony.) The inventory of Gravity Bombs for aircraft could be reduced, given the fact that air operations under the postulated Forward Defense concept would have mainly conventional missions.

Reduced levels of nuclear weapons are possible and, in some cases, desirable. The current inventory of largely obsolete nuclear weapons requires a large investment in manpower which could be beneficially applied to other areas. The short-range weapon systems require considerable manpower since they are widely dispersed to support tactical units. Some have criticized the security arrangements for this class of weapons. Removing and retiring these weapons would aid in the resolution of supposed security problems.

Another beneficial effect would be the availability of special nuclear materials for other uses. A heavy investment in fissile material is represented here.

Finally, the proposed reductions could be the basis for a sensible arms control initiative for NATO.

Strategy and Missions

Future NATO nuclear forces should have two deterrent purposes. First, to hold Soviet conventional and nuclear forces at risk which would thereby enhance NATO's conventional defense potential. Second, to provide a retaliatory capability if Soviet nuclear weapons are used. This modern and survivable nuclear force should have targeting options which emphasize threats against Soviet ground and air forces in Eastern Europe and the Soviet Union. *The highest targeting priority should be focused on the Soviet's most valuable asset — the Red Army.*

Other goals for this modern nuclear force would be to greatly increase survivability through providing longer-range weapon systems. The "mix" should be about 70 percent long-range systems versus today's 70 percent inventory allocation of short-range systems. This will allow rearward basing which should help survivability. Further, the major portion of NATO's nuclear forces should be mobile, which would allow survivability options emphasizing dispersal and deception.

A new military strategy for NATO is not necessary. The current strategy of Flexible Response is adequate for the proposed integrated conventional/nuclear modernization force. Any suggestion for a new strategy to encompass possible changing roles between conventional and nuclear forces should be avoided. History shows that to make even modest changes in official NATO strategy documents would lead to endless discussions which could only hinder the fielding of new conventional capabilities for NATO.

Other Issues

Dual-Capability Weapon Systems

Dual capability — the ability of a particular delivery system to use either nuclear or conventional weapons — has come under a great deal of criticism, particularly in the area of verification of arms control measures. Historically, dual-capable systems were foreordained when nuclear weapons were added to conventional forces in the fifties as extensions of conventional firepower. Thus, aircraft, battlefield missiles, and artillery shells were designed for both conventional and nuclear payloads. This, of course, aided in the economy of manpower and introduced a great uncertainty into Soviet offensive plans since it would have been very difficult to determine whether or not their forces would be faced by nuclear opposition.

Today, NATO has a wide range of dual-capable and single-capable systems as shown in Table 7.

Those who propose that future restructuring include eliminating dual capabilities must not forget that NATO is faced by a wide range of dual (or triple) capability on the part of Soviet systems. All of their weapon systems, missiles, and aircraft have the capability for delivery of nuclear, chemical, and conventional payloads. This is even true of long-range systems comparable to the Pershing II which have nuclear and chemical capability — the Scuds and Scaleboards.

If the notional concept for providing conventional alternatives for the missions of counter-air, interdiction, and attack on mobile forces is adopted, mission responsibilities could evolve as follows shown in Table 8.

Possible Soviet and NATO Reactions

What effect might the suggested integrated Forward Defense concept and these new conventional capabilities have on the Soviets?

TABLE 7

NATO DELIVERY SYSTEM CAPABILITIES (Including France)

Dual Capable	Single Capable
	Pershing IA
Short Range	Poseidon
8" Artillery Tube	Polaris
155 mm Artillery Tube	M-20 (France)
Honest John SSM	SSBS-3 (France)
Lance SSM	Atomic Demolition Munition
Pluton SSM (France)	SUBROC
	Pershing II (proposed)
Air Defense	GLCM (proposed)
Nike Hercules SAM	
Aircraft	
F-4	
F-104	
F-16	
F-111	
Buccaneer (U.K.)	
Jaguar (U.K.)	
A-6	
A-7	
Mirage III/IV (France)	
Vulcan (being retired) (U.K.)	
Super Etendard (France)	
Fleet ASW and Air Defense	
Aircraft — P-3, S-2, Nimrod (U.K.)	
ASW (Anti-Submarine Warfare) — ASROC (U.S.)	
AD (Air Defense) — Terrier (U.S.)	

TABLE 8

Dual-Capable Nuclear Components	Conventional "Equivalence" Alternatives*
Nuclear Artillery Short/Medium Range Rockets	MLRS/TGW CSWS
Aircraft: Counter-Air/Interdiction	CAM/BOSS
Aircraft: Attack of Follow-on Forces	CSW/SAW

*MLRS/TGW = Multiple Launch Rocket System/Terminally Guided Weapons
CSWS = Corps Support Weapon System
CAM = Conventional Attack Missile
BOSS = Ballistic Offensive Suppression System
CSW = Conventional Stand-Off Weapon
SAW = Short-Range Stand-off Attack Weapon

- Deterrence options for NATO at the conventional level will be vastly improved over those which have been available since the inception of NATO. Greater survivability for a force with long-range targeting and strike capabilities will put at risk the majority of Soviet follow-on and reserve forces. *This would be a qualitatively new threat to the Red Army.*
- It is postulated that the trend in the correlation-of-forces in their favor in conventional and nuclear forces would be stopped and perhaps reversed.
- A massive reappraisal of their forces, doctrine, and strategy to cope with NATO's new deterrence and defense options would be necessary. (Similar reappraisals occurred in the late 1960s when NATO started introducing precision-guided ground and air weapons. That took five or six years and resulted in some restructuring of their forces and acquisition programs.) New doctrine and tactics might be required for their concepts of offensive operations.

- More expenditures will likely be required in defensive systems, for example, the defense and hardening of aircraft Dispersed Operating Bases. Logistic methods and equipment would be extremely vulnerable to advanced conventional weapons. This could negate large expenditures the Soviets have made in their logistics network, particularly in heavy lift trucks.

What effects might this have on NATO?

- For NATO, some hopeful prospects might be in store. NATO might be able to buy another 30 years of deterrence. A focused approach to the upgrading of conventional forces would be available rather than the across-the-board approach suggested by the U.S. in the Long Term Development Program which has lost support.
- Public support for a concept which moves NATO away from a low-nuclear threshold is anticipated. Politically, the costs for new conventional options appear to be feasible for the Alliance.
- A focused effort which could help NATO get out of its current nuclear "fix" and into a sensible nuclear and conventional posture might restore some cohesion to the Alliance.

CONCLUSIONS

1. Available and demonstrated technology can be exploited to provide new conventional deterrent options and capabilities for NATO.

2. These capabilities would fill serious gaps in NATO's conventional posture and allow less dependence by NATO on possible early use of nuclear weapons.

3. The suggested conventional mission options in counter-air, interdiction, and defeating Warsaw Pact mobile ground forces — echeloned and in contact — could be made available in the period 1986 through 1988, given a timely decision.

4. The capabilities could be had within current and programmed NATO force levels.

5. With effective non-nuclear capabilities for executing the counter-air, interdiction, and counter-ground-force missions, a shift in roles for NATO's conventional and nuclear forces could occur. Modern nuclear forces would perform the "hold-at-risk" and retaliating functions. Modern conventional forces would constitute a formidable war-fighting capability in the event of aggression against NATO.

APPENDIX

Summary of Non-Nuclear Force Components and Costs for Four Important Missions

FIXED TARGETS

MISSION 1 — Counter-Air

Objectives: (1) Suppress approximately 30 Main Operating Bases for 3 days by missile attack; (2) Destroy Pact aircraft (1st and 2nd waves) on Dispersed Operating Bases by NATO aircraft attacks.

MISSION 2 — Interdiction

Objectives: (1) Interdict approximately 100 choke points by missile attack; (2) Attack of disrupted ground forces by NATO aircraft.

WEAPONS AND COSTS OF MISSIONS 1 AND 2

Weapon Systems: (1) Ballistic Missile/Terminally Guided Bus with Kinetic Energy Penetrators (KEP) for runway attack; (2) Manned Aircraft/ Unguided Area Submunitions with variety of unguided combined-effects submunitions (fragmentation, incendiaries, mines) for attack of aircraft and support facilities and personnel.

Costs: $2.3 billion for 900 missiles, 110 fixed shelters, and 10-year operation and maintenance. About 900 people required. Aircraft and air-munitions not included.

Availability: About 3 years (1986) after decision to proceed with completion of test and evaluation and action on acquisition.

MOBILE TARGETS

MISSION 3 — Attack of Echeloned and Follow-On Ground Forces

Objectives: (1) Attack of disrupted and follow-on ground forces, at ranges out to approximately 300 kms. (Includes destruction of supporting fixed and mobile air defenses); (2) Destruction of echeloned and follow-on ground forces (regiments and divisions), at ranges 30 to 100 kms.

Weapon Systems: (1) Air-delivered stand-off guided missiles with terminally guided submunitions, mines, and combined-effects munitions (fragmentation, incendiary, anti-materiel); (2) Ground-launched guided missiles with terminally guided submunitions, mines, and combined-effects munitions.

Surveillance and Targeting Systems Requirements: Airborne and ground-based real-time surveillance, acquisition tracking, and engagement systems with distributed ground-based information fusion centers. "Round the clock" operation in peacetime to avoid surprise and deception. Penetrating systems in wartime to provide battle-management information. Major portions of the sensors are all-weather.

Costs (total Central Region):

(1) Air-delivered Stand-off Missiles. About $1.5 billion for 200 missiles, support equipment and 10-year operating and maintenance costs.

(2) Ground Launched Missiles. About $2.64 billion for 3,000 missiles, vehicles, and 10-year operating and maintenance costs.

(3) Surveillance and Targeting. About $500 million for airborne optical, radar, and other systems for air operations and ground stations. About $1.2 billion for eight NATO corps in Central Region. Total acquisition and 10-year operating and maintenance costs for Central Region for attack of Pact ground forces is about $5.85 billion.

Availability: About 4 years (1987-88) after decision to complete development and acquisition.

MISSION 4 — Attack of Enemy Ground Forces in Direct Contact

Objectives: Destroy first-echelon regiments (armored companies, battalions, etc.) which may be on NATO territory.

Weapon Systems: Alternatives to short-range nuclear systems (artillery or rockets) having multiple kill capabilities.

Example: Multiple Launch Rocket System with terminally guided weapons. (Skeet) (See Figures 3, 4, 5, 6). Ranges 0-30 km. Targeting systems are available.

Costs: About $200 million to provide the conventional "equivalent" of 1,000 nuclear artillery shells.

OVERALL TEN-YEAR COSTS

Missions 1 and 2	$2.30 billion
Mission 3	5.85 billion (including surveillance/targeting)
Mission 4	0.20 billion
RDT&E* for all missions	1.05 billion
Total	9.40 billion
*RDT&E = Research, Development, Testing and Evaluation	

NOTES

1. *Bulletin of The American Academy of Arts and Sciences,* No. 6, March 1982.

2. One need only look at the communications technology for banking industry, automatic multi-node telephone switching (satellite, microwave land line) and the capabilities for national and global newspaper printing and distribution systems to see how far we have advanced. Contrast this to the NATO communications system which is largely the same as we've had for twenty years. NATO is spending $7 billion to upgrade the NATO Integrated Communications System with no increase in survivability.

3. See also Donald R. Cotter, "NATO Theater Nuclear Forces: An Enveloping Military Concept," *Strategic Review,* Spring 1981.

4. See the Workshop Report on The Soviet Threat in the 1980s in this volume.

5. For an earlier discussion of the concept, see Cotter (note 3 above).

6. Donald R. Cotter, James Hansen, and Kirk McConnell, *The Nuclear "Balance" in Europe: Status, Trends, Implications,* United States Strategic Institute, Report 83-1, January 1983.

7. See Senator S. Nunn's speech, "MBFR/Theater Nuclear Force Modernization," *German American Roundtable,* Washington, D.C., October 22, 1979.

8. A U.S. weapon now in development is a laser-guided surface-burst bomb. Other weapons soon to be available are the Federal Republic of Germany's STABO and the French Durandal and BAP-100 munitions. The U.K. has recently put into production the JP-233 runway attack system.

Index

A-6 aircraft, 248
A-7 aircraft, 248
Adenauer, Konrad, 84
Advanced non-nuclear technologies,
    24-27, 34-35, 200, 202-203,
    207-208. *See also* Non-nuclear mis-
    siles; Target acquisition
  cost and requirements for, 204
  counter-airbase mission of, 25, 201,
    236, 238-240, 251
  counter-ground forces mission of,
    25-26, 201-202, 240-243, 251-252
  force restructuring for, 244-245
  interdiction mission of, 25-26, 201,
    238, 240, 251
  issues on, 27, 204-206
  nuclear equivalence of, 24-25, 228,
    230-233, 249
  Soviet reaction to, 249-250
Andropov, Yuri, 69
Arms control
  and NATO force improvement, 11, 29
  and non-nuclear missiles, 206
Arms control negotiations, and Soviet
    policy, 95, 103-104n.93
ASROC, 248
Assault Breaker, 183, 241
Atomic demolition munitions (ADMs),
    245, 248
AWACS system, 179, 181, 223, 228
AXE (conventionally-armed ballistic
    missiles). *See* Non-nuclear missiles

Backfire bomber, 15, 211
Ballistic missiles, non-nuclear. *See* Non-
    nuclear missiles
Ballistic Offensive Suppression System
    (BOSS), 238, 249

Barriers, constructed, 203-204
Barriers, natural, 26, 29, 151-152, 160.
    See also Choke points
Biological warfare, by Soviets, 56
BP-755, 223
Brezhnev, Leonid, 93, 94
Buccaneer aircraft, 248

CAM-40 missile, 238, 239, 240, 243,
    245, 249
Central Region
  and other threat areas, 42
  primacy of, 10, 12, 116, 210
Chemical warfare
  NATO preparation against, 129
  NATO use of 206-207
  Soviet use of, 17, 56, 60, 206-207
Choke points
  and interdiction mission, 22, 151, 160
  and new conventional technologies,
    26, 201, 223-224, 240, 242, 251
Clausewitz, Karl von, 106
Command control and communications
    (C^3), NATO
  in development decisions, 165, 167
  improvements needed in, 23, 153,
    154, 155-156, 187-188
  low technology use in, 157
  for non-nuclear missiles, 204
  vulnerability of, 173
Command, control and communications
    (C^3), Warsaw Pact
  NATO disrupting of, 23, 154-155
  reliance on, 16, 18
  vulnerability of, 62-63
Communist Party of the Soviet Union
    (CPSU), nuclear-war impact on, 106

Continuous operations, by Soviets, 49
Conventional forces, NATO. *See* NATO
  conventional forces
Conventional forces, Soviet. *See* Soviet
  forces, conventional
Conventionally-armed ballistic missiles
  (AXE). *See* Advanced non-nuclear
  technologies; Non-nuclear missiles
Corps Support Weapon System (CSWS),
  160, 241, 242, 243
Costs
  for advanced conventional systems,
    30-31, 35, 204, 224, 238, 240-244,
    251-252
  for high-performance aircraft, 181-182
Crisis, Soviet management of, 112-114
Crisis stability, and NATO, 9
Cruise missiles, 152, 183-185, 238

Data handling
  measures to improve, 159
  need to improve, 20, 144, 147-149
Davey Crockett missile, 218
Deep attack
  air operations for, 180-181, 240
  considerations in, 151-152
  delivery systems for, 183-184,
    202-203, 228
  and Forward Defense, 22
Detente, Soviet view of, 74-75, 107
Deterrence
  and advanced conventional forces, 208
  by defeat of Soviet strategy, 41
  erosion of, 8, 209-210
  vs. gunfighter analogy, 133-134
  and reassurance, 8
  requirements for, 18, 28, 61
  Soviet posture for, 94-95
Document MC 14/3, NATO Military
  Committee, on Flexible Response,
  44
Drones
  need for, 149, 159, 182
  uses of, 182-183, 228
Dual-capability systems, 27, 247-249

8" artillery tube, 248
Electronic warfare, NATO
  need to improve, 154-155, 187-188
  and OMG neutralization, 156

Electronic warfare, Soviet, 15, 60

F-4 aircraft, 238, 248
F-15 aircraft, 187
F-16 aircraft, 248
F-104 aircraft, 248
F-111 aircraft, 238, 240, 248
Flexible Response doctrine, 9, 32, 94
  adequacy of, 141, 158, 217, 246-247
  and non-nuclear missiles, 199-200,
    208
  and OMGs, 16
  Soviet interpretation of, 71
  Soviet response to, 44, 48, 120
  Soviet weakening of, 43, 95
Forward Defense strategy
  adequacy of, 141, 158, 161, 169, 171
  air operations under, 246
  controversy over, 163-164
  enhancement of, 143
  need for, 10, 33, 163, 164-165,
    216-217
  and non-nuclear technology, 210
  offensive reinforcement of, 143, 190
  and OMGs, 16
  requirements for, 22, 141-142,
    225-226
  and surprise attack, 172
  weaknesses of, 120, 167, 197-198
Frog artillery rockets, 80
Frog/SS-21 short range missiles, 86

Garthoff, Raymond, 82
George, Alexander, 73
Gepard system, 187
Grechkov, A., 172
Ground Launched Cruise Missiles
  (GLCM), 238, 248
Gunfighter analogy, to Soviet war ini-
  tiation, 134

Hawk missile, 172-173
Hawk missile, Improved, 220-221
Helsinki Agreements (1975), 29
Honest John missiles, 86, 237, 248

Intelligence, NATO
  needs in, 49-50, 51, 146-147
  and OMGs, 54
  suggested improvements in, 148-149,
    185-186, 187-188, 226-228, 229

Intelligence, Soviet, importance of, 63
Intermediate nuclear force (INF), 219
Interoperability, need to improve, 28, 144-145, 158, 187-188, 213

Jaguar aircraft, 248
Jaruzelski, W., 113-114

Krupchenko, 123
Khrushchev, Nikita
   foreign policy and military doctrine under, 69, 79-84, 92
   and nuclear weapons, 94
   and Zakharov, 85
Kinetic energy penetrators (KEP), 238, 251

Lachiewicz, 124, 130, 131
Lance missile, 86, 160, 218, 236, 237, 241, 248
Lance missile, Follow-On, 149-150
Lee, W. T., 69
Leites, Nathan, 73
Lenin, V. I., 70, 73, 74, 106, 107
Long-Term Defense Program, NATO (1977), 90, 170
Long Term Development Program, 250
Low Altitude Dispensers (LADS), 223, 233, 240

M-20 system, 248
Malenkov, G., 69, 83
Marx, Karl, 105-106
Medium-Range Air-to-Surface Missiles (MRASM), 238
Michalak, Wojciech, 123-124
Mirage III/IV aircraft, 238
Missiles, non-nuclear. See Non-nuclear missiles
Mobile Groups, 53, 119, 121-122, 123-124, 125-128, 129-132, 171. See also Operational Maneuver Group
Multiple Launch Rocket System (MLRS), 159, 204
   costs of, 30-31, 252
   NATO need for, 21, 149-150, 202
   as nuclear equivalent, 228, 230, 231, 242-243, 249, 252
Mutual Balanced Force Reductions negotiations, 147

Mutually Assured Destruction, Russian attitude toward, 133. See also Deterrence
MW-1 dispenser, 223, 233

NATO (North Atlantic Treaty Organization)
   nuclear-dependence legacy of, 217-218
   nuclear vs. non-nuclear missile use by, 198-200, 207-208, 217
   political purpose of, 7-8
   and proposed advanced systems, 250
   Soviet perception of, 109-110
   threat to, 12, 42, 116, 158, 169-170, 171, 197
   war plans of, 120
NATO air operations
   alternative weapons systems for, 182-185 (see also Advanced non-nuclear technologies; Non-nuclear missiles)
   force ratios in, 216
   penetrations methods in, 180-182
   and surprise attack, 174-175, 178-180
   vs. Warsaw Pact airpower, 21-22, 25, 152-153, 160, 201, 220-221, 222-224
   vs. Warsaw Pact artillery, 150
   vs. Warsaw Pact ground forces, 188-189, 223-224, 226
   weaknesses in, 172-173, 244
NATO conventional forces
   and advanced technologies, 24-27, 34-35, 202-203, 204-206, 207-208, 244-245 (see also Advanced non-nuclear technologies; Non-nuclear missiles)
   C^3 of, 23, 155-156, 187-188 (see also Command, control and communications, NATO)
   compared with Warsaw Pact, 135, 211, 212, 213
   counter-C^3 by, 23, 154-155
   covering forces of, 176-177
   data handling by, 20, 144, 147-149, 159 (see also Intelligence)
   vs. follow-on attack, 22, 25-26, 150-152, 160
   improvement approach for, 143-145, 165-168, 170-171, 189-190, 205-206

improvements suggested for, 10-11, 24-29, 141, 145, 158-160, 210-211 (*see also specific performance areas*)
vs. initial attack, 19-21, 26-28
low-technology use by, 157-158
manpower prospects for, 28
operational strategy of, 176-178
performance required of, 18-19, 142
posture of, 161-164, 204-205
problems for, 168
shallow interdiction by, 188-189
and Soviet OMGs, 156-157 (*see also* Operational Maneuver Groups)
and Soviet surprise attack, 13-14, 47, 49-50, 108, 145-147, 174-176, 179
and tactical nuclear weapons, 199-200 (*see also* Tactical nuclear weapons, NATO)
target acquisition of, 147-149, 159 (*see also* Target acquisition)
and Warsaw Pact artillery, 20-21, 149-150, 159
NATO forces, overall
modernization of, 219
Warsaw Pact compared with, 85
NATO-Warsaw Pact standing committee, proposal for, 29-30
Netted Ground Surveillance Radar System, 229, 243
"Neutron Weapon" artillery shell, 230
New non-nuclear weapons. *see*
Advanced non-nuclear technologies;
Non-nuclear missiles;
Terminally-guided submunitions
Night warfare
and OMGs, 131
Soviet capability for, 51
Nike Hercules missiles, 172-173, 220, 245, 248
Nimrod aircraft, 248
Non-nuclear missiles. *See also* Advanced non-nuclear technologies; Precision-guided area weapons
costs of, 30-31, 224
counter-airbase mission of, 153, 160, 179-180, 201, 220-221, 222-224, 238
counter-ground force mission of, 201-202, 228, 241-242
interdiction mission for, 201, 222, 223
uses of, 182, 183-185

Non-nuclear missiles, Soviet, 153-154, 171-172, 180
North Atlantic Treaty alliance. *See* NATO
Nuclear deterrence
lessened reliance on, 29
undesirability of, 9
vs. upgrading NATO conventional forces, 24, 198-200
Nuclear forces
Khrushchev use of, 80-82
Soviet buildup of, 86-88
Nuclear Operation Plan (NOP), 227
Nuclear Quick Reaction Alert Forces, NATO, 222
Nuclear threshold
need to raise, 9, 32
and non-nuclear capabilities, 24, 32, 209-210, 219, 224

Ogarkov, Nikolai, 172
155 mm artillery tube, 248
Operational Maneuver Group (OMG), 16-17, 53-54, 63, 124-128, 156-157, 197
characteristics of, 129-132
and counter-C^3 operations, 154
employment of, 54
helicopters in, 59
missions of, 124
and Mobile Group, 125-128, 129-132
and NATO missiles, 236
problems in, 133
and second echelons, 49
and theater nuclear forces, 48

P-3 aircraft, 248
Patriot missiles, 179, 183, 241, 245
Peace movement
and Soviet declaratory efforts, 91
Soviet support of, 96, 111
Pershing missile systems, 86, 180, 218, 222, 245, 248
Pipes, Richard, 73
Pluton SSM, 248
Polaris missile, 248
Poseidon missile, 248
Precision-guided area weapons, 200, 219-220, 225. *See also* Advanced non-nuclear technologies; Non-nuclear missiles; Terminally guided submunitions

Pre-planning, NATO development of, 227-228
Psychological warfare, NATO use of, 65

Radio Electronic Combat (REC), Soviet capability for, 60. *See also* Electronic warfare, NATO
Rajmanski, 124, 130, 131
Rapier missiles, 220-221
Reassurance, as NATO goal, 8
Remotely piloted vehicles (RPVs)
  need for, 182
  utility of, 182-183
Roland missiles, 220-221

S-2 aircraft, 248
SS-4 missiles, 87
SS-5 missiles, 87
SS-12/22 missiles, 86
SS-20 missiles, 15, 87, 211
SS-21 missiles, 15
SS-22 missiles, 15
SS-23 missiles, 15
SSBS-3 system, 248
Scaleboard missiles, 247
Scud missiles, 80, 86, 247
SDV (Skeet Delivery Vehicle). *See* Skeet system
Single Integrated Operational Plan (SIOP), 227
Skeet system, 230, 231, 232, 233, 242-243, 252
Sokolovskii, V. D., 70, 72, 114
Soviet forces
  biological warfare by, 56
  buildup of, 67, 68, 69, 85-88, 95
  chemical warfare by, 17, 56, 60, 129
  in "correlation of forces," 73-75, 107
  modernization of, 15, 58-62
  purposes of, 68, 91-93, 95, 107-108
  readiness of, 56
Soviet forces, conventional. *See also* Warsaw Pact forces
  advanced technology for, 153-154, 171-172
  air operations by, 58-59, 64, 152, 214
  combat potential of, 211-213
  critical factors in, 61-65
  OMGs in, 16-17, 53-54, 124-128, 156-157 (*see also* Operational Maneuver Group)

purposes of, 12-13, 42-43, 44, 47, 79, 107
uncertainties facing, 17-18
vulnerabilities of, 18, 33, 54-55, 134-135
Soviet foreign policy
  assertiveness of, 67-68
  and "correlation of forces," 69, 72-75, 107
  declaratory efforts of, 88-91
  development of, 93
  Khrushchev era of, 79-84
  political-military methods in, 8, 12-13, 33, 93-95, 107
  Stalin era of 75-79
  three levels of, 77
  war as tool in, 106-107
  and Western Europe, 96-97, 106-107
Soviet military doctrine, 44, 70-71, 108-109
  crisis phase in, 112-114
  and declaratory efforts, 88-91
  definition of, 70
  on East-West war, 44
  expectations of victory in, 95
  initial war period in, 114-116
  under Khrushchev, 81-83
  offensive orientation of, 110
  opponents considered in, 109
  options recognized by, 109
  political rationale in, 8, 12-13, 78, 92-95, 107
  preparatory phase in, 47, 111-112
  in Stalin era, 77-78
  vs. strategy, 70, 71
Soviet military strategy and operations, 13-14, 46-55, 71-72. *See also* Operational Maneuver Group
  air warfare in, 131-132
  axes of advance in, 49, 51-52
  critical factors in, 62
  vs. doctrine, 70, 71
  follow-on system in, 50
  mobility and speed in, 50-51, 62, 63, 217
  and NATO tactical nuclear weapons, 55, 120-122, 123, 128-129, 134, 234-236, 237
  and nuclear weapons use, 13, 17, 45-46, 55

offensive structuring in, 16, 51-55,
    63-64, 118-120, 213-214, 215, 237
and Stalin, 78
surprise attack in, 13-14, 46-47,
    49-50, 55, 108, 145, 172-176
surprise vs. numerical superiority in,
    15-16, 57-58
Soviet Union
    future military investment of, 68-69
    improved relations with, 11
    and proposed NATO systems, 247,
        249-250
    risk-taking by, 68
    strategic objectives of, 44-45, 46, 116
    war initiation by, 13, 43-44, 48,
        133-134
Stability, in Soviet view, 74
Stalin
    foreign policy under, 75-79
    and nuclear weapons, 94
    and political design, 93
Stratmann, K.-Peter, 147, 157
SUBROC system, 248
Super Etendard aircraft, 248
Survivability
    of air force, 179
    NATO need for, 142, 210, 219
    and NATO nuclear decline, 218
    of non-nuclear missiles, 224

T-16 system, 241
T-22 system, 241
Tactical (theater) nuclear weapons,
    NATO
    and conventional capability, 24,
        198-200
    conventional equivalents to, 24-25,
        202, 228, 230-233, 249
    force restructuring for, 245-246
    future purposes of, 29, 234, 246-247
    and OMGs, 128-129
    original introduction of, 218
    Soviet readiness for, 17, 55
    and Soviet strategy, 45-46, 115,
        120-122, 123, 134, 234-237
Target acquisition
    for advanced systems, 243
    NATO need to improve, 20, 24-25,
        146, 147-149, 159, 186
    and non-nuclear missile missions, 224

and OMGs, 156
uses of, 144
and Warsaw Pact artillery, 149
Terminally guided submunitions (TGSM)
    effectiveness of, 26-27, 230
    against ground forces, 225, 226, 228,
        230-233, 242, 251, 252
    nuclear equivalence of, 202, 219, 230,
        232-233
    obstacles to, 184-185
Terrier system, 248
Theater information system (TIS),
    227-228, 229, 243, 244
Theater nuclear forces, Soviet im-
    provement of, 15, 58. See also Tac-
    tical (theater) nuclear weapons,
    NATO
Time frame
    for proposed non-nuclear systems de-
        velopment, 159, 160, 244, 251, 252
    for Soviet conventional offensive, 46,
        51, 108, 116, 213
    for Soviet mobilization, 15-16, 57
    for suggested NATO force im-
        provements, 27, 35
Tornado aircraft, 182, 187, 233, 238,
    240
Total Air Base Attack System (TABAS),
    238

Vulcan aircraft, 248

W-48 155 mm artillery shell, 230
Warsaw Pact forces. See also Soviet
    forces, conventional
    air warfare by, 222-223
    compared with NATO, 86-87, 135,
        211, 212, 213
    force ratios presented by, 214, 216
    mobilization capability of, 15-16, 57
Warsaw Pact forces, non-Soviet
    reliability of, 43-44, 64-65, 117
    utility of, 116-117
Werth, Alexander, 78
Western Europe
    importance of, 162-163
    Soviet efforts toward, 96-97, 106-107
"Wild Weasel" aircraft, 181

Zakharov, M. V., 84
Zhdanov, A., 77